THE **COMPLETE** **IDIOT'S** **GUIDE** TO

Strategic Planning

By Lin Grensing-Pophal

ALPHA

A member of Penguin Group (USA) Inc.

ALPHA BOOKS

Published by the Penguin Group

Penguin Group (USA) Inc., 375 Hudson Street, New York, New York 10014, USA

Penguin Group (Canada), 90 Eglinton Avenue East, Suite 700, Toronto, Ontario M4P 2Y3, Canada (a division of Pearson Penguin Canada Inc.)

Penguin Books Ltd., 80 Strand, London WC2R 0RL, England

Penguin Ireland, 25 St. Stephen's Green, Dublin 2, Ireland (a division of Penguin Books Ltd.)

Penguin Group (Australia), 250 Camberwell Road, Camberwell, Victoria 3124, Australia (a division of Pearson Australia Group Pty. Ltd.)

Penguin Books India Pvt. Ltd., 11 Community Centre, Panchsheel Park, New Delhi—110 017, India

Penguin Group (NZ), 67 Apollo Drive, Rosedale, North Shore, Auckland 1311, New Zealand (a division of Pearson New Zealand Ltd.)

Penguin Books (South Africa) (Pty.) Ltd., 24 Sturdee Avenue, Rosebank, Johannesburg 2196, South Africa

Penguin Books Ltd., Registered Offices: 80 Strand, London WC2R 0RL, England

International Standard Book Number: 978-1-61564-059-1
Library of Congress Catalog Card Number: 2010912363

13   12   11   8   7   6   5   4   3   2   1

Interpretation of the printing code: The rightmost number of the first series of numbers is the year of the book's printing; the rightmost number of the second series of numbers is the number of the book's printing. For example, a printing code of 11-1 shows that the first printing occurred in 2011.

Printed in the United States of America

Note: This publication contains the opinions and ideas of its author. It is intended to provide helpful and informative material on the subject matter covered. It is sold with the understanding that the author and publisher are not engaged in rendering professional services in the book. If the reader requires personal assistance or advice, a competent professional should be consulted.

The author and publisher specifically disclaim any responsibility for any liability, loss, or risk, personal or otherwise, which is incurred as a consequence, directly or indirectly, of the use and application of any of the contents of this book.

Most Alpha books are available at special quantity discounts for bulk purchases for sales promotions, premiums, fund-raising, or educational use. Special books, or book excerpts, can also be created to fit specific needs.

For details, write: Special Markets, Alpha Books, 375 Hudson Street, New York, NY 10014.

Publisher: *Marie Butler-Knight*

Editorial Director: *Mike Sanders*

Senior Managing Editor: *Billy Fields*

Senior Acquisitions Editor: *Paul Dinas*

Development Editor: *Lynn Northrup*

Senior Production Editor: *Janette Lynn*

Copy Editor: *Jaime Julian Wagner*

Cover Designer: *William Thomas*

Book Designers: *William Thomas, Rebecca Batchelor*

Indexer: *Johnna Vanhoose Dinse*

Layout: *Brian Massey*

Proofreader: *John Etchison*

Contents

Appendixes

Introduction

Strategic planning is often viewed as a necessary evil by small businesses. And that's the good news! Far too many companies fail to create a strategic plan. That is so unfortunate, because the process of creating a strategic plan—whether for the organization as a whole, for an important function (like marketing or human resources), or for a department—can provide a valuable road map to ensure that business resources—time and money—are being used effectively.

Strategic planning does not have to be a laborious, labor-intensive, academic process. It can be an invigorating, team-building process that helps all the members of a business get on the right track toward achieving some specific goal.

The Complete Idiot's Guide to Strategic Planning explains in easy-to-understand language how even the smallest business can use the power of strategic planning to chart a course, navigate that course, and achieve desired business results. You'll learn how to build a strong planning team, how to conduct the background research you'll need to guide your planning, how to create the plan, and how to build in evaluation methods to monitor success. Most importantly, you'll learn about tips and techniques to overcome a common strategic planning pitfall: failure to execute.

How to Use This Book

This book has 21 chapters organized in four parts, which we recommend you initially read from beginning to end and that will serve as useful points of reference for you as you embark on various strategic planning initiatives. The parts work together to provide you with the steps and tools behind successful strategic planning and offer practical advice that you can adapt to meet the needs of your business—regardless of industry, size, or level of familiarity with strategic planning. But you may also wish to keep the book on hand as you move forward with your planning process as a quick refresher about some of the key elements of the process or as a source of useful information to share with team members who may be new to the process.

Part 1, Laying the Foundation, provides some background on strategic planning and the use of strategy. You'll learn about the most common types of strategic plans, the importance of developing a strategic plan, and why we often resist formal planning. We'll cover the basics of strategic planning, including how long it takes, how much it will cost, and whether you should do it yourself or turn to outside resources. We'll also discuss how to select the people who will aid in the process.

Part 2, Gathering Key Information, covers the important step of making sure that you are relying on the right information—from internal and external sources—to guide the strategic planning process and help you make the right decisions.

Part 3, The Planning Process, provides an overview of the steps involved in actually developing the plan. Here we'll cover the role of the mission, vision, and values. We'll talk about how to develop and use a SWOT analysis. And we'll cover the four key components of a strategic plan: goals, objectives, strategies, and tactics. Mastering the information in this part is important because the proper use and alignment of these plan elements will improve your odds of success.

Part 4, Implementing and Updating the Plan, describes how to pull the plan together into its final format, distribute and communicate its contents to your company, track results, and make adjustments based on what you learn and changes in the environment in which you operate.

You'll also find four helpful appendixes: a glossary of the important terms used in the book, a list of additional recommended resources, some sample strategic plans, and a sample evaluation form you can use to assess your strategic planning process.

Extras

The following types of sidebars found throughout the book highlight specific items that can help you understand and implement the material in each chapter.

DEFINITION

These sidebars define the most important concepts in strategic planning. Use these words in meetings to impress your staff and your planning team—it will prove that you know what you're talking about!

MISSTEPS

These sidebars identify some potential pitfalls you should be aware of to make sure your planning efforts are most successful.

BEST PRACTICES

It's always a good idea to learn from those who have been there and done that. These sidebars provide quick, helpful, and easy-to-implement hints, techniques, and ideas to streamline your strategic planning activities.

DID YOU KNOW?

These sidebars present miscellaneous related information as well as interesting facts, history, and words of wisdom from experts and practitioners.

Acknowledgments

I'd like to thank all of the people at Alpha Books for their professionalism, skills, and good ideas. I can't express enough how excited I was to be able to work on this project and how grateful for the advice and expertise of all of those I encountered along the way.

I also want to thank the friends, colleagues, clients, and business connections who provided me with encouragement, ideas, tips, and examples along the way. Many of their stories show up in these pages and bring life to the strategic planning process.

Of course, I want to thank you, the reader, for purchasing this book. I'm passionate about strategic planning and hope that you will be, too—and that the process brings you a minimum of frustration and much success!

Finally, thanks to my two favorite people in the world: my husband, Dave, who reads my moods well and knows when I need another cup of coffee, more water, or something stronger, and my son, Justin, a law school/MBA student who will finally be graduating about the time this book is released. He's a good sounding board and a great source of factual information, data, and statistics—as well as much-needed comic relief every now and then. I couldn't do what I do without the two of them.

Special Thanks to the Technical Reviewer

The Complete Idiot's Guide to Strategic Planning was reviewed by an expert who double-checked the accuracy of what you'll learn here to help us ensure that this book gives you everything you need to know about strategic planning. Special thanks are extended to Gina Abudi.

Gina Abudi is a Partner/VP Strategic Solutions at Peak Performance Group, Inc. (www.PeakPerformanceGroup.com). She has a broad range of consulting experience in strategic planning, project and process management, business impact and return on investment (ROI), and general management/leadership, including succession planning and needs/skills/competency assessments. She has written a number of papers and articles on various management and project management topics, which can be found on her blog: www.GinaAbudi.com.

Trademarks

All terms mentioned in this book that are known to be or are suspected of being trademarks or service marks have been appropriately capitalized. Alpha Books and Penguin Group (USA) Inc. cannot attest to the accuracy of this information. Use of a term in this book should not be regarded as affecting the validity of any trademark or service mark.

Laying the Foundation

Strategic planning works—and it doesn't have to be the laborious, time-intensive, analysis-by-paralysis activity that many people believe it to be. In fact, strategic planning can be fun—really!

The chapters in this part will help you set yourself up for success from the very beginning. You'll learn about what strategic planning is and how it can help you gain focus and achieve results. I hope to convince you of the value of strategic planning and why you should use it for your overall organizational planning, special needs planning (like developing plans for marketing or human resources), and even department or single-purpose plans. You'll also learn how to choose your team members and understand the roles of people on the team, and you'll discover how facilitation tools can make a big difference in your strategic planning success. I'll also tell you where to look for outside help if you need it.

What Is Strategic Planning?

In This Chapter

- Understanding strategy and strategic planning
- Why have a plan?
- The different types of plans and how they're used
- The need for alignment from the top down

Whether you're taking a vacation, introducing a new product or service, or building a company from the ground up, everything begins with a plan. Most of us, when undertaking any task, will have a plan in our head, whether or not we actually commit that plan to paper—but not in all cases. We all know people who seem to work very hard, yet rarely accomplish anything of note. Chances are they don't have a plan.

Having a plan can make a difference in a big way even with something as simple as cooking dinner. When you have a recipe in front of you with specific ingredients listed and specific steps to follow to achieve the desired outcome, the odds of success are much greater than if you simply start to cook. The same is true of any planning effort, but, of course, the need to have a formal plan increases as the importance of the desired outcome increases. Consequently, planning for the introduction of a new product will be much more involved than planning for the addition of a new employee or the development of a newspaper advertisement. In both of these latter cases, while we may have a plan (even if it only exists in our head), it would not be defined as a strategic plan.

Taking the time to get this information out of the heads of a few and documented in a format that can be shared, referred to, and updated can help provide important guidance for the business and all of its employees. Here and in the chapters that follow, we'll cover those steps and provide an easy-to-follow road map for creating strategic plans that are results-oriented, actionable, and flexible enough to meet the changing needs of fast-moving markets.

A Road Map for Success

Strategic planning is a process used by business leaders to, well, plan. It's really as simple as that. A *strategic plan* is a management tool that helps an organization focus its efforts in support of some clearly identified final outcome. Once complete, it becomes a road map for success.

DEFINITION

A **strategic plan** is a document that outlines the steps that an organization, division, or department will take to achieve an overall goal or vision.

Most strategic planning efforts follow a three-step path:

1. Identify and evaluate the current situation.

2. Define the target—the goals or objectives you would like to achieve to make the situation more favorable.

3. Determine the path—outline how you will achieve the target.

Strategic planning can provide direction to help a company in several ways:

- Deciding which customers it will serve

- Deciding which products and services to offer those customers

- Determining how to attract and keep customers

- Determining how to produce products and services most effectively

- Identifying ways to reduce costs and, in the process, increase profits

- Identifying ways to streamline operations

Strategic planning is an ongoing process, not an event. That is an important concept to understand, because it can make the difference between a carefully crafted, beautifully designed, and expensively bound document that sits on a shelf somewhere and a living, breathing document that drives business performance. The planning process is never actually complete—it is, instead, initiated. As the plan is put into place, new information will emerge and business and market environments will change, which may require both wholesale changes and minor adjustments to the plan.

BEST PRACTICES

Effective strategic plans are designed to allow for ongoing evaluation and updates based on changes in the internal and external business environment.

A strategic plan is really nothing more than formal documentation of a set of related actions that a business, a department, or even an individual can take to achieve specific goals. Strategic planning involves setting up a strategy, or plan, that your business will follow over a certain period of time. It may be for your entire business, or for a portion of the business—a marketing plan, for example. Moving forward without a plan is folly. Let's look at a simple example.

For an in-class exercise in a public relations (PR) course, an instructor asked her students to come up with a communication plan based on a case study involving a small hospital in a rural community that was about to raise health-care benefit costs for employees. The students came up with a number of tactics, but when asked what their goal was, the students were unable to specifically articulate one.

The instructor asked, "Without a goal, how did you decide which tactics would work?" One student suggested that the goal was implied. The trouble is that if we select tactics without a clear idea of the goal that we're driving toward, the odds of us achieving any form of measurable results are pretty slim. Since few companies ever want to spend more than they need to in terms of either time or money, it clearly pays to be strategic!

Strategic plans can range from the large and very ambitious to the simple and easy to implement. A major health-care organization, for instance, recently announced the completion of its strategic plan: "a $580-million, 5-year vision for the future." The plan was developed over nine months and involved a 25-member cabinet of university and hospital leaders who met on a monthly basis. At the other end of the spectrum is a strategic plan that a nurse consultant developed for her business. Looking one year into the future, it focused on how she would use social media and other online tools to help raise awareness of her services.

When it comes to planning, there are no hard and fast rules in terms of what do plan for or how long the plan should be. The specifics of the plan are driven by the business and its unique needs.

What It Means to Be Strategic

There are widely divergent opinions about what it means to be strategic. When the question "What does the word *strategic* mean to you?" was posed in a social media forum, these were two of the responses:

> Strategy to me is the plan your company puts in place that guides the decisions being made on a daily basis. Having a good strategy usually requires all areas of the company to be making decisions leading toward the same outcome or goal.

> For us, it's really about sales. Marketing can help qualify leads, but then what? How are you perceived by your prospects? What are your unique values in the marketplace today? Who really is your target market? All of that should boil down to a solid positioning. Given the budget allocated to marketing, the plan nearly writes itself when you have a good basis of the brand strategy platform.

Both of these are a bit off the mark. A better definition comes from a student, who said: "In the end, I think strategy boils down to planning and predicting what you will do and what will happen. Of course, this doesn't mean things won't change. In today's world, strategy can be especially complicated because things can change so swiftly and plans can go down in flames so quickly."

Chapter 15 provides a thorough discussion of the definition and use of strategies.

DID YOU KNOW?

The word **strategy** originated as a military term and comes from the Greek word *strategos*, which means general.

Strategy involves planning and predicting—much like playing a game of chess—which is the example that most point to when attempting to define what strategy is. A good strategy will guide daily business decisions toward some predetermined and desired end. All of the activities involved in planning need to occur with a clear understanding of a target market and what that target market values.

So if we put these thoughts together, we could say that being strategic is all about having a goal, knowing your audience or market, and then planning and predicting the potential results of various actions you might take (and picking those with the greatest potential for your desired outcomes). Being strategic means thinking about what could happen in the future and coming up with plans to either increase or decrease the odds of that result, depending on your goal.

Strategic vs. Operational

The words "strategic" and "operational" are tossed around in the business world fairly frequently. "Strategic" is generally used to refer to activities undertaken by leaders; "operational" is generally used to refer to activities undertaken by front-line staff.

There are some additional important distinctions between being strategic and being operational, which can make the terms easier to understand and differentiate:

- Strategic = long-range; operational = day to day.

- Strategic = dreaming; operational = doing.

- Strategic decisions impact the ability of a company or business to achieve its core mission and guiding vision; operational decisions impact progress toward accomplishing specific tasks.

A strategic plan, therefore, is a long-range vision or dream created by senior management designed to assist the business in achieving its overall mission. The strategic plan indicates where you want your business to go and serves as the foundation for the development and implementation of operational plans that will ensure that you get there.

A strategic plan offers direction for the organization, division, or department based on mission and goals that are far-reaching. Operational plans provide the details of how these goals will be achieved based on specific things that owners or employees of the business will do to make the strategies happen. Operational plans are narrow and more specific than strategic plans. They support the strategic plan and outline specific action steps that will be taken.

Strategy in Action

Let's consider an example to help illustrate the difference between strategic and operational plans. An optometry clinic developed a strategic marketing plan to identify opportunities to grow the practice. The plan identified new markets that could be pursued and specific services that could be provided to these markets. The plan established goals related to specific increases in the numbers of patients that would be seen over the next year for each of the service lines offered and identified a number of ways (tactics) that the goals could be achieved. But the strategic plan stopped there—it didn't go into further detail on how each of the tactics would be achieved. That description would be operational and beyond the scope of the strategic plan.

While strategic plans are developed at higher levels of the organization, operational plans will be developed and implemented on the front lines by those who are actually doing the work. And, just as with strategic plans, sometimes these operational plans are formal and committed to paper, and sometimes they just exist in the heads of the people implementing the tactics.

In this case, for instance, one of the tactics was to increase the number of appointment openings available for patients each day. That required changes in scheduling that the clinic director needed to implement. She didn't need to develop a strategic plan to do this, but she did need to come up with an operational plan to make it happen.

MISSTEPS

The adage "failing to plan is planning to fail" can certainly be true. Yet despite the recognition that not having a plan is probably not a good idea, many businesses and business owners fail to take the steps involved in formal planning. Moving forward without a plan can result in lost opportunities and wasted resources.

Why We Resist Formal Planning

One of the reasons that many people resist formal planning is that they have too often been involved in planning processes that result in a beautifully bound plan that sits on a shelf gathering dust. They have memories of long, drawn-out processes that involved a lot of meetings but little in the way of actual implementation. In fact, many business people and business experts agree that it is not the development of plans that presents the greatest challenges for businesses but rather the implementation of those plans.

Even business scholars have challenged the traditional strategic planning process from the standpoint that the world can be unpredictable and not everything can be anticipated or planned for. Herb Kelleher, the co-founder and former chairman and CEO of Southwest Airlines, is said to have commented: "We have a strategic plan; it's called doing things." Of course, there's another popular comment that tells us that "even a blind squirrel finds a nut once in a while."

Some suggest that formal planning consumes time and energy that might be better spent responding more nimbly to the changes taking place in the business environment. Certainly Internet-based companies back in the 1980s and 1990s would have felt that this was the case. Unexpected changes in the environment can render even the most carefully and expertly prepared plan useless. And, as Kelleher's comment suggests, another reason for resisting formal planning is a sense of urgency—the need to be doing something. We need to act now! There is no time to plan! This tendency to want to move forward without a formal plan, however, is often referred to as "ready, fire, aim." Action is being taken, but that action is generally not well focused.

Finally, formal planning is often resisted or avoided simply because we don't know how to do it—we don't know what's involved, we don't know what the process entails, we don't know what the final product should look like, and we don't know how to actually implement the plan and monitor its effectiveness in achieving desired results.

Strategic planning does not need to be time spent unnecessarily; a well-developed plan will be specific enough to provide clear direction for both day-to-day and future activities. Planning also does not have to be excessively time-consuming and result in lost opportunities or delayed actions. In fact, effective planning can help identify opportunities that might otherwise be overlooked and help to avoid missteps that might take the business owner down the wrong path.

DID YOU KNOW?

One strategic planning professional says that he purposefully avoids using the "S-word" because of the negative reaction it often generates from small business owners and staff. Instead, he says, he talks about planning in general, often framed around the business plan. Focusing simply on planning can help to avoid the use of terms like *project management* or *strategic planning*, which often generate a negative response.

Ideally, your strategic plan should be focused enough that it provides members of your business with the direction they need to move forward appropriately, yet flexible enough that it allows for changes and adaptation as the environment changes. There are some simple guidelines that can be easily followed to ensure that the planning process will result in actionable steps that can be implemented to achieve positive results.

Types of Strategic Plans

Not all strategic plans have the same focus. There are various types of strategic plans ranging from the organizational plan, which focuses on the entire business and establishes business direction, to departmental and special purpose plans, which have a much more narrow focus.

It's important to note at the outset, however, the difference between a strategic plan and a *business plan*—two terms that are often confused. The strategic plan is used to drive the activities of an existing business, while a business plan is used as a starting point in establishing a new business and securing funding. A strategic plan takes a future focus and is designed to leverage strengths and overcome weaknesses while capitalizing on opportunities and avoiding threats. A business plan, on the other hand, is designed to assess and outline the potential for success for a business opportunity. Another key distinction between the two is that the strategic plan is intended to provide internal audiences with direction to achieve specific goals and objectives. The business plan is intended to provide external audiences with information upon which they can base decisions to financially support a business endeavor. While the two types of plans contain some similar elements, they are not the same. What we will be dealing with throughout this book is the strategic plan.

> **DEFINITION**
>
> A **business plan** is a document prepared for an external audience which is specifically designed to achieve funding and support for a new business initiative.

Organizational Plans

The strategic organizational plan is the broadest and highest-level plan. It is designed to direct the activities of the entire organization or business. The strategic planning process at the organization level will involve finding a fit between business goals and capabilities and the changing marketplace the business operates in. The organizational plan will define a clear company mission, establish specific objectives, and—most importantly—provide a broad overall focus and direction that will be used to coordinate all the functions of the business.

The company-wide strategic plan is developed at the board and senior leadership levels of large organizations and by the business owners and upper-level management team in smaller organizations. Once developed, it offers direction to other areas of the business and often drives the development of supporting strategic plans designed for specific functions, departments, or projects.

Financial Plans

The strategic financial plan provides an indication of how the organization's goals and objectives will be supported financially. It estimates and outlines plans for achieving the financing needed to implement the strategies of the overall organization or a specific project. The strategic financial plan will describe the actions required to achieve the financial objectives of the company and will quantify the resources—staff, equipment, and funding—needed to support the strategic organizational plan and the cost of these resources.

For example, suppose a small business is considering expansion and wants to develop a strategic plan for financing that expansion. The planning efforts would be focused on determining whether or not the idea is viable, where financial support for the effort might be attained, and what gaps or challenges might exist that might delay or cancel the effort.

Financial plans may also be created to support the introduction of new products or services or even to add staff. As with other types of plans, the scope can be very broad or very narrow depending on the overall goal of the planning effort.

Marketing Plans

The strategic marketing plan is driven by the overall strategic organizational plan. The objectives, strategies, and tactics of the marketing plan will be designed to achieve the specific marketing-related actions outlined in the strategic organizational plan. For example, if the strategic organizational plan includes an objective of increasing the number of new customers by 10 percent, the strategic marketing plan will include strategies and tactics designed to achieve that objective. The strategic marketing plan will detail the marketing goals to be achieved, the *marketing-mix strategy* that will position the company's products and services in its market, and the marketing and selling programs required to achieve marketing goals. The marketing plan outlines how the business will communicate with its various audiences—prospects and customers—to achieve the business objectives outlined in the strategic organizational plan.

DEFINITION

A **marketing-mix strategy** is a plan that indicates how a company will align all of its decisions related to product, price, place, and promotion activities to achieve maximum success.

Operational Plans

Operational or operating plans are not truly strategic plans, strictly speaking. As we've already seen, there are important distinctions between a strategic and an operational focus. Operational plans outline the things that need to be done in order to meet the goals and objectives outlined in the overall strategic plan. They indicate how the production or manufacturing processes will support the overall strategic organizational plan. In addition, operational plans consider the opportunities and limitations suggested by the financial plan and the sales estimates provided by the marketing plan. This information will be used to determine how the resources supported through the budget will be deployed to achieve overall organizational objectives. Operational plans may also be developed by specific departments to indicate how they will support the achievement of overall organizational strategic plan items through their actions.

Departmental/Special-Purpose Plans

Strategic plans may be created on a departmental level and even for special purposes. Strategic plans are commonly created by the human resources (HR) department within organizations, for example, to indicate how HR will support the overall organizational plan through its recruitment, retention, and placement efforts.

In some companies, each department is required to create a strategic plan in support of the overall plan. In others, department leaders may decide to create plans to help direct their own activities even though these plans are not required. Plans may also be created in support of specific activities—the development of a new product, the opening of a new branch office, or the implementation of a new process.

Alignment Between Plans

The organizational strategic plan should always serve as the basis or the reference point for the development of any other strategic plans within the company. Alignment should also occur between individual plans. Creating this alignment ensures that all elements of the business know what other elements of the business are doing in support of the overall plan. This awareness can help to ensure that activities are not duplicated (or overlooked) and also to identify areas of potential conflict that need to be addressed.

For instance, if the marketing plan indicates that sales of a particular product will be at a certain level, the department or area responsible for creating that product needs to know what projected sales figures are. In some cases, those projected sales figures may indicate demand that the product development group cannot meet. The knowledge of this discrepancy should prompt additional discussions stemming from the top of the organization and including impacted departments. These sorts of discrepancies often occur when the planning process is not coordinated and cascaded from the top down and when individual divisions, departments, or groups develop plans independently.

This happened at a small publishing company when the direct marketing manager identified high demand for annual updates of certain types of legal manuals. She created a plan that outlined the possibility for significant sales of a number of products but neglected to consider some key internal impacts:

- Would the editorial department be able to contract with authors to update these titles?

- Would the editorial department have adequate staff resources to create the new products?

- Would the printing department have the equipment, staff, and supplies to produce the books?

- Would the customer service department be able to manage incoming orders and effectively serve the needs of new and existing customers?

The biggest benefit of the strategic planning process from an organization-wide point of view is the ability to direct and align the activities of the entire organization. The larger the business is, of course, the more complex this process becomes—and the more important. Recognizing that strategic planning is a process and considering how that process can best be applied at your business is an important first step.

The Least You Need to Know

- A strategic plan is a road map or recipe that provides direction for the organization.

- The purpose of a strategic plan is to align the organization's resources toward the accomplishment of specific goals and objectives.

- The strategic organizational plan is the starting point for all internal planning activities, which may include financial plans, marketing plans, operational plans, and department-specific plans.

- Strategic plans should be developed from the top down, with each individual plan supporting the organizational plan.

Nuts and Bolts of Strategic Planning

In This Chapter

- Developing a planning process
- Assessing the amount of time required for planning
- Figuring the costs involved
- Can you do the planning yourself?
- Where to find help to streamline the planning process

Before beginning the process of strategic planning, businesses and individuals generally have questions about some basic elements of the process. When should planning occur? How often should planning occur? How long does the planning process take? Can I do it myself? If I choose not to do it myself, where can I find help?

These are all important questions, and while the answers vary based on the unique attributes of each business and each planning effort, there are some general guidelines that apply.

When Should I Create My Plan?

The answer to this question is "It depends." Since a strategic plan generally lays out how an organization, division, department, or project will unfold over the next year or so, it makes sense to plan on an annual basis; however, the timing for the development of the plan may vary.

For businesses with a strategic organizational plan that will be used as the starting point to drive the development of other plans, plenty of time needs to be allocated to allow for the completion of all of these plans. The goal is to have all plans in place, and aligned to coincide with whatever the *fiscal year* is for the organization.

> **DEFINITION**
>
> The **fiscal year** is the 12-month time frame a company uses to calculate its financial statements. For most companies this coincides with the calendar year, but not always. Companies may choose when their fiscal year begins and ends.

Let's suppose a company takes a calendar-year approach to planning based on its fiscal year. In this case, it makes sense to begin planning for the next year during the fourth quarter of the previous year—close enough to the end of the year so that adequate financial and sales data is available, but early enough that the plan can be available for all areas of the company to use to develop their plans in plenty of time for implementation by the first of the year. The smaller the company, the less complex this process becomes and the less time it will take. Larger companies can find the process more challenging as they attempt to balance the need for good information with the need to have plans ready for implementation.

One consultant who works regularly with small businesses on the development of their strategic plans says that a plan can easily be created in an afternoon, assuming the appropriate background information has been gathered and is available. Of course, the more people involved in the process, the more complex and time-consuming the process can become.

Creating a Timetable

A timetable can help establish goals and delivery dates for certain parts of the plan. The timetable can be adjusted as necessary, but it provides a good benchmark for planning activities so that all involved know what to expect. A timetable for the initial development of a plan might look like this:

Sample Strategic Planning Time Line—Initial Plan Development

Activity	Time Allotted	Month
Identify strategic planning goal	1 week	June
Assign team lead role	1 week	June
Assign facilitator role	1 week	June
Develop list of stakeholders	1 week	June
Select and invite team members	2 weeks	July
Hold initial meeting	2 weeks	July
Discuss mission, vision, values	1 day	July
Gather data and stakeholder input	4 weeks	August

Activity	Time Allotted	Month
Distribute data to team members	1 week	Sept
SWOT (strengths, weaknesses, opportunities, threats) analysis	1 week	Sept
Develop GOST (goals, objectives, strategies, tactics)	2 weeks	Sept
Write plan	1 month	Oct
Approve plan	1 month	Nov
Distribute and communicate plan	1 month	Dec
Plan reviews	monthly	Jan-Dec

Depicting the planning timetable in a calendar format can be a helpful way to visually communicate the planning process. A strategic planning calendar can easily be set up using calendar options in programs like Microsoft Outlook or Lotus Notes.

Keep in mind that there are no standards for the timetable that a strategic plan might take. The plan will be driven by the overall goal, the company culture, the sense of urgency the plan has, and the company's capacity and ability for performing the duties associated with the plan. Factors that can either lengthen or shorten the planning time frame could include the need to attain planning approval from a board or governing agency, the decision to hire an outside consultant or facilitator to aid the planning process, the availability of key team participants, and the approval process for the plan itself.

MISSTEPS

It is better to be realistic than aggressive when establishing the time frame for the initial strategic planning process. Overly aggressive time lines that participants can't meet will start the process on a negative note and can create negative perceptions about and frustration with the process.

Looking Ahead

In addition to questions about the length of time the planning process should take, businesses often wonder about the time frame that their plan should cover. In the past it was not uncommon for plans to encompass a 3-, 5-, or sometimes even a 10-year time frame. And while these time frames are still seen in strategic plans for government, nonprofit, and educational institutions, they are becoming less common today, particularly for small businesses. Why? Primarily because the business environment changes so quickly that a shorter time frame is much more practical.

How far the plan looks ahead will be driven by the business and the nature of the environment it operates in. A five-year plan in the technology industry would not make sense. A five-year plan for a funeral home might. In businesses where change occurs slowly, longer-range planning is appropriate.

One of the criticisms of strategic planning—and the reason that some plans simply sit on shelves gathering dust—is that the environment changes too rapidly for the plan to provide clear direction. That criticism, though, may suggest the need for a shorter planning cycle! It is possible, and often appropriate, for the plan to cover a three- to five-year time period but for the planning process to take place on an annual basis. The plan is simply rolled forward each year to cover a subsequent 12-month period. So, for example, in November 2011, a company might revise its 2011–2013 plan to cover 2012–2014.

In considering the appropriate time frame for your plan, consider both the environment you operate in as well as your ability to execute the plan. You must find the appropriate balance in terms of planning and doing and determine where your company might lie along a continuum that may range from government (on the slow-moving end) to technology firms (on the fast-moving end).

How Long Does It Take?

The amount of time required for strategic planning can vary significantly depending on the type of plan, whether it's the first plan or an update of a previous plan, the number of people involved, and the skill of the team leader and facilitator.

If this is the first plan, it will likely be developed over a series of several sessions, allowing time between sessions for participants to review information and complete any assignments. While strategic planning efforts can, and often do, drag on for weeks or even months, it is realistic to expect that an initial plan could be developed within a six-week period. Subsequent plan updates, which would typically occur on an annual basis, could be completed in a one- to two-week period. This assumes that supporting activities are taking place throughout the year—for instance, surveying of customers and employees, gathering sales data, and evaluating external factors impacting the business (I'll discuss these topics in detail in Part 2).

Once a strategic plan is in place, the planning process generally becomes part of ongoing business operations and occurs throughout the year. Here, for example, is a timetable that outlines the planning time frame and activities for one small business:

- January—annual needs assessment
- March—review needs assessment results, performance outcome indicators, and forecasts
- April—compile stakeholder recommendations
- May—create strategic planning documents
- June—prepare budget
- July—final changes to strategic planning documents
- August—release final strategic planning documents

This is just one example, however. For each business, the process will be different. It is important to remember that strategic planning should be considered a process, not an event. The process should be embedded into your business operations so that it creates a cycle that is repeated on a regular (generally annual) basis.

What Will It Cost?

It can be tempting to think that if you develop your own strategic plan, it will cost nothing. That is not the case. For businesses that conduct their own strategic planning activities, the primary cost is staff time required to gather information and participate in planning sessions. This cost is not insignificant and should not be downplayed simply because it is less visible than out-of-pocket costs that might be required to hire a consultant to help with the process.

Additional costs involved could include room rental (if the business doesn't have a room large or private enough to accommodate the planning group), supplies such as flip chart paper and markers, food and beverages to serve participants during the meetings, and the printing or producing of the actual plan document. In addition, some companies use software programs to help them manage and monitor their plans, and this would be an additional cost.

These costs can add up quickly and are often overlooked. Let's consider a typical planning process and associated costs in terms of staff time and expenses. We'll estimate a series of five 2-hour meetings involving 10 participants with an average loaded salary (wages + benefits) of $50,000 each—or about $24 per hour. We'll also assume that each of these individuals will spend an average of 10 additional hours outside of the meetings for general preparation, review of information, and completion of any specific assignments:

Meeting time = 10 hours × 10 participants × $24 = $2,400

Outside prep time = 10 hours × 10 participants × $24 = $2,400

Supplies and food = $50 per meeting ($50 × 5) = $250

TOTAL COST: $5,050

For an initial strategic planning session, this figure is likely to represent the low end of the scale in terms of cost. You can generate a more specific estimate based on your own business, including the number of people you would need to involve, the estimated time the process would take, and the amount of time involved in gathering and preparing information.

DID YOU KNOW?

The greatest area of expense for most strategic planning efforts is the time required of the participants.

Those businesses that choose to hire an individual or a firm to help with the process can then compare those costs to the costs of doing it themselves. Keep in mind, though, that even if you use an outside consultant, you will still incur staff time in terms of preparation and involvement in the process. Those costs will not go away. The expense of hiring a consultant, however, may be justified because of the outside expertise that the consultant brings about the strategic planning process.

The costs of hiring an outside consultant to help with the process can vary significantly depending on your industry, geography, and the size (and brand-name recognition) of the consulting firm you choose. One small consulting firm says on its website that it charges "$18,000 for a basic, 3-day strategic planning workshop for a small to midsize company. The cost may be more or less, depending on your specific needs."

It might also be necessary to conduct research as input to the strategic planning process (for example, customer or employee satisfaction research) if this information does not already exist. These costs could be considered part of the strategic planning process but might also be considered as part of ongoing business operations. For instance, if you don't currently conduct customer satisfaction or employee satisfaction surveys, these are key inputs to the planning process. This information is also valuable information that can be used to improve your products and services or employee relations, even in the absence of a formal strategic plan.

Can You Do It Yourself?

Can you do strategic planning yourself? You absolutely can. The process outlined in this book will give you the information you need to implement a strategic planning process. It is a straightforward process that relies primarily upon the value of the information gathered in support of the plan (see Part 2) and the skills of the team leader and facilitator to move the process along (see Chapters 5 and 6).

As with many business issues, there tend to be strong opinions on both sides. Many believe that the only way to effectively develop a strategic plan is to do it yourself. The reasons they offer are sound and include:

- The senior leadership needs to own the strategic plan—its creation, communication and execution.

- The industry-, company-, product/service-, and operations-specific knowledge held by those who know your organization best is critical and would be impossible to buy from the outside.

On the other hand, there are equally strong arguments to be made for the value of turning to outside resources:

- **Process expertise.** Unless somebody in your business has experience with strategic planning, it can take some time to simply become familiar and comfortable with the steps involved. An external resource can help make the process more efficient.

- **Outside perspective.** Those from outside your business will have broader viewpoints that can open your eyes to new opportunities and potential threats. An outside perspective can also help address the tendency toward *groupthink*. External resources are able to question assumptions that those on the inside may be hesitant to question.

- **Strategic perspective.** There can be a tendency for those within the business to become overly focused on the minutiae. An outsider can help ensure that the discussion remains at a strategic level.

 DEFINITION

Groupthink is a term used to define the tendency of groups that have worked together over a period of time and that are very cohesive to avoid critical analysis and conflict and accept raised ideas readily without adequate testing, analysis, or evaluation.

While, ultimately, ownership of the strategic planning process must rest with the owner(s) of the business, having the expertise necessary to actually develop and implement a sound plan is critical. One of the biggest mistakes made by businesses large and small is attempting to do this type of planning themselves and then falling prey to the tendency to be too internally focused, missing observations and opportunities that outsiders might see more readily.

If you're new to the strategic planning process, or if the results you're achieving aren't what you'd like them to be, bringing in outside help may be the right choice for you. (See the next section, "Finding Help When You Need It.") But regardless of which route you take, ultimately the plan—and its outcomes—will be yours alone.

In making a decision about whether or not to do it yourself, you should consider not only the cost (primarily in terms of staff time) that will be involved in the planning process, but also …

- **The nature of the plan.** A brand-new, organizational strategic plan will require higher-level competencies than a departmental plan. By the same token, updating an existing plan will be far less time-consuming and involved than developing a plan from scratch.

- **The skill levels of people in your organization (or who you otherwise have access to).** What level of knowledge or expertise in planning do you or others in your business have? Is that level of knowledge sufficient to move you through the process efficiently and effectively?

- **The culture of the organization.** Some businesses simply want to do it themselves. Only you can make that determination. And, ultimately, nobody understands your business better than you do.

- **The significance of the planning effort.** Developing a plan to provide some focus and direction to your small company, which is doing very well and does not have any significant changes on the horizon, might readily be done without outside assistance. A plan for a company that is struggling or that is interested in achieving significant growth might benefit from the expertise than an external resource could provide.

- **Potential lost opportunity costs.** For instance, while staff are involved in the strategic planning process, they will not be involved in other activities that may hold value to the business. The loss of that focus in some other area needs to be considered.

- **The need for a third-party facilitator or perspective.** If there are areas of significant disagreement in the business in terms of future direction, or if there is a sense that the perspective is too internally focused and could benefit from some external perspectives, it can be valuable to bring in a third party to help facilitate the process.

Finding Help When You Need It

For those companies that feel they could benefit from outside expertise in developing their strategic plan, there are ample resources available. A Google search for "strategic planning+consultant" turns up 2.8 million results! Clearly there are plenty of options to choose from. Those options may be available through large, well-known firms, smaller local firms, independent consultants, or even facilitators whose role would be to help manage meetings and team interactions.

The process of finding help involves the following steps:

1. **Determine what kind of help you need.** Are you looking for someone to guide you through the entire strategic planning process? Someone to help gather and review data and information? Someone to facilitate the process? Someone to assemble the information into a final product? Outline the tasks that you would want someone to perform and then prepare a written description of the project and your desired timetable.

2. **Assemble a list of potential firms and consultants to work with.** You can find names online, through local business resources such as the Chamber of Commerce or university business outreach departments, or through word-of-mouth recommendations from business colleagues.

BEST PRACTICES

When considering external candidates to assume the facilitator's role, it's a good idea to ask to observe a session the facilitator may be conducting with another company or group. This will give you a sense of the individual's personal style and personality in a group setting.

3. **Request proposals from these groups or individuals based on your project description and timetable.** Once proposals are received, you would proceed in much the same way you would when hiring an employee. You would evaluate the proposals against your requirements, select those that seem to represent the best fit, and schedule times to meet with potential consultants.

4. **Check references of previous clients.** This is a very important step! As you're checking the references that the firm gives you, consider asking these former clients if they know of other companies that have worked with the consultant you're considering.

As you evaluate the consultants you've selected, you will want to consider the following:

- Their strategic planning expertise

- Their experience with projects similar to yours

- Examples of successful projects they have completed in the past

- Their experience in your industry (this is not a deal breaker—but all else being equal, it can be a bonus)

Ultimately, your choice of a firm or individual to work with will be based both on their experience and ability to meet the requirements you've outlined as well as their fit with your company and those who will be involved in the planning process.

Once you're selected someone to help you with the process, you will create a contract outlining exactly what is to be done, by whom (the consultant or you), and by when. This is an important document that will not only help to guide the process but also to ensure that each person knows what is expected of him. The document should describe …

- The scope of the project

- The tasks to be done and who will do them

- The reporting process

- Desired outputs—written reports at certain time intervals, a final document, or a presentation.

- The time frame for the project

- Fees and payment schedule

Ultimately the decision of whether or not to use external resources should be based on consideration of both your internal expertise with planning and the cost of allocating staff time to the planning process versus having staff focused on other duties and priorities.

The Least You Need to Know

- The strategic planning time line and time frame will vary based on your business, industry, and how quickly change is occurring in your marketplace.

- Your company's fiscal year can be used as a starting point for developing your strategic planning schedule or calendar.

- The amount of time required for planning will vary for each organization or planning group, but can be aided through the use of a well-planned timetable.

- The costs involved in planning include the time of individuals involved as well as potential out-of-pocket expenses for consulting services, software, and supplies.

- It is possible to conduct the planning process yourself, particularly if members of the business have experience in planning.

- While strategic plans can be created using just internal resources, there are options and resources available for businesses that need outside assistance.

Building Blocks for Planning Success

In This Chapter

- Defining your strategic planning goal
- Creating ownership in the plan
- How to measure success
- A focus on getting things done
- Why communication is key

As you've seen, the strategic planning process requires a significant amount of time and effort for your business, your employees—and for you. You want to do everything you can to make sure that this effort is well spent and that the outcome serves to move your business forward to achieve positive results. To do this, there are some very important, foundational steps you should take that can help to ensure your planning efforts will be worthwhile.

It is no secret that many strategic plans go nowhere, and it's not surprising that business owners would be hesitant to invest time in a process that may not generate the result they're looking for. The problem doesn't generally lie with creating the plan—it lies with implementing the plan. In this chapter, we'll take a look at some very important, foundational must-do's that can make the difference between a plan that sits on a shelf collecting dust and a plan that drives positive and meaningful business performance.

Clarifying Your Strategic Planning Goal

The first step in ensuring success for your strategic planning efforts is defining your strategic planning goal. It seems simple, but too many skip this step or don't give it the attention it deserves. Your goal should be clear, measurable, and objective—something that, when the planning process is over, two independent observers could look back on it and say: "Yes, we achieved it," or "No, we didn't." You don't want to leave anything to chance.

All members of your planning team should have the same endpoint in mind. Gaining *consensus* on this endpoint and making sure that it is clearly stated is critical. In addition to being measurable and agreed upon, your strategic planning goal should be achievable. You don't want to assign yourself a task that cannot be achieved. Early failure will only serve to diminish the effectiveness of future planning efforts. So be specific, be measurable, and gain consensus but, above all, be realistic.

DEFINITION

Consensus means general agreement among a group. It does not mean unanimous agreement, which is often misunderstood. The challenge for teams is determining how they will define *general agreement*.

Actionable Goals

Here are some examples of actual strategic planning goals for various types of strategic planning efforts:

- To blend the best of old and new together in a vision for our future.

- To become a more engaged and integrated campus.

- To renew our focus on hospitality.

- To make our website a complete, interactive communication tool.

- To increase our revenue sources.

- To increase employee and company productivity.

Not all of these are good strategic planning goals. In fact, they are presented in order from least effective to most effective. Consider the first goal: "To blend the best of old and new together in a vision for our future." If you were a member of this planning team, what would this goal mean to you? How would you know if your company had been effective in meeting this goal? On the other hand, "To increase employee and company productivity" is a goal that can be objectively evaluated—each member of the planning team—and, in fact, each member of the business—could say whether or not this goal had been reached. This assumes, of course, that the company has a means of measuring and reporting employee and company productivity.

The key is that your strategic planning goal—whether for your company, a particular effort (like a marketing planning effort), or a department—have a measurable element to it so that you, and everyone else, will know when the goal has been met. (See the section "Establishing Measures of Success" later in this chapter.) Importantly, your strategic planning goal should not be to have a plan. Surprisingly enough, that does often seem to be the focus of many strategic planning efforts. The goal, though, should be related to some specific, relevant outcome that will impact the success of the business.

Questions to Drive the Planning Process

To help determine your goal, it's important to focus on what you ultimately hope to achieve. What's the endpoint? What will success look like? There are three vital questions that must begin the strategic planning process:

- What is our goal with this strategic planning process?
- Why are we conducting this planning process?
- How will we hold people accountable to ensure success?

It is not enough to simply say, "We need to develop a marketing plan for product XYZ," or "We need to develop a strategic plan for the HR department." What does that mean? What are the specific deliverables the team will be accountable for and what is the target date for producing those deliverables?

It is likely that there will be initial disagreement on the answers to these questions. Gather any group of people in your organization around a particular task, ask them to independently answer these questions, and you're likely to come up with as many answers as there are people in the room.

For instance, suppose you start with question number one: "What is our goal with this strategic planning process?" There are several possibilities.

- For an organizational strategic plan, the goal might be "to establish an initial framework for a strategic planning process that can be conducted on an annual basis to guide the budget development process and the development of supporting department plans."
- Other goals might be "to quantify staffing needs" or "to prioritize areas of focus for the year."

- For a strategic marketing plan, the goal might be "to identify specific markets that we will pursue and communication mechanisms that will be used to achieve specific, measurable sales goals."

- Other goals might be "to identify products to be discontinued," or "to determine how we could outsource our communication activities."

MISSTEPS

Unless specifically addressed, there is a good chance that multiple goals exist for the outcome of the planning process. At the outset, it is a good idea to make sure that all involved have reached consensus on what the intended outcome will be.

No one can tell you what your goal is or should be, and that can be part of the challenge. Ultimately, though, your goal is your goal. There are no right or wrong answers to what it should be. The goal that you come up with is likely to be different from the goal that another company very similar to yours would come up with. This is complicated by the fact that, even within your company, people may have different objectives for wanting to engage in the strategic planning process. When it comes to clearly defining your strategic planning goal, the focus shouldn't be so much on coming up with the right goal—there really is no such thing. The focus should be on ensuring that everybody going into the process has the same expectations about what the planning process is intended to achieve. Quite simply, you need to provide an answer—an honest answer—to the question "Why are we doing this?" An honest answer to this question is an important first step toward achieving ownership and commitment from those involved in both developing and implementing the plan.

Creating Ownership and Commitment

We have already seen that one of the dangers of creating a strategic plan is that it becomes little more than a historical document. Creating ownership in the plan and committing to implementing the plan from the very outset of the planning process can help to ensure that this doesn't happen.

Large organizations are most likely to fall prey to this issue because, very often, the planning process takes place at the very top of the organization, with little or no involvement from employees throughout the organization. No involvement equals no commitment. Large organizations, in fact, often suffer from internal politics and in-fighting that can slow or even halt the strategic planning process.

Commitment to the Planning Process

For many companies, strategic planning becomes little more than an exercise that is done on a regular basis that most of those participants fail to see the value in. For small business owners wishing to use strategic planning as a tool to achieve positive business results, creating enthusiasm and commitment to the process is key. Initially, the owner of the plan—we'll assume this is the business owner—needs to create commitment to the planning process itself. Members of the planning team and the organization at large need to believe that going through the planning process will be a valuable use of time. Even if the business owner of your organization isn't directly involved in the strategic planning process, it's important that all staff members see the business owner's commitment to the process.

Let's say that you're the business owner. You could just say, "This is what we're going to do—my way or the highway." But that is rarely the way to generate enthusiasm and commitment to anything. Your first step should be to have discussions with those you feel will be key to this process to determine their opinions about strategic planning—and, perhaps, their misperceptions. You're likely to find that you learn a lot in the process of gathering this feedback. Ultimately, what you're looking for is agreement that it makes sense for your company to engage in strategic planning and that the time it takes will be worth the effort in terms of benefits gained.

Commitment to Implementation

Beyond agreement that the planning effort itself is valuable, there must also be owner-ship and commitment to implement the plan. Those in the company who will play key roles in the process need to know who they are, understand the value of their contri-butions, and agree—explicitly—to uphold their commitment and meet their deadlines.

That, however, is easier said than done. What happens in many organizations is that the best intentions bump up against reality. Other things come up and divert attention from developing a plan while staff members focus on doing their jobs. Now doing their jobs is certainly a necessary activity and it's easy to see how attention can get diverted from planning to doing. But that's the crux of the problem. What are they doing? How does what they're doing contribute to or detract from the direction the company should be heading? It's impossible to tell without a focused planning effort.

Generally, when a company starts a strategic planning effort those involved start with the best of intentions. But as other priorities emerge, fires need to be put out, or inertia sets in, even the best planning efforts can fall by the wayside. Here's what it takes to minimize the risks that this will happen:

- A strong champion for the effort—preferably the business owner or CEO. The closer this individual is to the top of the organization, the better.

- A compelling reason to plan. The leader of the effort needs to clearly convey to the planning team and employees at large how the planning effort will benefit the company—and them.

- Clear—and clearly communicated—expectations.

- Explicit assignments. Individuals need to know that they, specifically, have responsibilities for achieving certain tasks.

- Consequences. Those who demonstrate their commitment and achieve results should be recognized—as should those who don't. All those involved in the effort need to be held accountable for what they do and don't do.

BEST PRACTICES

The commitment of the business owner or senior leader—and, in fact, all senior leaders—to the strategic planning effort needs to be visible. How do senior leaders demonstrate commitment? Through their words but also through their actions. They lead by example.

Here's an example. A small shipping company engaged in a strategic planning effort with the goal of evaluating the current organizational structure with an eye toward a change of some sort. The five managers in the company were involved in the planning process. Two of these managers felt very threatened by the process and what the impact might be on their own positions. Consequently, as they went about their daily work they criticized the process, questioned the value of the time spent in the planning sessions, and generally undermined the process at every step of the way. Shockingly, although the CEO was well aware of what these two were doing, he did nothing. Nothing is also what happened with the plan.

As this example shows, sometimes plans can be derailed during the planning process. It is more common, though, for plans to fail after the planning process is complete. The plan is created and assignments may be made, but lack of follow-through and accountability lead to inertia and inactivity. If you work with your business to create a plan and then never refer to that plan again, what kind of message are you sending?

Establishing Measures of Success

It's a good idea to establish measures of success for the planning process at the outset. This should not involve simply setting a target date for completion of the plan and regular review sessions for the planning team. The plan must not become just a document—the plan is not the outcome, the planning process is the outcome. Measures of success should focus on how the planning process will be used to monitor performance.

One woman who has been involved in a number of strategic planning sessions over the course of her career, all in very large organizations, says that she can think of none that she would call a success. While, in each case, the process resulted in a completed plan, she says that the plans were never fully implemented. Each subsequent planning cycle created a new set of priorities and actions, but the planning process never included a thorough review of results achieved. To her, this represented a failure for the planning process.

A quality manager at a technology firm recalls the planning process her company engaged in prior to and after becoming involved in the *Malcolm Baldrige National Quality Award* process. Before participating in the program, she says, planning was more of an exercise that was focused on the creation of the plan. The Baldrige process helped the company focus more on measurable outcomes and realize that the plan was simply a tool to help achieve those outcomes.

 DEFINITION

The **Malcolm Baldrige National Quality Award** is a government program that helps companies focus on achieving measurable business results by focusing on six process areas (leadership, strategic planning, customer focus, measurement, workforce focus, and process management) through a series of specific criteria-based questions.

Focusing on Execution

It is sad but true that far too many planning efforts fail. They fail for various reasons, but primary among them is failure to execute the plan. Now there may be times during the strategic planning process when you might feel like executing somebody, but that's not what we're talking about here! Execution, from a strategic planning standpoint, means getting things done.

One employee at a communication firm says: "You can have a good planning session, a good plan, and an all-star team, but if you can't execute then it's all for naught." And, he adds, you can also execute miserably. "Everyone thinks that every plan they come up with is going to be a success—they're not. Successful execution is the hardest part of the process."

He's right. Sometimes people think that the main challenge of strategic planning will be coming up with ideas, but that's far from the truth. The trouble that most companies face in terms of execution is not having too few ideas. In fact, the reverse is true—they have too many! A strategic plan—when developed and implemented effectively—can be a salve for that particular problem by providing focus and direction. Ultimately, it is far better to develop an average plan that is well executed than an exceptional plan that goes nowhere. Strategic planning is not about good intentions.

Each year the Conference Board, an independent membership organization that delivers knowledge about management and the marketplace, conducts a study of key issues among top executives and, invariably, the issue of execution shows up in the front of the list. Business leaders recognize the importance—and the difficulty—of executing or, as Nike would say, "Just doing it." There are a number of reasons that plans fail to be executed. These include:

- There are inadequate resources—time, money, and talent—to achieve the plan.

- The plan is not well communicated—people don't know what's expected of them and, consequently, don't meet those expectations.

- The actions required to achieve the plan's strategies and tactics are not well defined.

- Accountabilities are not clear—no one knows who is doing what.

- The culture of the organization is not driven toward execution—there are no incentives or disincentives tied to achievement or non-achievement of the plan elements.

- Nobody is tracking whether or not the plan elements are being worked on or achieved.

- There is a lack of commitment, follow-through, and holding people accountable by the plan owner and business leaders.

Strategic plans lose their value when the strategies they outline are not implemented. A challenge that planners frequently encounter is tying the plan to action. A focus on execution should start during the planning phase, and the tone should be set from the top of the organization. The business owner or CEO must hold the organization accountable to work the plan; this means establishing regular periods for review, having meetings, and holding people accountable for completing their assigned tasks and achieving targeted results. Nothing less will lead to success.

A small educational services firm embarked on a strategic planning process, paying several thousand dollars for a consulting firm and software that was intended to manage the planning process. The planning team involved all of the managers from the small company, and they were each assigned specific aspects of the plan to be responsible for. For several months nothing happened—then the CEO decided to review a section of the plan each month at the management planning meeting. At first, the only notable result was that the online template began to be filled out each month. But as the CEO maintained a focus on deliverables and began to hold the managers accountable, progress started to be made. There is a saying that "What gets measured gets managed." Nowhere is this more true than with the implementation of a strategic plan. If nobody is paying attention, nothing will happen. The concerted focus of a CEO or team leader can make all of the difference in the world.

Communication Is Key!

When you first embark on your strategic planning effort, it's important to communicate to the entire company what you're doing and, most importantly, why you're doing it. What are the anticipated benefits for your company? How will employees know that these benefits have been achieved? What role will they be expected to play? How will they be kept informed of progress along the way? Will they have the opportunity for input, and how will they provide that input?

DID YOU KNOW?

Robert Kaplan and David Norton, renowned experts on strategy and the authors of *The Balanced Scorecard* (see Appendix B), say that their research indicates that 95 percent of a company's employees are not aware of, or don't understand, their company's strategy.

Plans should not be created in a vacuum. This is critical and leads directly back to earlier points about execution. When employees are aware of and engaged in the planning process, they are more likely to recognize how their efforts can impact success. They understand why planning takes place, how the plan impacts the business, and, in turn, how their own actions can make a difference. The planning process should not take on an aura of secrecy and exclusivity. It should be an open process that is widely and regularly communicated.

The following table offers some suggestions on the types of communication that might be used at various stages in the process and the frequency of communication. As you'll see, communicating frequently and through many channels is recommended.

Communicating the Strategic Planning Process

Stage	Communication Tools	Frequency
Planning to plan	Staff meeting; manager to employees; newsletter; e-mail	Once
Formation of team	Staff meeting; manager to employees; newsletter; e-mail	Once
Selection of team	Newsletter; e-mail members	Once
Planning process	Special planning newsletter	After each meeting
Plan approval	Company meeting; special newsletter update	Upon approval
Plan progress	Staff meeting, newsletter	Monthly updates

Having a formally defined communication process will help to keep the importance of communication front and center with the planning team and ensure that employees are kept informed over the planning process. What can happen otherwise is that team members may have the best intentions of communicating about plan progress but they may forget. Or one team member may share more or different information than another team member. Or team members may share information prematurely—before formal decisions have been made. A formal process can help to avoid these issues and ensure that employees are receiving regular, consistent, and accurate information about the planning process.

BEST PRACTICES

Give some thought to how input from employees who are not active participants in the planning process will be solicited and responded to. Maintaining an open process will help avoid a tendency for the planning process to feel secretive or exclusive.

Each company will come up with its own specific plan for communicating depending on the tools available, the size and structure of the company, and the planning process itself. What is important, though, is that there is a commitment made to communicate at the very outset. No plan will succeed if all of the people needed to contribute to the plan's success are not involved from the very beginning and don't receive ongoing communication about the plan's progress and results.

The Least You Need to Know

- The strategic planning effort should have a goal related not to the completion of the plan but to some measurable outcome that will benefit the business.
- Those who have been involved in planning efforts will confirm that planning is the easy part—execution is what is most difficult.
- Creating ownership in the plan is a critical step for ensuring accountability and plan execution.
- Success of any strategic planning efforts requires commitment, communication, and accountability.
- Strategic planning should be an open, inclusive process, not something that is done behind closed doors by the business leaders.

Selecting the Right Team

In This Chapter

- Pulling together the right people for your strategic planning effort
- Characteristics of an effective team leader
- The benefits a skilled facilitator can bring to the process
- Other important team roles
- How to keep members engaged

The team you pull together to help you develop and implement your strategic plan will play a critical role in ensuring that the plan is a living, breathing document that actually generates results. Team members should be carefully chosen and should clearly understand the expectations you have of them. They should also have a clear understanding of what their involvement will mean in terms of both time commitment and serving as a champion for the strategic planning effort with others in your business.

Each participant in the planning effort will have specific roles and tasks—this includes individual team members as well as the team leader, the facilitator, and the recorder. In this chapter, we'll take a look at the various roles, how to select team members, and some critical skills and tasks that must be performed to ensure a positive outcome.

Who Has the Information You Need?

When forming your planning team, your focus should be on the outcomes you hope to achieve. You will want to involve those people most likely to be able to help you achieve these outcomes. You don't want to overlook people whose perspectives will be critical, but neither do you want to involve people whose time might be better spent elsewhere.

Pulling in Your Internal Experts

In some cases, it will be obvious who you need to include as part of your planning team. If you're creating a marketing plan, for instance, and you have a marketing manager, you will want to have that person involved. But who else might have valuable perspectives? Well, perhaps one or more of your salespeople—their interactions with customers and prospects may provide important insights. Or someone from your accounting team—their knowledge of the costs and returns associated with marketing efforts might be useful. In addition to technical criteria that may help to identify participants, there are other more cultural issues you will want to consider:

- Whose support will you need to ensure that the plan is actually put into place and that results are achieved?

- Who has the potential of being a detractor to the plan if not involved?

- Who might have strong administrative or facilitation skills that would be helpful throughout the planning process?

- Who has expressed interest?

While the cost of staff time to be engaged in the planning process can be significant, it is generally best to be more inclusive than exclusive. Consider the cost to be an investment toward future success. Involving someone now who has strong interest and is likely to be able to positively contribute to results is better than overlooking that person and risking that they might feel alienated and less inclined to put forth effort later on.

BEST PRACTICES

When pulling in team members from other departments, make sure to gain the support of the employees' supervisors before asking the staff member to devote time to the planning process. It's a courtesy that can help to avoid resentment later.

Don't overlook contributors who may be new to the organization or in entry-level positions. One communication executive looking back on his career recalls the frustration of being left out of important strategic planning sessions that he felt he could have contributed to effectively. "It often seems that the people invited are at a senior level and may not, necessarily, be the best to provide good insights about customers and other operational issues. They're sometimes disconnected from the business and don't have the perspectives that frontline employees can bring about what's actually happening with the customer or the community."

Don't overlook those who may be perceived as potential detractors to or critics of the process, either. Sometimes these people can become your strongest allies! The old saying "Keep your friends close and your enemies closer" can certainly be true in this case. A woman charged with implementing a strategic plan for the introduction of a CRM (customer relationship management) system at a utility company chose a very vocal opponent of the project to be a member of the team. When asked why, she said: "I'm better off dealing with him now than dealing with him later. If he's part of the process all the way along, he's less likely to be a barrier later." That perspective is well-founded and should be a consideration as you select team participants.

Of course, another important consideration is the willingness of people to commit to the process, so it may require some arm-twisting along the way. Those who are initially in opposition, however, are often eventually eager to be part of the process.

When selecting team members, make sure that ...

- Key decision-makers are involved. You don't want the process to be held up because the members of the team don't feel comfortable making decisions and moving forward.

- All key stakeholder groups have been covered. These include those who will be most affected by the plan as well as those who will be most instrumental in implementing the plan.

- You have included someone who can facilitate the administrative aspects of the process—arranging meetings, keeping minutes, and so on.

Do You Need Outside Assistance?

As mentioned in Chapter 2, there are times when you may choose to call in outside expertise to be part of the planning process. Sometimes this can be to provide consultation on the strategic planning process itself, or it might be to provide facilitation skills. Some organizations also involve vendors or contractors that may be very involved with the company, familiar with its operations, and integral to its future success. Others involve key customers or community leaders.

The Team Leader and Facilitator

Two critical roles for your planning efforts are the roles of *team leader* and *facilitator*. The team leader should be the individual who has the highest level of ownership—or the most to lose or gain—through the process. For an organizational strategic plan, this would likely be the business owner, CEO, or highest-ranking official. For a strategic marketing plan, it would likely be the person in the highest-level marketing position. For a strategic department-level plan, it would be the department leader. For a project plan, it would be the person responsible for the project's success. The team leader must have subject matter expertise relative to the project.

The role of the facilitator, on the other hand, does not require subject matter expertise related to the strategic planning goal. Instead, the facilitator should be somebody who is skilled at leading a group, eliciting and managing input, and dealing with conflict.

> **DEFINITION**
>
> The **team leader** is the person who is ultimately responsible for the successful completion, and often implementation, of the plan. The **facilitator** is an individual who is responsible for leading a meeting or discussion. The role of the facilitator is to move the discussion forward; the facilitator is not an active participant in the discussion.

Sometimes these roles are assumed by a single person. Ideally, though, the roles should be separate. When the same person serves in both roles, there is no neutral party to facilitate situations where there may be disagreement among team members or, particularly, between the team leader and team members.

The Role of the Team Leader

The role of the team leader is to champion the strategic planning effort and, ultimately, to own the process and the outcome. The team leader should be the person who will own the plan. Business owners or CEOs often try to avoid this role because it may seem too administrative and time-consuming; however, if the business owner or CEO is the one who will be driving the plan toward completion, this person needs to lead the process.

In Chapter 3 you learned about the balance between planning and execution—planning is, believe it or not, the easy part. Execution is the most difficult part of the process and the reason that many planning efforts fail. They fail because after the plan is developed, nothing happens. Literally. That may seem difficult to believe, but it is true in many organizations. To improve the odds that something will happen, it helps to have the natural owner of the plan lead the process. This doesn't mean that if the business owner is also the owner of the plan he or she can't call upon others for assistance. The key, though, is that the business owner be visibly engaged in and committed to the process. That will go a long way toward ensuring commitment and engagement of the others involved in the planning process and in the actual implementation of the plan.

The team leader is a critical position and does exactly what the title suggests—leads the process. An effective team leader will lead an effective process and improve the odds that the plan will be well executed—although the team leader will need to continue to lead the process well after the planning sessions have ended.

Clear Vision

Most importantly, an effective team leader will have a clear vision of what needs to be accomplished and why. It is the team leader who will choose the team members to work on the strategic planning process, clarify for them what the goal and outcome of the process will be, engage them in the process to gain their commitment and support, and, ultimately, lead them through the successful implementation of the strategic plan.

Having a clear vision of what you want to achieve through the strategic planning process can benefit from having a good understanding of what others may want. Engaging in conversation with key players prior to declaring your ultimate vision can help to avoid changing direction later.

MISSTEPS

A weak team leader will be ineffective and doom the success of the planning process. In a situation where the natural person to lead the effort lacks strong leadership skills, it's a good idea to assign a co-leader who has those skills.

Strong Management Skills

The role of the team leader in a strategic planning process is a critical one. It's a big task and one that many are not formally trained in. However, the same skills required of effective managers come into play here. These include:

- The ability to articulate a clear vision.

- The ability to demonstrate how this vision will positively impact participants.

- Visible enthusiasm and support for the process.

- A willingness to be a leader—not a dictator. Effective leaders are able to capitalize on the inputs of the team rather than simply assert their will.

- Strong communication skills.
- The ability to motivate and hold people accountable.

Looking back over his years of participating in strategic planning processes, one team member says that the best leaders ask, "What do you recommend, why, and how will you implement?" The worst, he says, are "autocratic control freaks." They tend to give orders: "These are my strategies. This is what I want. I have decided and you will do it my way, or else." Not a great way to gain support and commitment from team members!

Consistent Direction

The team leader must also be consistent. In the best of all worlds, the strategic planning process will proceed from a clear mission through conclusion without any changes in direction along the way. Changes in direction can quickly result in lost credibility for the team leader, lack of trust in the process, and lost commitment among team members. This is not to say that the team leader should not be prepared to change course if absolutely necessary. However, these changes should be related to events outside the control of the leader, not due to lack of preparation up front.

Open Mind

It's important that the team leader have an open mind and that he or she creates an environment for the planning process where participants believe they can be honest and straightforward.

One strategic planning participant says, "I've been on teams where the team leader will say 'Let's be open and honest—let's be critical and take a really critical look at our operations," but then will react negatively or defensively to any critical input given. If you're going to say you want open and honest feedback, you have to really prove to the team that you can handle open and honest feedback."

Another participant on a strategic planning team for an investor-owned utility says, "I'm on a team right now where the president and CEO is really a tough cookie. At the first meeting she said 'I want this to be different—I want people to come and collaborate and work together.' She said all of the right things, but it just hasn't worked out that way. She just beats people down—it's her way or the highway—and it's not collaborative. Actions speak louder than words."

Being authentic, being inclusive, and being open to hearing information that may be negative, challenging, or threatening is critical to being successful in the role of the team leader in a strategic planning process.

The Role of the Facilitator

While the boss can, and sometimes should, serve in the team leader role, the boss should not serve as the facilitator of the planning process. The dictionary definition of facilitate is "to make easy or easier," and that is exactly what the strategic planning facilitator is charged with doing. The facilitator has three broad objectives when facilitating the strategic planning process:

1. Moving the group toward the pre-identified outcome.

2. Initiating and sustaining an efficient process that encourages collaboration and interaction between all participants.

3. Involving and showing positive appreciation for the contributions of all participants.

The facilitator should typically not be the team leader or the boss of a significant number of other people involved in the strategic planning process. This is, in fact, the part of the strategic planning process that is most often outsourced to someone that is not part of the company or process. The reason for this is that the process will benefit from an unbiased facilitator who has no strong opinions about the process, the company, or the outcomes. In fact, it is not even necessary for a facilitator to have subject matter expertise about the issue the plan will address. The facilitator of a strategic marketing planning process, for instance, does not need to have expertise or background in marketing.

What a facilitator must have is the ability to lead a group of people through a series of discussions that may involve sensitive issues, disagreement, and conflict. The facilitator must be dispassionate in managing sometimes passionate exchanges of information and opinion and have the ability to channel these strong emotions into productive problem-solving.

You may want to use an outside facilitator if:

- This is your first strategic planning process and nobody within your business has had experience with strategic planning.

- You have attempted to conduct strategic planning processes before, but these efforts have not been successful.

- The issue you are dealing with has the potential to create significant disagreement and tension and you have neither anyone internally who could skillfully handle that tension nor anyone internally who does not also have strong opinions about the issue.

- Nobody internally is interested in, or has the time to commit to, facilitating the strategic planning process.

Key Facilitation Skills

Whether selecting someone from within or turning to someone outside the organization to facilitate the process, there are some key skills you should look for. Skilled facilitators will have knowledge and expertise with various types of group processes and facilitation tools (see Chapter 5) and will be able to effectively use these tools to move the process along. Strong facilitation skills are used in many settings other than strategic planning. For instance, sales, training, mediation, and even hostage negotiation have these skills in common:

- The ability to remain calm and unflappable under pressure.

- Exceptional communication skills, including the ability to listen carefully and intently to inputs, to draw out comments from quieter participants, and to deflect the inputs from overbearing participants.

- The ability to respond non-defensively to angry, defensive, or challenging participants.

- A solid understanding of group process and the ability to apply leadership, team development, and facilitation concepts to a live situation.

- Good organizational skills and the ability to move the planning process forward.

- The ability to be flexible, when necessary, to ensure that important points and inputs are covered.

In addition, the facilitator in a strategic planning setting should have experience with strategic planning—he or she should know the steps involved in the process, understand the intended outcome, and have familiarity and experience with the various issues and interactions that would be unique to this type of interpersonal setting. An effective facilitator will lead a group of people through a process toward an agreed-upon goal by encouraging participation, involvement, and commitment from all participants.

In larger organizations it may be possible to find someone inside the organization who is far enough removed from the issues involved in the planning process, and who has the appropriate interpersonal and facilitation skills to manage the process, to serve in this role. In smaller organizations this can be difficult because there are fewer people to choose from, and it is less likely that these facilitation skills will be present. Additionally, it is more likely that internal participants will have opinions, background, and baggage that they bring with them to the process.

MISSTEPS

One of the important elements of effective strategic planning is that participants feel free to raise issues, question the status quo, and challenge strong beliefs in an open environment. If the facilitator is someone who is known to have strong opinions on certain issues, participants may be less likely to voice their true thoughts. This can occur regardless of whether the facilitator is considered to be an opinionated or a very accommodating individual.

Facilitation Tasks

The responsibilities of the facilitator will include following an agenda, keeping the group on track, clarifying and summarizing points made, managing individual personalities and conflict, facilitating teambuilding, outlining next steps, and ensuring follow-up. The facilitator will work closely with the team leader, who will be establishing the agenda and providing feedback on how the process is going and what changes, if any, need to be made.

At the outset, it will be important for the facilitator to work with the planning group to establish some ground rules that will help to direct the session. Some important ground rules that will serve as a starting point are:

- Everyone should participate.

- Everyone will be given an opportunity to speak.

- Feel free to build or expand on the ideas of others.

- Don't edit yourself. Even if an idea seems too expensive, too far-fetched, or too complicated, get it out there!

- The session is a brainstorming session—ideas should be shared but not debated.

In addition to these ground rules, the facilitator should ask the team if they have any additional rules they would like to guide the discussion. These might include such things as:

- Starting and ending on time.

- Hats are left at the door—meaning no individual's input is more important than another, regardless of formal title.

The facilitator will work closely with and take direction from the team leader and will support the team leader in helping to move the process forward efficiently.

Other Team Roles

The team leader and facilitator roles are the most critical in the strategic planning process, but other roles have value as well. These include team members, ad hoc members (those who may participate on an as-needed basis), and the recorder.

Team Members

Team members will be the workhorses of the strategic planning effort, during both the planning process and implementation. The importance of their roles and commitment to the process should be made clear to them at the outset. All team leaders have had experiences with team members who want to be part of the process but who aren't committed to actually doing anything. When team members are asked to be part of the planning effort, they should be informed that:

- They have been chosen because of their ability to provide insight and input in some specific way.

- Their agreement to participate requires that they be committed to attend all meetings, complete any pre-work for those meetings, and be active participants during each meeting.

- They will be supportive of the planning effort outside of meetings, raising any concerns they have with the team, not with other non-participants.

- Their honest input is required, but this input should be grounded in facts and data, not just personal opinion.

Being explicit with these expectations at the outset can help to avoid breakdowns later. As the planning process moves forward, the team leader and facilitator should continue to reinforce these expectations—and be willing to provide course correction, as necessary, along the way. Team members who prove to be unable or unwilling to fulfill these expectations should be removed from the process.

Ad Hoc Members

Participation in the planning process represents a cost for your company, so you want to make sure that you're including those people who are most critical to the process. There may be other people who have input to offer in less-critical areas that you may wish to call upon on an ad hoc basis. They may not be invited to every meeting, but their input and expertise may be useful during certain parts of the process. Ad hoc members should be expected to follow the same guidelines as permanent team members in terms of the expectation for their participation and their support of the effort with others in the company.

The Recorder

The activities of the planning process should be documented by a recorder—somebody whose primary responsibility will be to document the activities of the meetings. One woman who has been involved in numerous design and planning meetings over the years says that one thing that tends to trip up the process more than anything else is the notion that the facilitator or team leader can also take on responsibility for being the note-taker, or recorder, for the meetings.

The team leader who takes on the responsibility for taking notes is in a precarious position. There is a certain amount of power that comes along with being the recorder—after all, you document what has occurred. In fact, one vice president at a health-care organization admitted to one of his team members that he liked to be the recorder because of the control it gave him. While there may be some truth to this, it is not a good way to gain the trust of team members. Team leaders have plenty of important responsibilities related to the planning process—taking notes should not be one of them.

Being a good facilitator requires the full attention of the person in that role. If that attention is divided by trying to record ideas, they can quickly lose focus. Facilitators may be tempted to take on recordkeeping responsibilities to expedite the recording of the minutes, but it is best to assign this task to someone else.

BEST PRACTICES

While the facilitator should not serve in the role of recorder, this doesn't mean that the facilitator should not make good use of white boards and other tools to help facilitate the communication of ideas during the planning sessions. This does not, however, take the place of note-taking by the recorder.

The recorder's responsibility will be to ensure that the ideas and inputs of the group are not lost. They will follow the flow of the meeting and ensure that important details are captured, documented, and, later, distributed to members of the team and other interested parties.

When the Boss Is Involved

There is another important role that has the potential to either positively or negatively impact the planning process—the role of the boss. Even though the boss may say—and may truly feel—that he or she is unbiased and open to hearing honest, open inputs from team members, there is always the tendency for participants to defer to the boss. This may be observed through quick support of the boss's ideas or through quickly backing down on an issue that the boss disagrees with.

As one strategic planning consultant notes, "One challenge that I have experienced during client engagements is the natural reserve that some staff display in front of company leaders. One or two unfortunate comments could lead to quite a freeze in the room."

This, again, is where the facilitator can plan a key role. A strong facilitator will be alert to these incidents and can call a break in the meeting, as necessary, to coach and counsel the boss, as appropriate. A facilitator who works with companies often on strategic planning initiatives says, "One of the most frequently encountered hurdles is to overcome the reluctance to be perceived as foolish in front of the CEO or boss." To help minimize this, the facilitator clarifies the role of the CEO or boss to indicate what he or she can and cannot do. The CEO or boss can:

* Challenge the team's thought process.

* Advise the team of changes or challenges they may not have been aware of or may not have considered.

* Provide the necessary resources to accomplish the plan.

* Obtain a commitment from the team to achieve the plan.

But the CEO or boss may not:

- Arbitrarily or independently make changes to the plan.

- Withhold the resources necessary to complete the plan.

These commitments are obtained up front, before the planning process begins.

Keeping Team Members Engaged

Throughout the planning process, both the team leader and facilitator should be focused on ensuring the free flow of ideas and communication among group members. In recalling her experiences with various team leaders during strategic planning processes, one woman in the construction industry says, "The most effective team leaders I have worked with were very knowledgeable but had the ability to participate in a discussion without imposing their own opinions. The most frustrating team leaders were recorders who did not inspire creative thinking—these are followed closely by the know-it-alls who only wanted the end result to represent their ideas."

MISSTEPS

Cancelling or rescheduling meetings too often can lead to disengagement among team members. Develop a set schedule for meetings and stick to it.

Team leaders and facilitators can engage team members through thought-provoking questions and what-if scenarios. They can take multiple ideas and create concise statements that reflect the collective input of the team. They focus on team, rather than individual, contributions while still recognizing individual efforts. The woman in the construction industry says, "One of the best team leaders I've ever worked with had everyone thinking way out of the box. We actually talked about flying saucers! Yet our strategic plan, at the end, came back to Earth with goals that challenged us to incorporate change without abandoning reality or our identity."

At the conclusion of an effective strategic planning process, the group will feel exhausted yet exhilarated. At the conclusion of an ineffective process, the group will feel frustrated and fatigued.

A successful strategic planning process requires a fully functioning team. Keeping the team on track, engaged, and committed to working together effectively to achieve the strategic planning goal requires a combination of administrative and interpersonal skills that we will review in the next chapter.

The Least You Need to Know

- While the team leader has an important role, the facilitator is the most critical player in the strategic planning process.
- Team members should be carefully selected based on a balance between the knowledge and insights they can contribute and the value of their time.
- The team leader's consistent vision for the work of the group ensures focus and commitment.
- The involvement of the boss in a strategic planning effort is often unavoidable, but it must be managed by the facilitator to ensure open and honest input from all team members.
- Team members can be kept engaged through free-flowing communication and openness to new ideas and differing opinions.

Pulling the Team Together

In This Chapter

- Meeting times, making assignments, and other details
- Helpful facilitation tools to generate input and manage conflict
- Effectively managing the stages of team development
- Managing changes in the team

The success of your strategic planning effort depends on the skills, abilities, and commitment of your team members. Most importantly, as you saw in Chapter 4, success depends on the abilities of the team leader and facilitator. In this chapter, we'll take a look at the administrative and interpersonal issues that must be addressed to ensure the effective functioning of the planning team and a successful planning outcome.

Administrative Issues

There is a great deal of administrative work involved in a strategic planning initiative. That work involves communicating with team members, coordinating meetings and schedules, organizing meeting activities, and creating and managing documents that team members need prior to meetings and that are created during meetings. These administrative tasks may often be assigned to the same individual who will be serving as the recorder for the meeting. If they are not, it should be made clear who will be responsible for these tasks, and processes should be put in place so that the team can be assured that these important details will be handled effectively.

Setting a Meeting Schedule

Initially the group will need to decide when, where, and how often it would like to meet. These decisions will be based on the time line developed for the completion of the planning process (see Chapter 2), the competing priorities of the team members, and the availability of meeting space. This can be a pivotal point where the team leader can set the tone for the importance of these meetings.

Let's assume the team leader is the business owner. She has selected a group of individuals who she has asked to serve on the team, and she's called them together for an initial meeting to discuss next steps, including the meeting schedule. The following discussion is one that is likely to occur among the 12 people that have been chosen to participate in this process:

> I won't be able to make meetings on Mondays—that's when I file the XYZ report.

> I won't be able to meet on Friday afternoons; I leave early on Fridays.

> June is out for me—I'll be on vacation.

The team leader needs to determine—and communicate—where the strategic planning process falls in line with other priorities, both personal and professional. If she falls on the side of allowing most everything else to take precedence, that sends one message. If she falls on the side of not allowing anything to interfere with the strategic planning priority, it sends an entirely different message. Where your particular planning effort lies along this continuum sends a clear and important message to participants. There are no right or wrong answers—it will depend on the culture of your organization. It is important, though, that you recognize that taking an attitude that is too lax can minimize the importance and urgency of the process.

Establishing a standing meeting day, time, length, and place can help to minimize these conflicts. Ask all team members to put the dates on their calendars as firm and establish the expectation that they be there.

Considerations about the location of the meeting are also important and will, again, depend on the company culture and environment. A small company with open spaces and a lot of activity can be a challenging environment for holding a meeting where participants' full attention is important. On the other hand, using an off-site meeting space can raise costs and require more time for travel between work and the meeting site.

It's up to the team leader to set the stage for the sanctity of these meetings. If held on site, will the team leader require that participants turn off phones and pagers? How will that impact the ability to deal with other responsibilities? With customer interactions?

Making Assignments

In smaller companies, where the business owner is everybody's boss, making assignments is clear-cut: the owner makes the assignments. In larger companies, where managers and supervisors come into play and may not be part of the planning process, conflicts can arise when strategic planning activities interfere with other job responsibilities.

It's important at the outset to address these issues. This again will mean that the team leader or business owner will need to make a decision about the priority of the strategic planning activities compared to other activities and provide direction to team members and their supervisors or managers about which take precedence. It may also be necessary to establish some process for navigating conflicts that may arise and create concerns as the process moves along.

MISSTEPS

Failing to take steps to hold team members accountable for their assignments may mean that work doesn't get done. Include assignments in the agenda and minute items to ensure that those responsible for getting tasks done will feel a sense of accountability.

Again, the team leader plays a pivotal role here and sends messages—through words and actions—that impact that all-important stage of execution. If team members begin to get the impression that just about anything else can come before strategic planning activities, the chances that the plan's development—and implementation—will be successfully executed are definitely impacted.

Sharing Input Outside of Meetings

The majority of the work of the team will take place during team meetings. However, there will also be work that needs to take place outside of these meetings—for example, reading materials that will be used as input to discussions or finding the answers to questions raised during a meeting. There are some important considerations to be addressed here:

- There should be a clear expectations established at the outset that team members will be held accountable to complete outside work on time so that they are prepared to contribute during meetings.

- There should also be a clear distinction between the work of individuals and the work of the team. In other words, it is perfectly appropriate for the sales manager to gather sales data to report back to the team at a team meeting; however, it is not appropriate for the sales manager, the team leader, and another team member to discuss strategy as a subgroup separate from the overall team.

- There should be agreement on what process will be used to communicate the work and progress of the team to the rest of the organization and what role individual team members will play in that process.

While the planning process should not develop an aura of secrecy or exclusiveness, it is also important to avoid inadvertently sending mixed or inaccurate messages back to the rest of the company through the actions of individual team members. A team member who shares information based on his or her own perspectives before formal communication is shared by the team leader may be missing—or misinterpreting—key points, which results in confusion or, in some cases, unnecessary concern.

These are all important issues that must be considered and addressed before the team begins its work.

Team Facilitation Tools

I've already discussed in Chapter 4 the importance of the facilitator role and the value of having a strong and experienced facilitator who can effectively guide the group through the planning process. Skilled facilitators are excellent communicators and interact with others effectively—but they interact with purpose. There are a variety of tools that facilitators use to help a group through the work of planning. Let's take a look at these tools, their purpose, and when and how they can most effectively be used.

Brainstorming

Brainstorming is probably one of the most common team facilitation tools, and most people have been involved in a brainstorming session. It is a technique that has been used since the 1950s to encourage the generation of creative ideas. The concept seems easy enough—consider a particular topic or issue and throw out ideas around that issue.

The idea behind brainstorming is that it separates two central problem-solving activities—having ideas and testing ideas. By focusing on generating ideas, the thinking goes, people are more likely to come up with surprising and fresh thoughts and perspectives.

BEST PRACTICES

Anything goes in a brainstorming session—the idea is that when our minds are left to think freely without the constraints of worrying about whether our ideas are good or bad, the great ideas will readily emerge. Be bold!

While that idea is sound, it can be difficult to achieve. Brainstorming is used to generate and build upon ideas from a variety of perspectives—that is its value. Unfortunately, in most brainstorming sessions, more time is spent evaluating and critiquing the ideas than coming up with new ones. Consequently, the primary role of the facilitator in a brainstorming session is to keep the ideas flowing and to keep participants from engaging in more critique than creation.

This means that as ideas are raised and generated, the facilitator should caution participants from saying things like "That won't work!," as well as things like "Great idea!" There really should be no evaluation involved—positive or negative—during the brainstorming process. In fact, the facilitator can be most effective by laughing at and encouraging even the craziest of ideas and squelching those who attempt to challenge or critique ideas by saying something like, "Remember, no critiquing—let's come up with more ideas!" To brainstorm most effectively, facilitators should …

- Have a very narrowly defined and specific focus. For instance: "We're going to brainstorm new product ideas," or "We're going to brainstorm new ways of attracting employees."

- Go for quantity, not quality. This can be a good way to keep the focus on idea generation, not discussion. Having a specific number in mind can also help to focus on rapidly coming up with ideas. "In the next 30 minutes, let's come up with 100 ways we could communicate about our strategic planning process to our employees."

- Encourage participation from all. Be mindful of those who haven't contributed as well as those who seem to dominate. Call upon the quieter participants to draw them out.

- When energy and ideas begin to wane, focus on a few key points and ask participants to build on those.

• Capture everything. Often brainstorming inputs are captured on flip chart paper or a whiteboard. This is something the facilitator could do, but it may also be helpful to call upon the planning team's recorder as a backup to make sure all inputs are captured effectively.

Only after the fresh ideas of the group have been exhausted should the process turn toward evaluating those ideas. At this point the group can discuss criteria to be used in deciding how to narrow the list. These might include such things as cost, use of existing resources, or time required to implement. Once criteria are established, the group can continue to narrow the list to come up with the top items. One common technique for doing this is nominal ranking, which I'll discuss in more detail in Chapter 12.

Mind-Mapping

Mind-mapping is a form of brainstorming popularized by Tony Buzan, an author and educational consultant, in the 1970s. Mindmaps incorporate a visual component that allows participants to actually see how one concept branches off from another. Mind-mapping can be used to help branch off additional ideas from the top items generated from the brainstorming process.

One of the benefits of mind-mapping is that, due to its visual nature, it can help participants remember and visualize the ideas generated and their relationship to each other much more easily than a long list of ideas. The value of mindmaps is that they depict not only facts, but the structure of a topic of the relative value of related points.

The process starts with an initial question or problem, which is written in the center of a large piece of paper, on a whiteboard, or—most recently—on a computer using mind-mapping software and projected so the entire group can see the output.

BEST PRACTICES

Software applications like mindomo.com, mindmeister.com, and mindgenius.com can be used to easily create mindmaps. Individuals can also benefit from the use of mind-mapping to brainstorm on their own!

In a traditional mind-mapping session, the facilitator would write the title of the issue being explored in the center of a page and draw a circle around it. The initial related items to the main point would then be indicated on the map by drawing a line out from the circle and labeling it. Subpoints would be indicated by drawing additional lines out from those original lines. Lines can continue to be added at any level of the diagram depending on whether the idea relates directly back to the original question, or whether it is related to a subpoint or sub-subpoint. To keep it simple and not overly clutter the page, single words or simple phrases should be used. Symbols or drawings can also be used to illustrate points and ideas.

Multi-Voting

Multi-voting is a great alternative to traditional majority rule voting and can be especially effective in strategic planning settings where a number of people are involved and where votes may be cast over a variety of options.

Let's consider an example. Suppose we have 12 people participating in our strategic planning process and we're voting on two options. Four people vote for Option #1 and eight people vote for Option #2. It's pretty clear that there is a preference and we're fairly comfortable selecting Option #2. But suppose there are four options on the table and the vote breaks down like this:

- Option #1 - 2
- Option #2 - 3
- Option #3 - 4
- Option #4 - 3

Option #3 has a slim margin, but if we were to select that option there would be 8 of the 12 participants whose preference was not chosen.

When group consensus is important, multi-voting can be used to more effectively narrow down a list of options to the one that is preferred by the majority. Here's how it works:

1. Each participant receives a number of votes to be cast. To determine the number to assign, divide the number of total options by three. So, if there are 15 options, each participant would receive 5 votes.

2. Participants are given sticky dots or sticky notes to indicate their preferences.

3. Participants vote simultaneously. So if there is a list of the options on a flip chart, participants come up to the flip chart and begin casting their votes. Participants can use all of their votes on a single item if they choose, or divide their votes among two or more items.

4. Those options receiving the highest number of votes rise to the top of the list.

The Delphi Method

In the voting methods just described, it's easy for one member of a group to be influenced by one or more members of the group. This tendency often leads to groupthink, which I discussed in Chapter 2. To avoid the tendency of individual group members to be unduly influenced by others, and to ensure the value of all ideas and inputs, techniques such as the Delphi method can be used. This method is based on the assumption that group judgments can be more valuable than individual judgments and uses anonymity to ensure that people are comfortable sharing their opinions.

> **DID YOU KNOW?**
>
> The Delphi method was developed during the 1950s as part of the Air Force-sponsored Rand Corporation study as a means of gaining perspectives from a group of experts on the probability of possible enemy attacks. Experts could offer their opinions, along with support for those opinions, anonymously. The larger group would then review the results and recast their votes. The process continued until consensus was reached.

The method involves a number of cycles of anonymous input managed by a facilitator who consolidates the information. Here's how it works:

1. A questionnaire is distributed to the group and answered anonymously and individually.

2. Responses are gathered, summarized, and sent back to the group members along with another questionnaire.

3. The process continues until a clear group consensus is reached—requiring anywhere from two to six cycles.

Each round results in a new list of options that is prioritized based on the responses from the previous round. Polling software applications can be used to simplify and streamline this process.

The Delphi method can be effective when face-to-face meetings of the required experts are not possible or when face-to-face meetings are being dominated, or have the potential to be dominated, by one individual. They can be a good way to minimize the impacts of having a boss involved in the strategic planning process where a contentious or controversial issue is being addressed and participants might be less likely to share their true feelings.

The Fishbowl Method

The fishbowl method is a good tool to use when an issue is *polarizing* the planning team or strong opinions on one side of an issue exist in the group. It is a process that forces team members to listen to the perspectives on both sides of the issue and, in the process, move closer to an understanding of alternative ways of viewing the issue.

DEFINITION

Polarizing occurs when two opposite positions are taken and held strongly between members of a group. Once the position has been taken, it can be difficult to find neutral ground.

Here's how it works:

1. The issue is defined. For instance: "Do we need to consider outsourcing our IT services?"

2. The planning group is arbitrarily divided into two groups. One group is arranged in an inner circle of chairs and the other group is arranged around this group. The inner circle becomes the fishbowl.

3. The participants in the middle are assigned a perspective to take—in this case it might be: "Yes, we should outsource our IT services." They are given some time to consider the reasons why this would be a good idea—regardless of their actual personal opinions—and then asked to begin their group discussion.

4. The individuals in the outside circle are not allowed to provide any input—verbally or nonverbally. They must simply listen to the conversation.

5. Roles are reversed and the outer circle moves to the inside and discusses the opposite perspective while the new outer circle listens in.

6. The larger group is then divided into two camps based on their actual, individual opinions and the process is repeated.

A variation of this approach is the open fishbowl method. In this process, any member of the inner group can choose to leave the inner circle and a member of the outer group may enter. The goal is to encourage new perspectives and the results can be quite interesting as even those with very strong opinions find themselves beginning to understand the compelling perspectives of others.

All of these tools can be used to help generate discussion, reach consensus, and defuse polarizing situations. The skilled facilitator will have experience with these techniques and more; they will also have the ability to spontaneously implement the appropriate tool at the appropriate time depending on group dynamics.

Stages of Team Development

Skilled facilitators know that dynamics change over time as the group becomes more comfortable with its mission and with each other. Understanding the stages of team development can help facilitators anticipate challenges and manage the expectations of the group. The stages are predictable and require different types of facilitation skills. All groups go through these changes, so facilitators, leaders, and team members should not be frustrated or disheartened when they find themselves engaging in significant disagreement or conflict over issues. It's to be expected!

Bruce Tuckman, a psychologist, developed the most commonly used framework for team development in the 1960s—forming, storming, norming, and performing.

Forming: Coming Together

The forming stage occurs, as the name suggests, as the team is being formed and members are first coming together. Roles and expectations are being defined and team members are getting to know each other. During this stage, the facilitator should …

- Allow time for team members to socialize and get to know each other in an informal way.
- Be alert to any interpersonal tensions and take steps to defuse them.
- Identify participants who hang back and take steps to draw them into discussions.
- Focus more on interpersonal team development than the work of the team.

Storming: Anticipating Early Conflict

Once a team becomes comfortable with its role and its members, the facilitator can anticipate conflict. This is the storming stage and that is what behavior during this stage looks like. Team members are beginning to identify the strong and weak members and finding their position along this continuum. Stronger members may be more vocal in stating their opinions and concerns. Weaker members may withdraw. Key steps for the facilitator to take at this stage include:

- Draw upon the participation and talent of the strongest team members to serve as positive role models.

- Draw out those team members who are withdrawing and take steps to bring them into group discussions, encourage their comments, and intervene, as necessary, when their ideas are being attacked.

- Respond quickly to negative interpersonal conflicts and channel these conflicts into more positive behaviors. (Some of the tools described earlier in this chapter can be helpful here.)

BEST PRACTICES

A facilitator whose team has gotten stuck in the storming phase may make inroads by meeting individually with team members to find out what issues are causing the conflict.

The important thing for both the facilitator and team members to recognize is that the storming stage is a normal part of the process of team development. These behaviors are to be expected and can be effectively managed.

Norming: Pulling Together

After going through the stage of dissension and turmoil, the team moves into the stage of norming, where they pull together as a cohesive group to achieve a common goal. There will still be—and should be—disagreements among the group, but members are becoming more adept at managing these disagreements, listening to each other, and resolving conflicts on their own. The facilitator may have a tendency to breathe a sigh of relief and relax a bit at this point, but it is still important to …

- Monitor group behaviors and interactions to encourage involvement and model positive communication.

- Manage both the team members who contribute too much and those who contribute too little.

- Give positive as well as constructive feedback on team and individual performance.

From here it should all be downhill—but we'll soon see that it's not!

Performing: Achieving Results

Finally, the team has pulled together and weathered some storms, and team members have acclimated to their roles and are now able to contribute effectively to team success. The group is performing! Unfortunately, the team is at risk for a couple of problems at this stage:

- Because of the cohesiveness they have achieved and their resistance to moving back into a storming stage, members may become overly—and inappropriately—agreeable. This is called "groupthink."

DID YOU KNOW?

Irving Janis, a research psychologist who did a great deal of research on groupthink, strongly believed that groupthink was to blame for the failure of the ill-fated Bay of Pigs invasion in 1961.

A change in team dynamics may occur when any member of the team changes—but most notably when the team leader or facilitator changes. A change in direction can also set the team's performance back to an earlier stage.

Facilitators faced with these issues should do the following:

- Play devil's advocate from time to time, encouraging the team to consider both the pros and cons of the ideas they're generating—what could go wrong as well as what might go right.

- Be prepared to move and use some of the techniques from earlier stages of team development as changes in the team occur.

- Remain flexible and alert to team dynamics, recognizing that no team ever remains the same and that progress through these stages moves in both directions.

It is unlikely that any team will move through each of these stages in a linear fashion. There will be bumps and setbacks along the way. This commonly used model is generally presented in a linear way, suggesting that one stage ends as another begins; however, in truth there may be overlap between the stages as, for instance, the group moves from storming to norming and then back to storming again.

Managing Team Changes

Managing the team process and team changes is an important task for the facilitator. Knowing what to expect and the techniques to employ at each stage of team development is key. Any change in team membership, mission, or environment will cause a change in team dynamics, and this is something that the team leader and facilitator need to be aware of and prepared to address. It will be important for the facilitator to continually assess the team's stage and use the techniques appropriate for that stage to help manage the process. For example, if new members are added, time will need to be devoted to resocializing with less focus on the work of the team for a brief period of time.

Eventually, the team's work will be done—at least for this cycle. For the team leader and facilitator, an important consideration will be whether the work of the strategic planning team will begin and end on a regular cycle—generally annually—or whether the same team will be charged with planning in subsequent years. The decision will impact the management of the team and the process, and there are benefits and drawbacks to both approaches (See Chapter 21).

In any event, the culmination of the team's work represents another stage in its development and a stage that should not be ignored. In fact, Tuckman, jointly with Mary Ann Jensen, updated his model in the late 1970s to add a fifth stage—adjourning. Not surprisingly, this stage can create a sense of loss for participants. It can be helpful to have some type of commemorative or celebratory event at the end of the planning process to recognize the contribution of the members and to allow them an opportunity to revisit and reflect upon their experiences.

The Least You Need to Know

- The administrative tasks associated with your planning effort are important and should be considered and addressed before the meetings begin.
- The team leader lays the foundation for accountability and execution through actions.
- The facilitator's ability to effectively use various team facilitation tools will help to manage conflict and move the team forward.
- Changes in team makeup and the planning environment can be expected and will have an impact on team dynamics and process.

Gathering Key Information

Strategic plans can't be created in a vacuum. Effective plans require input from a variety of internal and external sources. That data-gathering process may seem intimidating, but it doesn't have to be. You'll find that much of this information you already have on hand; learn how to establish a process for making the data-gathering process even easier in subsequent years.

In this part, we'll cover the process for conducting a situation analysis and the important pieces of information you'll need to support the decisions you'll make. You'll learn about a tried-and-true model for seeking information, and how to conduct industry, market, competitive, and internal analyses. And you'll discover sources of information that can help streamline your data-gathering process.

Situation Analysis

In This Chapter

- Understanding how to use situation analysis
- Deciding what data and information you need
- Gathering primary and secondary data
- Qualitative vs. quantitative data
- How to conduct your own research
- Developing a process you can use during each planning cycle

You've decided that you need to embark on a strategic planning effort, you've identified your strategic planning goal, you've pulled together a team, and your team leader and facilitator are chomping at the bit to move forward. But you can't gather in a room to start working on the plan without some important background information. You're going to need data and information to help you make informed decisions about the right objectives, strategies, and tactics to meet your strategic planning goal.

In this chapter, we'll take a look at the broad categories of data available to you, how to access data that already exists, and how to gather new data if you need it.

How Situation Analysis Is Used

While you obviously know a lot about your business, and you've gathered other people together who also have a lot of information and knowledge, you should never go into the strategic planning process without taking the time to conduct a *situation analysis*.

Based on data gathered from a variety of sources, a summary will be created to provide an overview of the market, the industry, and critical elements of the company. The situation analysis provides a snapshot of the current situation for the company, business unit, or department that is engaged in the strategic planning process backed up by information that has been gathered from internal and external sources. The type of information you will need depends on the type of plan you're putting together and, to a certain degree, on the information that is available to you. This information then becomes the factual basis for the next step in the planning process—the SWOT analysis (discussed in Chapter 12).

Deciding What You Need to Know

It's true that businesspeople can suffer from analysis paralysis—the inability to move forward until they feel they have uncovered every rock and searched in every narrow cranny for all of the information they need to make the right choices. Let's shoot down that notion right away. You will never gather all of the information you need to make choices that will be 100 percent right. In fact, there is no such thing as being 100 percent right. Instead, your goal should be to minimize risk to the degree that makes sense considering the costs and benefits involved. It can be easy to get caught up in attempting to gather a lot of data—and spending a lot of time and money—when sometimes the answer might have been much easier, and cheaper, to find.

Here's an example: a direct mail company had an idea for a new program that it felt would appeal to its market of business attorneys in a particular state. The company didn't know, though, how interested its audience might be in the topic so it considered doing some market research. There were 10,000 potential attendees in the market and the firm had access to their addresses through a list they could rent. They estimated that it would cost about $5,950 to do the survey, including the cost of the list, postage, printing, and staff time. It would take about a month, on the low end, for the survey to be developed, distributed, returned, and analyzed.

On the other hand, if they were to just do it—just develop the program and promote it to this same list—they estimated that their costs would be about $7,950. The list, postage, and printing costs would be the same, they would need to reserve a room for the program (about $1,000), and there would be additional staff time involved, about twice as much as they estimated for the survey.

So the risk of moving forward without the data would be about $2,000. The reward would be a faster answer (after all, the survey might indicate that they should move forward, but we all know that surveys don't always reflect what people will actually do—only what they say they will do) and would probably be associated with a certain amount of revenue because some percentage of the target market might sign up for the program. The firm decided to just do it.

The moral of the story? Sometimes more data is not better.

As you're considering the data you will gather, ask yourself: "What is the value of the information I will attain and how will I use it compared to the time and cost involved in gathering it?" If the balance is skewed toward more cost (time and money) and less value, it may not be worth the time and effort to gather the data. Some types of information are more valuable than others. For example, the decision to franchise your business is significant and could undoubtedly benefit from a lot of reliable data. A decision about adding a new salesperson, on the other hand, would require less data and analysis.

Ultimately, you must decide between "need to know" and "nice to know." Just because you can measure it doesn't mean you should—but you can't manage what you can't measure. So you must be continually making choices about what is important for you to be able to manage—and, hopefully, improve—and what you will simply need to do based on the best business assumptions and decisions that you and your team can make. Everything is not worth measuring.

MISSTEPS

Planning teams may fall victim to what has been referred to as "analysis paralysis"— the tendency to over-analyze or over-think an issue to the point of diminishing return. The team's facilitator can play an important role in making sure that does not happen.

What Questions Do You Need Answered?

At the outset, you will need to determine what questions you need or would like to have answers to. The first time you go through the strategic planning process, this step will take some time. In subsequent years, though, you will have a foundation established that you will only need to review and update on an annual basis.

There will be some big buckets that the data you need will fall into:

- **Market data**. Information about your market area and the prospective customers in that area—who they are, how many there are, where they live, etc. (see Chapter 8)

- **Customer data**. Information about your customers—who they are, their levels of satisfaction, etc. (see Chapter 10)

- **Sales data**. Your own internal sales data (see Chapter 10)

- **Employee data**. Years of service, turnover, satisfaction data, etc. (see Chapter 10)

- **Competitor data**. Information about your competitors—who they are, what they sell, how much they sell, what their customers (and yours) like or dislike about them, etc. (see Chapter 9)

- **Industry data**. Industry growth and trends, innovations, etc. (see Chapter 7)

Within each of these buckets there will be different types of information you wish to collect depending on your planning goal, data availability, cost, and time. Not all of these buckets will always apply or apply at the same level. For instance, if you are working on a strategic marketing plan, customer and market data will be very important, but employee data may not be as important. On the other hand, if you're developing a strategic HR plan, customer and market data may not be as important, but employee data will be very important.

A good first step in deciding what information you need is to poll your planning group. This can be done quite simply—even via e-mail. Just send a quick e-mail saying, "In thinking about our upcoming planning process and our goal of X, what information do you feel you will need?" Then gather up all of the inputs and determine which data to go after. You'll note some commonalities and some unique inputs. To make a final determination, you may want to ask for the group's input, or the team leader may decide which inputs are most appropriate as a starting point.

BEST PRACTICES

Don't fret over your data choices at this point; just put a stake in the ground. If you find that you're missing important information as you move forward, you can always gather it and add it to your list. Start with the information you feel will be most important to you in this process.

Once you've come up with your list, you can start to assemble the data. Some you will already have on hand, some may be available through other sources, and some may require additional research.

Primary and Secondary Data

The information you use during the strategic planning process will consist of both primary and secondary data. Primary data is data that you have gathered yourself. It can include sales data, employee data, or data generated from surveys you have conducted (employee or customer satisfaction surveys). Secondary data is data that others have gathered. Some examples of secondary data would be census data collected by the government, surveys done by trade and professional groups, or research done by consulting firms for other companies similar to yours (research done by consulting firms on your behalf would be primary data).

Just because secondary data was not specifically gathered by you does not mean it has no value. Secondary data can often be very useful to you and can save you a lot of money if the information is pertinent. It will generally cost more to generate your own primary data than to access information that is already available through other sources, like trade associations or the Internet.

You probably already have a great deal of primary data available to you, although you may not be using it as aggressively as you could. You may have data that tells you what kinds of customers buy certain products from you. You might be able to break down this data by where they live, how they made the purchase (for example, in a store or online), how much they spent, or when their last purchase was. You can determine how many current customers you have and at what rate you are losing or gaining customers. These all represent important bits of information that might drive certain objectives during your planning process. For instance, if you find that the number of new customers you are attracting each month is declining, you might develop an objective to increase the number of new customers each month by a certain percentage.

Secondary data can be useful to see relationships between your own performance and the performance of other businesses in your industry—or in other industries. That will help you compare, for instance, whether your level of sales is greater, about the same, or lower than others in your industry, or if your employee turnover rates are higher, lower, or about the same. Secondary data can also provide information about potential consumers—many surveys are conducted of consumers by trade and professional associations annually and these surveys are often available at no cost, particularly if you are members of the trade group.

Qualitative and Quantitative Information

The highest level of reliability occurs when you have an actual experience, as we saw in the direct mail example earlier in this chapter. But there are times when it will not make sense to actually do something to see what happens. In those cases, and in cases where you need to make a decision and are missing important information, the availability of sound data to help you make a good choice will be critical.

Once again, you can never have information that is 100 percent reliable—never. There will always be some element of chance involved. Your goal, therefore, is to minimize that element of chance based on the importance of or risk involved with the decision.

Both primary and secondary information can be either qualitative or quantitative. Qualitative data is informative, but not *statistically significant*. In other words, you should not rely on it heavily when making decisions that involve a lot of risk. Quantitative data, on the other hand, is statistically significant. It gives you a very good (but not perfect) indication of some situation. Quantitative research uses mathematical calculations to both define an existing situation (descriptive statistics) and to predict a future outcome (predictive statistics).

DEFINITION

Statistical significance is the degree to which you can rely on the information you gather to accurately predict an outcome.

Risk is removed as you move along the continuum ranging from qualitative information on one end to quantitative information on the other.

We've talked about decisions you will need to make about what information to gather and how your decision will be based on a comparison of cost and benefit. A similar decision you will need to make when conducting your own research is what level of statistical significance (or reliability) you need to make good decisions. The more important, and potentially risky, the decision is, the higher level of reliability you will want.

In general, the higher the level of statistical significance, the more expensive it will be to gather the information. Fortunately, while there are many companies that conduct market research for companies, large and small, you may also choose to conduct your own research.

Conducting Your Own Research

If you need information that you don't have on hand and that secondary sources can't adequately provide, you may decide to do your own research. But in fact, you are doing research all of the time, whether you realize it or not. Each time you ask a customer about their experience, you are doing research. Your web traffic statistics represent research. Your observations of employee behaviors and attitudes represent research. If you do employee or customer satisfaction surveys, those represent research. Research simply involves gathering information. Some of the most common methods of conducting research involve observation, focus groups, surveys, and polls. Observation is ongoing and informal. It's the kind of research we tend to refer to when we say things like "Customers really seem to like the new layout of the store," or "Employees seem to be gathering in the break room together more often." Observation is a qualitative form of information.

Focus groups are also qualitative—they provide useful information, but you are not able to conduct mathematical calculations based on the information you gather, and major decisions should not be based on the information gathered. Surveys and polls are quantitative—you can conduct mathematical calculations on the information gathered—but not always statistically significant. Much depends on whom you included in the survey or poll and how well these individuals reflect the entire population. That's where sampling comes in; sampling is a science far beyond the scope of this book. You should recognize, though, that the decisions you make in terms of how many people to choose from certain audiences and the methods you use to choose them will have an impact on the validity and reliability of the information you gather.

Focus Groups

A focus group is an in-depth interview conducted with anywhere from 6 to 10 people in a group setting. The input from participants in the focus group session is based on their personal opinions and preferences and is often influenced by the discussion that occurs during the focus group session. These inputs are intended to provide a source of general insight or direction and should not be used, without additional quantitative research, to make decisions of any significant importance. For example, it would not be a good idea for a 1,000-member organization to make a decision about a new benefit plan based solely on the input of 7 employees from across the organization.

But while focus groups shouldn't be considered a form of quantitative research, they can provide value. Focus groups provide an opportunity to generate qualitative input from individuals in a setting that allows them an opportunity to talk about their attitudes and perceptions. The depth of the information obtained can be richer, for example, than information gathered through a survey.

Focus groups can be especially effective when you don't really know what it is you need to know. Clearly it can be tough to develop a formal survey when you really have no idea of what questions to ask in the first place! A focus group can help you get a sense of what people are thinking and can often help to clarify questions or point to areas of questioning that you might otherwise not have thought of. For example, a health-care organization decided to use focus groups when it wanted to get an idea of how the public perceived its advertising slogan "There Is Only One." Asking questions on a survey would have provided information, but it would not have provided much depth in terms of why people responded the way they did. Focus group sessions provide an opportunity to probe further to get at the meaning behind a response.

In this case, the health-care organization was concerned that the public might think its slogan was too arrogant. In fact, comments from employees suggested that employees felt that way. However, in focus group sessions, the organization learned that, while the statement was considered bold, the claims were backed up by facts, data, personal experiences, and word of mouth. A total of about 36 people were involved in four focus group sessions. Based on these sessions, a decision was made to continue with the slogan but to include questions related to the validity of the claim being made in the organization's annual consumer research survey—a quantitative survey.

DID YOU KNOW?

While focus groups appear to the casual observer to be simply a group discussion, they are more carefully structured than listening sessions or employee or customer meetings. More than an opportunity for employees or customers to just share their thoughts, effective focus groups are designed around a specific research goal (for example, what do customers think about this new product idea?) and guided through the use of a prepared discussion that will be used by the focus group facilitator to lead the discussion.

Focus group participants are chosen based on how well they represent the overall population whose input would be valuable to you. Getting maximum value from a focus group depends heavily on the skills of the facilitator.

Successful focus group facilitators stay on target, focus on the discussion guide, and do not take part in the conversation; they merely facilitate it and are skilled at calling upon the inputs of all participants—encouraging input from quieter participants and tactfully controlling participants who may try to monopolize the conversation. The input of the focus group participants is generally gathered both through audio- or videotaping the sessions (with participants' agreement).

Again, be mindful of how these inputs should and shouldn't be used. Focus group inputs can help to provide a *sense* of opinion or perspective and may guide additional research efforts. Focus group inputs are not, however, intended to serve as a quantitative or statistically reliable source of information.

Polls

Basically, a poll is just a quick survey designed to get a sense of the opinions or feelings of a group of people. Many computer-based applications include the ability to conduct quick polls. In fact, you can even conduct very simple polls through some e-mail packages. Polls can be either qualitative or quantitative. The polls we are all familiar with around election time are statistically significant. They are gathered from population samples that have been selected based on certain criteria and in numbers that reflect an appropriate sample size. The types of polls most often used by businesses, though, tend not to be statistically significant—they are just a quick snapshot of what some group thinks about an issue. Often the question is just thrown out to the group with no consideration of selecting a statistically significant sample or ensuring that individuals aren't able to cast their vote multiple times. As with focus groups, this kind of qualitative research can be informative but should not be relied upon to make significant decisions.

Two examples of quick poll questions that might be used during the strategic planning process are:

- A poll to determine whether employees feel they understand the purpose of the strategic planning sessions: "Do you feel you have a good understanding of why we are embarking on these strategic planning initiatives?"

- A customer poll about their service experience: "Please rate your service experience with our company over the past three months on a scale of 1–5, with 5 being excellent."

Surveys

Like polls, surveys may be either qualitative or quantitative, depending on how the sample was selected and its size relative to the overall population. The following examples are commonly used in surveys designed to get a sense of how an organization and its products and services are viewed in comparison to competitive offerings:

- When you think of other financial institutions in the area, what names come to mind?

- For each of the names mentioned in the answer to the previous question, please indicate on a scale of 1–5, with 5 being high, your perception of their (service, products, complaint management, array of products, etc.).

- How important do you consider each of the following factors when selecting a financial institution? (Factors could include such things as price, quality, service, etc.)

The responses to these types of questions will give you an indication of what is important to your customers and how what you have to offer compares to your competitors. The resulting gaps can help you determine where you should focus your efforts.

MISSTEPS

Drawing conclusions from qualitative information can lead to bad decisions that can be very costly. Even survey results can be called into question if the proper sampling techniques have not been used.

Surveys look deceptively easy to develop and implement. Come up with the questions, develop the survey, and send it out. But there are some important tips that you can follow to increase the level of reliability of any surveys you may choose to do:

- **Start with clear objectives.** Before you conduct any survey, know what you want to know—and what you will do with the information after the survey is completed. What information do you hope to obtain? How will you use that information? Don't ask questions just for the sake of asking. Make sure your surveys are focused and actionable.

- **Make sure to choose an appropriate sample.** While you can obtain statistically valid results by surveying a segment of an entire population, you may, when it's possible, want to include all members of the group whose feedback you're seeking in the survey. Employees are a good example—if you have 1,000 employees, a sample may be the best option. But if you have 50, why not survey them all? Employees not included in a sample may feel left out and resentful. On the other hand, don't survey your entire employee population if the information you're seeking can be obtained from specific employee segments. For example, if you're concerned about high turnover in a specific department, focus on that department.

- **Consider the timing of your survey.** Don't survey customers during the holidays or employees during extremely busy work periods. At the same time, if you're surveying in response to an immediate need or to gauge response to a specific issue, conduct the survey as quickly as possible after the event or issue.

- **Don't ask what you already know.** If you know that your service call response time is too long, don't ask customers if they think your service call response time is too long. Along the same lines, don't ask for feedback or input on things you are not willing to change. If your hours of service cannot be changed, don't ask customers if they would be interested in other hours of service—that may raise an expectation you are unprepared to meet.

- **Test your survey before distributing.** It's easy to overlook the obvious when developing a survey. Before rolling out any survey instrument to your survey population, test the survey on a smaller group; 10 to 12 samples should give you a good idea of whether the survey was easy to understand and follow, whether questions were meaningful, and whether you inadvertently missed a key point.

- **Consider automating your surveys.** Intranet- or Internet-based surveys not only provide convenience for those taking the survey but for those compiling and analyzing the responses as well. Online surveying can be a good way to take the pulse of an audience quickly.

DID YOU KNOW?

Since it was launched in 1999 by Ryan and Chris Finley, the online survey tool SurveyMonkey (www.surveymonkey.com) has grown exponentially and is used by large and small companies. About 80 percent of the Fortune 100 are SurveyMonkey subscribers.

> • **Use benchmarks to determine what the results you've gathered mean.**
> If 65 percent of your employees say they are "highly satisfied" with your
> benefit plan, what does this mean? Is this a high percentage or a low percent-
> age? You can't tell unless you have a way of benchmarking your data against
> your own or others' results. Benchmarking simply involves asking others to
> provide you with data on their experiences as a basis of comparison for your
> own results. Gathering benchmarks will help you determine whether you are
> lower than, about the same, or higher than other organizations on whatever
> measure you are using.

Using Secondary Data

You can, and should, take advantage of data and information that has already been
gathered by others when conducting research. Secondary data is another readily
accessible source of information that can serve as a valuable input to your planning
process. Secondary data is available through a wide variety of sources—the government, trade and professional organizations, consulting firms, the media, etc. This
data can be particularly useful to you when you do not have the time or money to
gather information on your own, and often it can provide just enough information for
you to make informed choices.

The Internet is a great source of secondary data, but it is important for users to
consider the source of the information they are gathering. When searching for
information on the Internet, the domain can give you a clue about the validity of the
information:

- **.com**—a commercial site. The information you find here is generally being
  presented by a company to promote its products and services.

- **.org**—an organizational site. While the information is not as commercial as
  the .com sites present, the information is still being presented by an organization and may be somewhat biased; these sites may also be associated with
  trade and professional organizations.

- **.edu**—an educational organization site. The information you find here generally has more credibility than the .com and .org sites.

- **.gov**—a government agency site. These sites can be a very good source of
  background information on laws, regulations, and survey or census data on a
  variety of issues.

Developing a Process to Use Year to Year

The first year you develop your plan will be the most labor-intensive in terms of identifying and gathering the background information you will need and what levels of performance you can and should expect. Here are some steps to follow to initiate a process that can be repeated in subsequent years:

1. Develop a list of the data you are looking at, organized by major category (industry, market, competitor, internal) and whether it is primary or secondary data.

2. Indicate what the source of data is for each item. Be specific. If sales data came from Joe, in marketing, indicate Joe, in marketing, as your source. If you contacted Ms. Haversham at the Association of Builders, 555-555-5555, mhaversham@ab.org, indicate this as well.

3. For primary data, indicate whether the data comes from existing records (like sales data) or from research that must be conducted each year (like employee satisfaction data). If a survey was used, include a copy of the survey and an indication of where the electronic file for the survey resides.

4. Indicate who will be responsible for obtaining each piece of information, the date they should acquire it by, and who they should give the information to. (These dates can then become part of your annual planning document.)

5. Update and change this document as new sources of information are identified.

6. Include this information with other information relevant to your planning process where it can easily be accessed.

In the next chapters, we'll talk about the broad categories of background information and the different types and sources of data that are available to you, along with some options and opportunities for gathering that data.

The Least You Need to Know

- Situation analysis involves gathering and analyzing information about your market, customers, competitors, sales, employees, and the industry you're in.

- Much of the data you will need for the planning process can be found internally but is often overlooked.

- Data quality can vary. Is it primary or secondary, qualitative or quantitative? Or in the case of data attained via the Internet, what is the domain associated with the site?

- A variety of do-it-yourself research options are available, including focus groups, surveys, and polls.

- Defining and documenting a process for conducting the situation analysis can save time for subsequent planning sessions.

Industry Analysis

In This Chapter

- The value of doing an industry analysis
- Determining where you fit
- How to use Porter's Five Forces analysis
- Evaluating the challenges and opportunities that impact your business

While the prospect of conducting an industry analysis may at first seem somewhat daunting, it is not as bad as seems. In fact, you probably already have a good sense of the industry you operate in—you just may not have formalized your understanding in a way that can be readily shared with others. Fortunately, this is an area where the government can definitely be your friend! The government has an exhaustive classification system it uses to classify businesses into different sectors and has massive amounts of information available on each of those sectors that can provide you with valuable information. Most importantly, the information is available at no cost (well, as a taxpayer you actually have paid for this information, but it will feel like it doesn't cost anything).

Because of the massive amounts of information that is available, it can be challenging to know what to gather and how to use it. Fortunately, there is a standard process many companies use that can be very helpful to you as you try to get your arms around all of the information out there about the industry you operate in.

In this chapter, we'll take a look at the process for determining where your business fits, how to use Porter's Five Forces analysis, and how to evaluate industry challenges and opportunities.

How Industry Analysis Is Used

No company exists in a vacuum, and rarely is a business the only one of its kind. Businesses operate as part of an industry that includes other businesses doing the same type of work and offering the same types of products and services. Using *industry analysis* to learn about and understand industry impacts can help businesses identify important opportunities and challenges.

DEFINITION

Industry analysis is the process of evaluating the factors that are impacting a particular industry—the industry the business conducting the planning activity is in—by looking at data and information related to the size and number of businesses, their sales, and the regulatory and other issues that may impact them.

What Industry Are You In?

The first step in conducting an industry analysis is determining what industry you are in. It may seem straightforward; if you have a laundry, for instance, you might assume that you are in the cleaning industry—and that would be, in part, correct. However, you may be surprised to know that the government has actually categorized all businesses into a series of very specific industry segments.

SIC and NAICS Codes

For many years the Standard Industrial Classification (SIC) system was used to categorize businesses into industry segments. That system was replaced by the North American Industry Classification System (NAICS). This change actually increased the number of classifications formerly available but is said to be easier to use, more accurate, and more frequently updated. The major flaw with the SIC system was that it identified the output of a business rather than the business processes. This meant that the lists were not as clearly defined as they might be. *NAICS codes* are used to identify processes, making them more specific and more detailed—six-digit classifications compared to four-digit classifications under the SIC system.

DEFINITION

NAICS codes are six-digit classifications created to represent businesses in North America—Mexico, the United States, and Canada. They provide a framework that allows businesses, as well as the general public, to access and apply comparative statistics and data relevant to the business they are in.

The highest level of classification is called "sector" (similar to the previous SIC "division" classification). The first two digits of the NAICS code define the sector. Industries are grouped into 20 broad sectors that are, in most cases, similar to familiar SIC divisions (new divisions are indicated with *). These categories are listed in the order they are numbered:

- 11—Agriculture, forestry, fishing, and hunting

- 21—Mining

- 22—Utilities

- 23—Construction

- 31-33—Manufacturing

- 42—Wholesale trade

- 44-45—Retail trade

- 48-49—Transportation and warehousing

- 51—Information

- 52—Finance and insurance

- 53—Real estate and rental and leasing

- 54—Professional, scientific, and technical services*

- 55—Management of companies and enterprises

- 56—Administrative and support and waste management and remediation services

- 61—Educational services*

- 62—Health care and social assistance*

- 71—Arts, entertainment, and recreation*

- 72—Accommodation and food services

- 81—Other services (except public administration)

- 92—Public administration

The NAICS uses a hierarchical system for numbering that starts with the two-digit Economic Sectors (as shown in the previous list). Digits 3-5 allow for more specific identification of various sectors processes. The first five digits are fixed for use in the

United States, Canada, and Mexico. The sixth digit is optional for each country and may be used to reflect economic and information differences. More detail on the classifications and their use can be found at www.census.gov/eos/www/naics/.

For example, the NAICS number for potato chips is:

> 31 Manufacturing
>
> 311 Food Manufacturing
>
> 3119 Other Food Manufacturing
>
> 31191 Snack Food Manufacturing
>
> 311919 Other Snack Food Manufacturing

How the Codes Are Used

What is the importance of these numbers? They are used by federal statistical agencies to aid in the collection, analysis, and publishing of statistical data. The NAICS system, which was developed jointly by the United States, Canada, and Mexico, allows for a high level of comparability between these countries—basically helping to ensure that apples-to-apples comparisons can be made. For business owners this means that, once you have identified the category your business falls under, you can then access a wide range of statistical information to help you conduct an industry analysis.

So let's consider where our laundry business might fit in this classification system. It would fall under 81232—Dry Cleaning and Laundry Services (except Coin-Operated). The description of this industry is:

> This industry comprises establishments primarily engaged in one or more of the following: (1) providing dry cleaning services (except coin-operated); (2) providing laundering services (except linen and uniform supply or coin-operated); (3) providing drop-off and pickup sites for laundries and/or dry cleaners; and (4) providing specialty cleaning services for specific types of garments and other textile items (except carpets and upholstery), such as fur, leather, or suede garments; wedding gowns; hats; draperies; and pillows. These establishments may provide all, a combination of, or none of the cleaning services on the premises.

In years gone by, you would have had to look in a very large book—or books—and drill down from the very broad general category of personal services until you found the code that represented your business. Today, it's much easier. Simply enter: "NAICS+laundry" into a search engine and let the computer do the rest! Another option is to go to www.naics.com/naics2-6page.htm, where you'll find a chart with links that allow you to quickly drill down by the categories described earlier.

Enter the search term "NAICS 81232+data" and you'll get a list of 94,000 potential sources of data and information about laundry services. You probably didn't realize just how much information you had access to, how inexpensive it was, or how quickly you could find it!

Where Do You Fit?

An understanding of the industry you operate in will help you determine how your company is positioned in terms of size and success when compared to others in the same industry. The industry analysis will also give you some initial indications of competitors within the same market.

Important Industry Factors

During the industry analysis, you will be considering:

- The size, trends, and outlooks for your industry
- Geographic area—this can range from local to international
- Product or service provided
- Target market
- Legal or regulatory environment

These considerations are reviewed in terms of three critical components of any company's success—the value of the product or service to customers, the level of competition the business operates in, and the bargaining power the business can bring to bear with its suppliers. Within this framework, the industry analysis also considers broader environmental impacts on the business.

Finding More Information

Information about the size, trends, and outlooks for your industry are readily available through government and industry sources. Once you've determined your industry classification code, you can find information about the status of your industry through a wide range of sources—many at no cost through the government, such as:

- The Economic Census (factfinder.census.gov/), which can be broken down by geography to the local level

- The Statistical Abstract of the United States (www.census.gov/compendia/statab/), which provides statistics on the social, political, and economic organization of the United States.

- Current Industrial Reports (www.census.gov/manufacturing/cir/index.html), which provides specific information by industry

Other commonly used sources of industry information may not be free to own but can be accessed through local public or university libraries either in hard copy format or through databases that the library may subscribe to. Some examples:

- **Business Source Premier**—U.S. and international market research and industry reports from Datamonitor and other publishers.

- **Gale's Small Business Resource Center**—focuses primarily on the consumer goods and services industries, broken down into trade and industry reports.

- **Encyclopedia of American Industries**—profiles of manufacturing and services industries. (other similar sources are: Encyclopedia of Emerging Industries and Encyclopedia of Global Industries).

- **Value Line Investment Surveys**—one-page overviews of various industries.

- **Standard & Poor's Industry Surveys**—comprehensive reports on a number of major industries.

Industry websites and trade organizations can also be useful sources of in-depth information about an industry. There are literally thousands of associations serving virtually every industry niche. Becoming a member of the trade associations that serve your industry can provide you with access to research reports and proprietary information that can aid the industry analysis process.

Articles published in business magazines and trade journals are another good source of information. Again, your local library can be a great source of this information. And, speaking of libraries, your reference librarian can be a great friend and ally in the industry analysis process. Reference librarians love data and information and they know where to find it. Don't be afraid to ask—you'll make their day!

BEST PRACTICES

If you or family members are enrolled in classes at a university or technical college, you may have access to proprietary databases that you might otherwise have to pay for.

Porter's Five Forces Analysis

The problem you will face as you begin to gather information for the industry analysis is not finding enough information, it's figuring out what to do with the information you gather and how to make sense of all of the data. There is, fortunately, a model that can help to provide a framework for this analysis: Porter's Five Forces.

In 1979, Michael E. Porter, a Harvard Business School professor, developed a framework for industry analysis, which is now referred to as *Porter's Five Forces analysis*. It uses five forces to examine the competitive nature of a market in terms of the market's attractiveness or potential for profitability of a business. In an unattractive industry, the combination of these five forces would drive down overall productivity—just the opposite would be true in an attractive industry.

DEFINITION

Porter's Five Forces analysis is a framework for analyzing industry impacts based on five key forces designed to provide an indication of the competitive environment, and consequently, the overall profitability potential for the business. The combination of the five forces will either support or drive down profitability.

The five forces are:

- Threat of new entrants
- Power of suppliers
- Power of buyers
- Availability of substitutes
- Competitive rivalry

Let's examine each of these and how they provide input for the strategic planning process.

Threat of New Entrants

In evaluating the threat of new entrants to your market, you need to be thinking from the perspective of the potential entrant and, from that perspective, identifying the barriers that exist to determine where they fall along a continuum of inconsequential to prohibitive. Obviously, the easier it is for others to enter an industry, the more competition there will be. Some industries have high barriers to entry—these might include high fixed costs, scarce resources, high costs to customers to switch companies or a high level of government restriction or legislation. The threat of entrants for a seafood restaurant are likely to be higher than for a medical device company.

In looking at the threat of new entrants to a market, we consider various barriers to entry. These include:

- Loyalty to existing brands or companies
- Incentives available from other companies (for example, discounts for volume purchases)
- High costs to produce the product or service
- The need for resources that may be scarce
- High costs to customers for switching from their current provider
- Government restrictions or laws that impact the ability to do business

Suppose my seafood business has been serving the lakeside community for 20 years and has a loyal following. As I analyze the industry in preparation for the strategic planning process, I would first consider the potential threat that might exist in terms of new entrants to the market. I know that there are not significant start-up costs involved in establishing a seafood restaurant. And, because I'm currently the only restaurant in the area, I know that the market may be attractive to new entrants. I have a big benefit because of the loyalty of my current customer base and their positive word-of-mouth, but I also recognize that a big-brand entrant to the market (Red Lobster, perhaps) will represent a potential threat to my business. Competition from other sources might be hindered, however, by the oil spill in the Gulf of Mexico, which may create scarcity for certain types of seafood (it has a potential impact on my business, too, of course).

If I'm the medical devices company owner, I would use this same analysis to consider the barriers that exist for others to enter my market. Certainly the high cost of producing these products is going to be a factor that makes it prohibitive for competitors. Governmental regulations are also a consideration in the medical devices industry. Switching costs would also be a consideration – the hospitals I currently provide these devices to would incur significant costs if they were to decide to begin using another manufacturer. The risk of a competitive entrant to the market for my medical device company is likely to be significantly less than for a seafood restaurant.

MISSTEPS

Try to avoid the tendency to believe that nobody else could possibly offer your product or service in a way that would be more attractive to your customers. Be open-minded and realistic about the possibility of new and better ways to do what you do.

Power of Suppliers

The power of suppliers is the second consideration in Porter's Five Forces analysis, in which you would consider the possible threat of pressure from your key suppliers in terms of access to or price of the supplies you use. The oil industry is a good example of an industry where the power of suppliers is significant—the factors that impact companies in this industry include:

- Few suppliers of the product
- No (or very limited) substitutes
- High switching costs
- Importance of the product to buyers
- Higher profitability for the seller than the buyer

Business owners want to be on the other end of this spectrum in terms of the suppliers they rely on. They want to have many sources of the supplies, readily available substitutes, low switching costs, lower levels of importance of the supply, and higher profitability for their services than the supplier has. A company that has successfully managed the supplier relationship and placed itself in a position of strength relative to suppliers is Walmart. The less reliant you are on a limited group of suppliers for key inputs needed to produce and distribute your products and services, the better your position.

Power of Buyers

The buyers of our products and services may also exert power over us that must be analyzed to determine our level of risk. Again, Walmart is a good example. As a customer of companies that produce various products, Walmart exerts significant pressure over its suppliers—and, in fact, has the ability to negotiate terms that are more favorable to itself than to the suppliers, driving down costs significantly.

Your customers may be able to exert similar influence over you if the following conditions exist:

- You have a small number of buyers.

- You have buyers that purchase large volumes of your products or services.

- There are many other options available to them, and switching would be easy.

- The product or service you offer is not that important—customers could do without it if they had to.

- Your customers are very price sensitive, meaning that they would readily switch to another supplier for a minor price shift.

Availability of Substitutes

If you offer a product or service that has no—or limited—substitutes (like the oil industry), it is far more difficult for customers to leave you and choose another supplier. In considering your business and the level of risk for losing customers to other options, you would want to consider what the substitutes are for your product or service and how readily available they are.

DID YOU KNOW?

Many believe that the newspaper business is doomed because of the advent of online media and the wide availability of information through alternative channels. But some in the industry are redefining the definition of what business they're in. Reframing the business from "the newspaper business" to "the business of providing information" creates new possibilities for disseminating information beyond the traditional print format.

For instance, other types of restaurants could serve as a substitute for the seafood restaurant. Or customers could buy and prepare their own seafood instead of going to the seafood restaurant. Consequently, the risk of losing customers through switching is relatively high. For the medical device company, on the other hand—assuming that the device is unique and offers a benefit that can't be found through other options—the risk is much lower.

Competitive Rivalry

In considering the competitive environment, you should consider both your own competition and also the competition that occurs in the industry overall. The more competitive the industry, the lower the availability of profits for individual businesses. Competition tends to exist when there are many businesses of about the same size offering about the same thing in a mature industry where there is limited opportunity to gain new customers and growth is possible only by stealing customers away from other competitors. An example of a mature industry where this is the case would be the soft drink industry.

Industry-Wide Challenges and Opportunities

The industry analysis will provide you with a high-level perspective of the broad issues impacting your business. Of course, not all businesses will be equally concerned with the broad impacts on their industry. Much will depend on the market area you choose to serve. If your market is national (or international), you will clearly have many more impacts and will need to do significantly more analysis than if you serve a narrow, local market. The main things you will be concerned about are:

- **What is the economic outlook for the industry I'm in?** For example, the outlook for videotape rentals may be grim, but the outlook for hospice services may be pretty good.

- **What competitive forces exist in my industry?** As we've seen, the more attractive the industry and the better the outlook, the more opportunity there will be for competition.

- **What factors may create change in my industry?** For example, the Gulf Coast oil spill in 2010 is likely to impact the seafood and tourism industries in that part of the country.

- **Who are the key players in my industry?** Again, if you're focusing on a local market, you will want to consider this from a local point of view. If you're in an international market, you will need to consider a much broader range of potential competitors.

- **What moves might my competitors be thinking about making?** This is a strategic consideration that requires speculation and creativity. "If I do X, what will the competition do? Then what should I do? Then what might they do? ...," and so on.

- **Given what I know and have learned about my industry and my competitors, what are the most important factors that will contribute to my success?** These factors can suggest opportunities to position your business in ways to take advantage of these success factors in product development and service delivery as well as through marketing communications.

The market, competitive, and internal analyses that you will conduct next will help you become much more specific as you explore the relevant factors that represent opportunities and challenges relative to the strengths and weaknesses of your business.

The Least You Need to Know

- An industry analysis gives you an indication of the trends impacting the business you're in and how you stack up against other businesses doing the same type of thing that you do.

- Every business is part of a specific industry; identifying where your industry fits can lead you to a wealth of important information.

- Using Porter's Five Forces analysis as a framework for industry analysis can help simplify and focus the process.

- Identifying challenges and opportunities helps position your business relative to its key competitors.

Market Analysis

In This Chapter

- Accurately defining your target market
- How satisfied are your customers?
- How to calculate market share
- How to expand market share

For any business, understanding your customers—or your market—is critical. Businesses have a wide range of choices to make when it comes to deciding who they wish to serve. The important thing is to clearly understand the needs of the market so that what you have to offer can be provided in such a way that it meets the needs of those individuals.

Surprisingly, many companies are very internally focused. Business owners come up with what they believe is a great idea for a product or service, and they believe in that product or service very strongly. They then attempt to convince a group of potential customers (their market) that what they have to offer is what the market needs or should want. While that approach can sometimes work (with a new product, for instance), in most cases it is a backward approach. Instead, businesses should be seeking to understand their market as thoroughly as they can so that what they provide can be aligned with the customers' needs in terms of product attributes, price, place (location or access), and promotion (how you communicate with customers).

Market analysis is an important part of any strategic planning effort but, of course, will be especially critical when creating a strategic marketing plan. In this chapter, we'll take a look at the steps involved in conducting a market analysis.

How Market Analysis Is Used

Market analysis is used by businesses to identify the potential demand for their products and services. By first identifying a market area to be served, based on geography, and then examining factors that are specific to that geography, businesses are able to estimate market demand. These estimates of demand are important inputs for decisions related to the volume of product to produce, where to locate services, and more.

> **DEFINITION**
>
> **Market analysis** is the process of identifying and analyzing factors in a specific geographic area to forecast market demand and identify issues that may either positively or negatively impact sales.

Defining Your Market

Before you can begin to thoroughly understand your market, you need to determine who it is. It's entirely up to you! You may choose to serve a local market, a regional market, a national market, or an international market. You may choose to serve teenagers, young families, women between the ages of 25 and 55, or men over 60. You may choose to serve low-income, middle-class, upper-class, or extremely wealthy individuals—or any combination of the above, and more.

Effectively defining your market is important for two reasons:

1. It helps you focus your communication efforts to reach just those individuals who are most likely to generate sales.

2. It gives you a focus for market research efforts.

Let's take a look at how you can most effectively analyze your market.

What Is Your Market Area?

What is the geographic area that you wish to serve? Within that area, which customers are you targeting? The answers to these questions are important and bear consideration. Looking at this information incorrectly can cause you to make faulty decisions.

For example, a dentist hoping to expand her practice was focused on a market area that represented a 30-mile radius from her office. She was readily able to get census data about the population in that area. To keep the calculations simple, let's say there were 10,000 people in the age range that she was targeting; she had 1,000 patients. She calculated her market share at 10 percent, and, on the surface, that would seem to be accurate. But this number is based on a couple of flawed assumptions:

- While she did not wish to target Medicaid patients because of poor reimbursement, their numbers were included in the overall population count. This would inaccurately reflect her actual market share. Let's say the removal of the Medicaid population would reduce the market to 8,000 individuals—with her 1,000 patients, her market share would then be 12.5 percent.

- While she had defined her target market area as a 30-mile radius from her office, some of her patients actually came from outside this radius. Again, they should not be included in the market share calculation because they do not reflect her defined target market. Again, let's say her market area has 8,000 individuals and she has 1,000 patients. But upon closer evaluation, she learns that 500 of those patients actually reside outside what she has defined as her market area—reflecting an actual market share of 6.25 percent.

When defining your target market, make sure the definitions are clear and that you're using those definitions to develop numbers to represent your market potential as well as your own market data.

Who Are Your Customers?

If you are not already gathering information about your customers, you should take steps to do so. The more you know about your customers, the more information you have to find additional customers that are like them. Sometimes businesspeople have a general idea of who they will serve. For example, a boutique opens in a small community and thinks it will draw customers primarily from the small businesses around it. As time goes on, though, the owner learns that the boutique is becoming a destination spot for people living in the community, as well as those living in surrounding communities. She knows this through her own observations of who frequents the boutique and through the information she's able to capture through in-store surveys, credit card slips, and asking customers for their zip codes.

Direct marketing organizations and online businesses have a ready-made opportunity to gather information about their customers through the questions they ask during the ordering process. While you don't want to make the ordering process cumbersome by asking for too much information, you should be capturing some basic information about customers to help in your market analysis. Even non-direct marketing organizations and traditional brick-and-mortar businesses can take steps to gather information about customers through the simple channels described above.

Once you've begun gathering information about customers and have access to this information, you can begin to analyze and learn more about them. This knowledge will serve as input to the planning process. For instance, suppose you find that 80 percent of your customers are coming to you from within your city limits. This information might suggest that you focus more communication efforts within this radius to attract the customers that have not yet tried your product or service. Or it might suggest that you take steps to expand your market outside this area by reaching out to consumers in other locations.

In addition to *demographic information* about your customers, and information you might gather through observation, various types of surveys can provide additional insights.

DEFINITION

Demographic information is information that defines the observable or quantifiable characteristics of a customer—gender, age, income, where they live, etc.

We talked about different types of surveys and how to use them in Chapters 6 and 7. Surveys can help you gather information about customers that can give you direction for your marketing efforts. You can use surveys to find out about customer characteristics and preferences (how often they purchase a certain type of product, how they spend their time, or where they typically shop), what they think about your products and services, or what they think about competitive products and services. This feedback can indicate areas where you have strengths to build on and areas for potential improvement.

It's important to pay attention to the information you are gathering from your customers and to avoid a common tendency to think that, instead of taking steps to meet customer needs, you should try to convince them that what you have to offer is what they should want or need. An example of a young restaurant owner illustrates the danger of this tendency.

This young restaurant owner was operating his third restaurant in a small community near a golf course. His dream was to deliver an upscale dining experience to the community—the type of experience that others, he felt, were not meeting. But after three years in business, he found that he simply wasn't generating the demand that would allow him to stay in business. At a closing event for his restaurant, he shared his disappointment with those gathered—primarily family and friends, but also some loyal patrons of the restaurant—and remarked, "I was just unable to convince the people in this area of the value of my style of cooking. I can't tell you how many times over the past three years people would come into the restaurant and say: 'Do you have a fish fry?' No, no, we don't do fish fries here!" Clearly the restaurant owner was failing to listen to his customers and missed an opportunity to make modifications to his menu to meet the needs of a ready market.

When and What Are They Buying?

Sales data can provide you with a wealth of information about your customer: when they buy, what they buy, and how much they buy. By combining these various bits of information, you can learn quite a lot. For instance, you might find that traffic to your website is highest on Monday mornings and that most purchasers during that time frame are young men living in urban areas. You might find that your deli and boutique draws most of its business during the workweek, less on weekends. This type of information can help drive decisions about hours of operation, location, and which customers to target through various communication channels.

There are a variety of different scenarios that might play out based on what you're learning through this sales data. You might find that lower-priced items are selling at higher rates than higher-priced items. You might find that certain items sell much better than others—and some sell very poorly. You may find that certain items sell best during certain times of the year. All of this information will be important as you move forward with your strategic planning efforts.

Assessing Customer Satisfaction

Information about your customers' levels of satisfaction can provide you with indications of areas where you need to focus more attention and areas where you are performing well (you might want to focus on these areas in your marketing communication materials).

Monitoring Is an Ongoing Process

While formal surveys of customers are often used to determine customer satisfaction, this is really something that you should be monitoring on an ongoing basis. Put processes in place to make sure your employees are collecting this information from customers that they know what to do with the information they receive.

> **MISSTEPS**
>
> Don't ignore or avoid your most unhappy customers. It is from them that you can actually learn the most about what you need to do to make your business a success. Actively soliciting feedback from *all* customers, even those who may not be entirely happy, can be a valuable source of information.

TARP Worldwide (www.tarp.com), a consulting firm in Arlington, Virginia, specializes in measuring and managing customer satisfaction and loyalty. Based on research originally conducted in the 1970s and repeated over the years in virtually every industry and in 20 countries, TARP has found a number of important facts that hold true:

- In business-to-business environments, 75 percent of customers will complain to a frontline person (compared to 50 percent across all industries). If the frontline person is an employee of a distributor or retailer, chances are good that the problem will go no further. Only 1 to 5 percent of these customers will escalate their complaint to a local manager or corporate headquarters. That's bad news, because you can't fix what you don't know.

- Complaint rates vary by type of problem. Problems that caused the customer to lose money had high complaint rates (50 to 75 percent). Problems related to mistreatment, quality, and incompetence resulted in frontline complaints only 5 to 30 percent of the time. Again, this is bad news—you need to be hearing about the problems that customers are encountering.

- Only 20 percent of dissatisfaction is caused by employee actions. Other sources include the company's products and processes (40 percent), and customers' own mistakes or incorrect expectations (40 percent).

- Customers who complain but have their concerns satisfied are up to 8 percent more loyal than if they had no problem at all. Again, it pays to pay attention!

- Companies can be more effective in getting employees to share the negative feedback they receive if the focus is on punishing the process, not the people. That's important, because in order to make sure employees are sharing this information with you, you need to make sure they don't feel they will be punished for doing so.

Using Customer Feedback

The feedback you gain through various sources related to customer satisfaction can provide you with information that can help you ...

- Identify areas where training may be needed—how employees should answer the phone, how to deal with customer complaints, etc.

- Identify areas where processes or procedures could be improved—eliminating long lines at checkout, speeding up shipping of products, etc.

- Identify areas where standards need to be put in place and communicated to employees—standards may relate to order turnaround time, phone transfers, response times, etc. What are your customers' expectations for these key processes and how can you establish standards to ensure those expectations are being met?

In addition to considering feedback from customers gathered through employee interactions and surveys, businesses can learn a lot from analyzing their own data about lost customers. Understanding why, and how many, customers are leaving you will both give you a good leading indication of the potential for declining sales down the road and help you take steps to improve products, services, and procedures to eliminate these defections in the future.

For many companies it can be difficult to tell when a customer has left. Unless the product or service is sold on some sort of membership basis (magazine subscriptions, for instance), it can be tough to know whether the customer is actually no longer a customer or just spending less on the type of product or service you have to offer. In tight economies, this can be particularly true. A simple survey of customers who haven't done business with you for some time can give you an indication of whether they've actually left—and why.

BEST PRACTICES

If you're not doing so already, take steps to gather customer e-mail addresses, making sure that you have their permission to communicate with them through this channel. The ability to communicate with customers via e-mail instead of through the post office or by phone can save both time and money.

For example, a women's boutique sends the following survey, in the form of a mailed postcard, on an annual basis to customers that have not bought something in the store the previous year:

We miss you! We haven't seen you in the store for a while and miss your business. Please help us continue to provide high-quality products and services by providing some feedback for us. Check one of the boxes below:

❏ I still consider myself one of your customers; I just haven't had a chance to shop lately.

❏ I no longer stop at your store because my needs have changed.

❏ I no longer shop at your store because I have left the area.

❏ I no longer shop at your store because I have been unhappy with the pricing of your products.

❏ I no longer shop at your store because I have been unhappy with the service provided.

❏ I have found another store that provides me with better options to meet my needs.

Please include additional comments below:

_____

_____

_____

The information you receive from a simple survey like this will give you an indication of the number of customers you may be losing as well as some clues into why they may no longer be using your services. To be able to do this, of course, you need to make sure that you are collecting contact information for your customers and are also tracking sales. Consider offering a discount or some other incentive to boost response rates.

BEST PRACTICES

In an electronic environment, businesses should think broadly about the type of information they collect about customers. For instance, e-mail addresses and mobile phone numbers are becoming increasingly important in an e-communication environment.

Market Share

Market share is the percentage of sales that a business is generating from a defined market. It can be difficult to calculate because it can be difficult to get good information about exactly who is buying what; however, estimates can be made based on general knowledge about buying habits for certain types of products and services.

DEFINITION

Market share is the percentage of the total available market that a business serves. It may be measured based on number of customers, revenue, or unit sales.

Measuring Market Share

To measure market share effectively you will need …

- **A specific definition of your market.** This might vary by product or service, so you might actually have several pieces of data reflecting market share across multiple items.

- **Reliable and up-to-date information.** Whatever source of information you use, be sure to use it consistently. Look for the most recent data available.

- **Agreement on what to measure.** For instance, will you measure market share based on overall number of customers, revenue, or number of items sold?

The decision you make about how to measure market share will result in different answers.

Suppose you operate a spa business that sells hot tubs. There were 100 hot tubs sold in your market area last year. You sold 50 of them—you would then have a 50 percent market share. But you could also calculate your market share based on revenue instead of units. Suppose the total sales volume for hot tubs in your market area was $500,000, and your sales were $350,000. In this case, your market share would be 70 percent. Quite a difference! How do we explain that difference? Very simply, actually—your hot tubs obviously sell at a higher price point than your competitors'.

Which gives you the best reflection of the market? It is really up to you and what is most important to you. A business, for instance, that is new to a market and interested in establishing a presence might focus on quantity—an established business might be more concerned with revenue.

What Market Share Tells You

In addition to helping a business determine how it is positioned compared to the competition in its service area, market share can be used to monitor the progress of the business over time. Are the market share numbers increasing or decreasing? What are the trends?

Businesses go through predictable stages of growth, as do their products and services. Which products are positioned for growth? Which are dying? The trends that you monitor can help you answer these questions and identify where you need to be focusing—or pulling back on—resources to support various products and services.

In the 1970's, Boston Consulting Group came out with a model—the Growth-Share Matrix—that is widely used today to categorize products into one of four categories: cash cows, dogs, question marks, or stars:

- **Cash cows** are products with slow growth but high market share. They require little investment to keep them going and generate a high amount of contribution to the bottom line.

- **Dogs** are products with both low growth and low market share. They contribute little to the business and are basically just kept around, because they do not consume a large amount of cash.

- **Question marks** are products with low market share but high growth potential. Because market share is low, investment is needed to boost their growth, but the business can't be certain whether this investment will ultimately pay off and move the question mark product into a different category.

- **Stars** are those products that are generating both high growth and high market share. Ultimately, of course, as the product matures, the star product is likely to become a cash cow. If, on the other hand, they begin to lose share, they may become dogs.

Using this framework to examine a company's product mix can help to make suggestions about where to continue to invest time and effort and where to pull back. For instance, should resources continue to be allocated to dogs, or should those resources instead be used to invest in question marks?

DID YOU KNOW?

The category "dogs" was originally called "pets" by Bruce Henderson, the Boston Consulting Group employee who originated the matrix. The term "dog" has become more commonly used in recent years.

For small businesses, market share is not necessarily the best gauge of success both because it may not measure the metrics that are most important to the business and because access to accurate data may prove challenging. Because market share is a commonly used concept in marketing, though, it's important to understand.

Sources of Information

Gathering information to help you calculate market share can be challenging. Often, estimates must be used based on national data that provides some indication of market share across industries and geographies. Your best source of market share is likely to be the library—particularly university libraries. There you can get access to directories such as:

- **Market Share Report:** available in both print and electronic formats. Offers market share data on companies, products, and services in both consumer and industrial segments at the company and brand level.

- **IBISWorld:** an electronic database with in-depth, industry-specific reports on American industries based on NAICS codes.

- **Global Market Share Planner**: a print reference with somewhat limited information (only 12 sectors covered), but a good source for international data—51 countries are covered.

- **MediaMark Internet Reporter:** a database that contains detailed consumer product usage and media information collected from a national sample of U.S. consumers, including demographics, lifestyle, product usage, and media exposure.

Increasing Your Market Share

The only way to increase your market share is to generate more customers, more sales, or more revenue from the market area you have defined. Many businesses— even very large businesses—fall prey to the thinking that if they expand their geographic or demographic reach, they will be expanding market share. That's not necessarily true.

Here's why: if you currently define your market as a 10-mile radius from your location (which includes 50,000 people), measure your market share based on number of customers, and have 10,000 customers, your market share is 20 percent. If you expand to serve a 20-mile radius and build your number of customers to 20,000 customers, your market share has not increased to 40 percent. It has changed to some other percentage relative to the new, expanded size of the market. The population is no longer 50,000, but some higher number. The same issue applies if you were to expand the demographics of your market (for example, expanding to serve an older or younger demographic).

MISSTEPS

Don't make the mistake of assuming that you can expand your market share by opening up a branch office or a new store in another community. The only way to increase market share is to increase overall sales as a percentage of a defined market area.

Neither expanding your market area nor going after a new type of customer will increase your market share unless your overall sales go up proportionately. You may increase market potential because you have a number of new customers to target, but you will not necessarily increase market share. Quite simply, increasing market share always requires selling more. This may mean selling more products, selling to more people, or generating higher revenue amounts. That is not to say that expanding geographic or demographic reach is not important—just that it is not a reflection of market share.

One way that you can increase market share that doesn't involve expanding service area or market demographics is by introducing new products or services. Introducing new products and services can help you increase market share if you measure market share based on number of customers (your new product may attract new customers in your market area) or revenue (your existing customers may buy more from you because of the new products offered).

It's important to note that increasing market share is not always the best strategy for a business. In fact, increasing market share may require investing in more advertising or decreasing prices—both of which will negatively impact your bottom line. Many companies really don't care about market share. In fact, most small companies would likely not be able to deal with the demand that would be generated from significantly increasing market share; it's simply not their goal.

Consider all of the restaurants in your community—the large chain restaurants and the small, family-owned or specialty restaurants. While the large chain restaurants may be focused on capturing market share, chances are the smaller restaurants are more concerned with generating a certain amount of revenue and margin to meet their financial needs.

The Least You Need to Know

- Market analysis involves analyzing your customer needs and preferences as well as defining your market position.
- By understanding who your customers are, what's important to them, their levels of satisfaction, and at what rate they may be leaving you, you can develop targeted strategies and tactics to boost sales.
- Accurate market analysis requires a clear definition of the market in terms of both geography and customer demographics.
- Companies must decide if market share is an important measure for them and, if so, how they will define and measure market share.
- Introducing new products or services is an effective way to increase market share.

Competitive Analysis

In This Chapter

- How competitors are defined
- Identifying current and potential competitors
- How do you stand out from the competition?
- Identifying areas of risk and opportunity

Every business must understand who its competitors are. A good understanding of the options that your customers have can help you make sound decisions about how to position your products and services in terms of product attributes, price point, distribution, and communication.

In this chapter, we will take a look at the definition of competition (you may be surprised!), how to gather information about competitors to develop a competitor profile, and how to position your products and services so you capture a greater share of mind among your target audience than your competitors.

How Competitive Analysis Is Used

Competitive analysis is used by businesses to determine where they fit in and how they might be able to both capitalize on unique attributes they have or minimize potential weaknesses. Understanding all of the options available to potential customers can help businesses position their products and services in ways that make competitors less relevant.

> **DEFINITION**
>
> **Competitive analysis** is the process of identifying direct and indirect competitors, determining their strengths and weaknesses, and developing ways to position a business and its products and services to take advantage of opportunities and overcome potential threats.

Who Are Your Competitors?

Who do you compete with? That's an important question and, as you'll soon see, not as straightforward as you might think. Businesses have a tendency to underestimate both the number and the impact of the competitors they have. This is a factor of pride in the product or service, the tendency to believe that there are no other alternatives, and a lack of understanding of the difference between direct and indirect competition.

Direct Competitors

Direct competitors are those that offer basically the same thing that you offer. A direct competitor for McDonald's, for instance, would be Burger King. Virtually all businesses have direct competitors—or quickly will. Consider Apple's iPad, for instance. When introduced it was unique, representing a new product that initially had no direct competition. Shortly after its introduction, though, other technology companies began working on similar products that would soon enter the market and represent direct competition.

The same phenomenon takes place on a smaller scale in cities across the country. A coffee shop goes up on one corner in town and soon other coffee shops are popping up throughout the city. You introduce a shopping service for harried mothers and soon another shopping service is introduced.

Competition is inevitable and, ultimately, good for the end consumer. Competition results in improved product quality, pricing, access, and service to meet consumer needs. For the business, of course, competition is often not viewed in a favorable way. Competition represents risk. In assessing this risk in preparation for the strategic planning process, businesses need to consider …

- Who their direct competitors are.
- The level of potential threat the competitors represent.
- The level of opportunity that competitors may represent.

Here's an example to help illustrate this point.

A home medical equipment company in a mid-sized community identified direct competition from large, national providers of home medical equipment—Walgreen's and Apria. These were formidable competitors with significant resources, and they represented a threat in terms of the potential for existing customers to shift to these services due to the lower costs and broader product choices they could provide. On the other hand, the owners of the smaller business determined that it had something to offer that the larger providers could not compete with—local, personalized services. The company had both a potential threat and a potential opportunity represented by these competitors. During the strategic planning process, both of these points would be raised and considered relative to the company's other strengths, opportunities, weaknesses, and threats.

In this case, the competitors identified represented direct competitors—they filled basically the same need in the same way. But companies must also consider the impact of indirect competitors.

Indirect Competitors

Indirect competitors represent any alternative choices customers have to fill an identified need. Indirect competitors are often overlooked as companies tend to focus more on the direct competition for their products and services. They do so at their own peril, however.

MISSTEPS

Failing to consider all of the options customers have for obtaining what it is you have to offer them can result in overlooking not only threats to your sales but also opportunities you may have to provide new types of products and services.

Let's dive a bit deeper into the definition. We've already seen that McDonald's and Burger King represent direct competition for each other. But they both face a significant amount of indirect competition:

- Any other restaurant, even outside the fast-food realm

- Staying in and cooking at home

- Going to a friend's or relative's house for dinner

These alternative choices may seem silly and not worth considering, but the impact can be significant. Consider the effect that the declining economy in 2008–2009 had on consumers' choices to dine out versus eating at home. Consider the emergence of the word *staycation* to represent consumer choices to vacation in their own backyards instead of staying in hotels or flying to other destinations.

It's easy, and quite common, to ignore the impact of indirect competitors, but this can leave you blindsided, as this next example illustrates.

A webinar company that developed webinars for trade associations that, subsequently, sold the webinars to their members found that its sales volumes were declining at an alarming rate. Not only was the level of new customers rapidly declining, but the number of programs scheduled by existing customers was dropping and the number of registrants signing up for these programs was also on the decline. While the company had long considered other companies that provided the same services to associations as its competition, it discovered that these companies were also realizing a decline in numbers of customers, programs, and volumes. What was going on? Ultimately, the company recognized that it was experiencing indirect competition from the rapid growth in the availability of no- and low-cost information online, including free webinars on a variety of topics. The company had overlooked a primary source of competition from indirect competitors and its strategies failed to take these into account.

Indirect competition, in fact, represents the primary source of *disruptive innovations* that can threaten the existence of a business.

DEFINITION

Disruptive innovation (sometimes referred to as disruptive technology) describes an unexpected change in the market that results in a new product or service that takes the place of an existing product or service. For example, Blockbuster would consider Netflix to be a disruptive innovation because it introduced a new option to consumers that made Blockbuster's offerings obsolete.

In considering the competition that may impact your business, it's important to think broadly and to consider any other alternative customers have that might mean a lost sale for you. Paying attention to sources of indirect competition can be a good way to stay ahead of market changes that could negatively affect your business.

Profiling the Competition

Developing a deep understanding of competitors—whether direct or indirect—is important so businesses can develop plans that position what they have to offer in ways that are more attractive to consumers than what the competition has to offer. The more you know about your competition, the better. You must assume, as well, that the competition is taking steps to learn as much as they can about you. (In fact, one small-business owner that marketed seminars and had two local competitors doing the same thing was convinced that they went through his trash at night—he may have been right!)

A common means of tracking competition is to create profiles for each of your key competitors. These profiles provide detailed information about your competitors' services, markets, staff, and—to the extent possible—their finances and strategies. The type of information commonly included in competitive profiles include:

- Year formed

- Location of stores or branches (and, now, online presence)

- Key players (founders or owners, key staff members)

- Products and services offered including pricing and sales information, as available

- New products or services that may be under development

- Market served—geographic and demographic

- Promotional mix—budget, advertising themes, and positioning strategy

- Financial information—profitability, capital position

- Recent changes of significance—new product introductions, market expansion, or changes in ownership or staff.

Identifying top competitors (including indirect competitors), establishing a standard format for these profiles, and assigning someone to be responsible for developing and keeping profiles up to date is a good starting point. Profiles should be reviewed and updated on a regular basis and will serve as an important input to the strategic planning process.

Depending on the type of business you have and the industry you're in—and whether your competition represents for-profit, not-for-profit, publicly held, or privately held organizations—there is a great deal of *competitive intelligence* that is readily available. This may include organizational structure, profiles of key executives and employees, products or services and their pricing, advertising strategies, and market share. Other information can be harder to come by, such as profit information, customer retention data, and new product strategies. But all of these types of information are worth seeking out and there are ample sources available to provide insights into what the competition is doing—or thinking of doing.

DEFINITION

Competitive intelligence involves gathering and analyzing information about competitors and their products and services.

Competitive intelligence is legal—industrial espionage is not, but the line between the two can often be blurry. While competitive intelligence involves gathering publicly available information, industrial espionage involves gaining access to information that is not publicly available, and which is considered proprietary by the business, through means that are at best unethical and at worse illegal. For example, digging through a competitor's trash bins or hacking into their computer systems is a form of industrial espionage.

Gathering Data

Three broad categories can provide useful information about your competitors:

- **Recorded data** is data that is available through annual reports (for publicly held companies), news releases, media coverage, etc. Identifying these sources of information for your competitors and developing processes to monitor these sources regularly can help you stay on top of what's happening.

- **Observable data** is information that you have access to through a variety of means. Perhaps you have access to pricing information or price lists. You can monitor the type of advertising and promotion that your competitors do. You can even buy products and services from your competitors to learn firsthand about what they do and how they do it.

- **Incidental data** is data that you come across through luck or chance. There are many stories of businesspeople picking up copies of marketing plans and other competitive information in restrooms and other unlikely places. So, incidental data is another source of competitive information—clearly it pays to be observant! Other sources of incidental data can come from:

    Suppliers and vendors

    Trade shows

    Employee recruitment interactions

    Friends, relatives, colleagues, and other connections

Two popular options for gathering competitive data on companies are:

- Dun & Bradstreet, which provides financial performance and other information

- Lead411.com, which provides key executive names, information on new hires/ terminations, funding sources, and other information

One woman who was recruiting a media relations staff person tells of a candidate who left behind—purposefully—a folder filled with details about her current employer's media relations activities. The interviewer was shocked, and while she did read the information, she didn't follow up with the candidate—after all, if the candidate would share information about this employer, the odds were pretty good she'd share it about her new employer as well!

DID YOU KNOW?

In March 2010, an Apple software engineer accidentally left an iPhone prototype he was testing on a barstool. Although the phone was disguised, it ultimately ended up in the hands of Gizmodo, a technology weblog, which discovered what it really was and quickly shared the story online.

Mystery Shopping

Another interesting source of information is available through a research technique known as mystery shopping. Mystery shopping involves sending someone into a business to act in the role of the customer and then report back on the experience.

The mystery shopper might also simply call businesses and ask questions to gather information. In a medical clinic, for instance, the marketing staff regularly conducted mystery-shopping activities that included:

- Calling area primary care providers to find out how soon a new patient could be seen and comparing this data with their own.

- Checking into LASIK eye surgery offerings in the area and comparing the response time, value of information provided, and sales techniques between the various businesses.

- Gathering informal information from employees who had family members or who might themselves seek treatment from other competing providers.

In short, it pays to be creative—and sometimes sneaky! There are ample opportunities to gather competitive data in casual, incidental, and entirely legal ways. You can be assured that your most savvy competitors are also gathering this information about you.

Getting Information Online

The massive amounts of, and ready access to, information on the Internet represents significant opportunities for companies seeking to learn about their competition, as well as significant risk for companies whose competitors are seeking to learn about them! It's a two-way street, and it pays to be traveling faster down that street than those you're competing with.

There are some simple ways that you can monitor the activities of your competitors online. These include:

- Simple searches in any search engine using your competitors' business or product names.

- Tools like Google Alerts, which allows you to enter search terms and phrases and get updates on an immediate, daily, or weekly basis about references to the terms you select.

- Social media tools like Facebook, LinkedIn, and Twitter, which allow you to follow the postings of competitors and track comments about competitors— and your own business—being made by people online.

BEST PRACTICES

The transparent nature of the social media environment makes it easy to track and follow the competition. Becoming a follower on Twitter or a fan on Facebook can give you access to not only what your competitors are saying and doing but the interactions they have with customers as well.

The problem you'll face in analyzing the competition isn't in finding information—there's a wealth of information available, much of it at no cost—but in determining how to most effectively use that information.

What Makes You Stand Out?

The purpose of gathering information about your competitors is to determine how they are the same—and different—from you. This information can help you identify opportunities to stand out and offer something unique to the market. It can also provide you with early indications of areas of potential risk when competitors' offerings begin to compete more directly with yours or when they are planning to expand their services or market area. In evaluating this information, it can be helpful to develop a means of quantifying the things you've gathered to help you identify areas of both opportunity and threat.

Using a Matrix to Determine Your Position

One tool that can be very helpful is a competitive analysis matrix. A matrix allows you to compare yourself and your competitors against a list of key attributes that are important to your target audience. The ability to produce such a matrix, of course, requires that you have effectively gathered accurate information about your customers' requirements and preferences and about your competitors. We'll assume this is true.

A basic matrix can be produced simply by identifying your key competitors and the attributes that you feel represent competitive factors. Let's say you're thinking of opening a locally owned fast-food restaurant. You know that you will face a lot of competition from national chains, but you've decided that you can compete with them on the primary attributes customers are looking for and provide something more—a local connection, locally grown food, and community support. You identify the main competitive attributes as friendly and helpful staff, quality of food, efficiency of service, and price. You then create a matrix with your competitors listed on the left side and the competitive attributes listed across the top, and you rank each competitor, on each of the factors, using a scale of 1–5, with 5 being high. You consider each individual category as well as an overall average rating for yourself and each of your competitors.

The matrix might look something like this:

Competitor	Staff	Food	Efficiency	Price	Score
McDonald's	3.5	3.7	4.3	4.0	3.875
KFC	2.7	3.2	3.2	3.2	3.075
Taco John's	1.8	2.7	2.8	4.0	2.82
Pizza Hut	3.0	4.5	3.8	3.0	3.575

So this simple analysis tells you that based on your own subjective assessment, your greatest competitive threat will come from McDonald's and you would be least worried about Taco John's. But what this analysis fails to take into account is the weighted importance of each of the criteria. The final score is just an overall assessment of everything rolled into one score.

With just one more step, though, you can develop an analysis that gives you an indication not only of an overall average score but an overall weighted score. It also provides an indication of where each of your competitors falls on attributes that have the most importance to the market. To do this you will need data, information, or your best guess about the relative weight of the attributes you've identified in the minds of the target customers.

BEST PRACTICES

You can gain data about consumer perceptions through a consumer market assessment, where you ask consumers to rate you and your competitors on an array of attributes. That will give you a much more statistically significant result.

For a weighted competitive analysis matrix, you would follow these steps:

1. Identify the elements of success that are most important to you.

2. Identify the attributes that are most important to your customers.

3. Identify your key competitors (don't overlook indirect competitors).

4. Give a weighting (Wt.) to each of the items that are important to you and your customers (the total of all rankings should equal 1.0).

5. Rate each competitor on each of these factors.

6. Multiply the rating of each competitor by the weighting of the success factor.

The following table shows how this would work. The chosen factors are listed down the left-hand side of the table. The weighting (Wt.) for each factor is provided and each competitor is assigned a rating (C#1-r, C#2-r, C#3-r). Ratings are multiplied by the weight to develop a weighted score (C#1-w, C#2-w, C#3-w). The final two columns show your ratings and weighted scores.

Factor	Wt.	C#1-r	C#1-w	C#2-r	C#2-w	C#3-r	C#3-w	You-r	You-w
Quality	.4	3.5	1.4	3.0	1.2	4.5	1.8	4.5	1.8
Service	.3	4.0	1.2	2.5	.75	4.2	1.26	4.8	1.44
Location	.1	4.5	.45	3.0	.3	4.5	.45	3.0	.3
Totals	1.0		3.05		2.25		3.51		3.54

r = rating   w = weight

These results tell you that you have scored the highest, with a slight margin over Competitor #3 (we'll assume you used actual survey data to come up with these numbers!). In addition to this overall score, though, the weighted analysis gives you an indication of what goes into that overall score relative to the areas of most importance to your market. So, for example, based on the weighting factors, quality is the most important factor. Here you are neck and neck with your next closest competitor. You can also see that while location is a factor, the weighting of the factor is so slight that it doesn't really provide a competitive edge for those two competitors that scored relatively high here.

If you don't have actual data to use in this type of assessment, you will need to be as objective as possible in rating both your competitors and yourself, which can be challenging to do. But give it your best shot. While the ratings themselves will be somewhat subjective, the resulting relative rankings should provide at least some indication of where you stand relative to your competition and give you a good idea of where you need to place your focus.

Monitoring for Potential Competitors

It's easy enough to evaluate the competitors you know about. But businesses always have to be prepared for the entrance of new competitors. New competitors may emerge regardless of how long you've been in business or how established you are, and their entry can be devastating.

A woman who had owned a trendy wine and beer bar next door to a popular restaurant in a resort community for several years, and had a loyal and well-established following, found herself suddenly faced with a competitor. The entry of that competitor, coupled with a tight economy, almost caused her business to shut down. The new entrant wasn't able to capture enough market share to make a go of the business and ended up closing. But the result obviously could have been much different.

Remember, no business is immune to the impact of competition—even the mighty fall. If you're alert, though, and taking steps to monitor the competitive environment, you may be able to identify early risks that you can address through your strategic planning process. There are certain factors that can increase the odds that a competitor might enter your market. These include:

- The potential for high profit margins

- Demand that is not being met by existing businesses

- Opportunity for competitive advantage (existing businesses are not providing quality, service, or access at levels that are meeting market needs)

- No major barriers to market entry

If these conditions exist in your market, you should be on your toes. The steps that you should take to thwart the entry of competitors represent the basics of running any business. However, business owners sometimes take these factors for granted or become complacent about when they feel they are the only option available to customers. These include meeting demand through your products and services; focusing on providing high quality, service, and access; and remaining innovative in your development and delivery of products and services.

The Least You Need to Know

- There are two types of competitors—direct and indirect; both have implications for businesses in terms of how they position what they have to offer.
- A variety of resources is available to evaluate current competitors and identify the potential for new competitive market entrants.
- Once competitive attributes have been identified, identify opportunities that will allow your business to stand out from the competition.
- Identifying areas of risk and opportunity can help companies compete effectively with existing competitors and stave off new competition.

Internal Analysis

In This Chapter

- The value of core competencies—and how to determine yours
- Understanding your company's financial position
- Key issues related to employees and staffing
- Evaluating internal systems and processes: what's working and what's not

In an analysis of the internal environment, you will consider how your business creates value for customers and how you deliver this value in a way that is profitable and that reflects a business model that works.

There are multiple internal factors that you will consider during this process. Chief among these are your core competencies (the things you do best), your financial position (including sales volumes), employees (primarily related to hiring, turnover, and satisfaction), and system or process issues (areas of efficiency or areas that need to be improved). The good news is that you probably already have all the information you need to conduct your internal analysis. All you will need to do is identify what information is important to you and develop ways to make the gathering and reporting of this information part of your ongoing planning activities.

Your internal analysis will help you plan for the future by documenting how you currently operate. During this analysis, you will identify your core competencies and consider trends, limitations, and opportunities. You will gather information about your company's strengths and weaknesses, products or services, staffing, and finances.

In this chapter, we'll take a look at the type of internal information that can aid in the strategic planning process.

How Internal Analysis Is Used

Internal analysis is used to provide an assessment of the business in terms of critical factors such as level of sales, types of customers served, employee satisfaction, and operational impacts that may include access to funding and the condition of buildings and equipment. While much of your situation analysis to this point has been on the outside world, the internal analysis involves taking a look at yourself.

DEFINITION

Internal analysis is the evaluation of factors internal to a company, and under its control, that may impact its future success. Internal analysis generally focuses on customer, employee, and financial considerations.

Core Competencies

In their 1990 article, "The Core Competence of the Corporation," published in the *Harvard Business Review*, C. K. Prahalad and Gary Hamel defined *core competencies* as the important variables within an organization that are …

- Durable.

- Difficult to duplicate.

- Of significant customer value.

DEFINITION

Core competencies are the things that you do better than anybody else. They are things that hold great value for your customers and that competitors would have a difficult time replicating.

All businesses must have a range of competencies, but not all of these competencies are core. For instance, common business competencies include marketing, production or operations, management of human resources, administration, and research and development. In considering the competencies that may be core to your business, it can be helpful to look back on your competitive analysis (see Chapter 9) to identify those areas where you have strengths that the competition lacks and, particularly, areas where these strengths also align with areas customers highly value.

Companies that have core competencies have a competitive edge. The core competency sets them apart and strengthens their brand. For instance, FedEx built its business based on its ability to deliver packages quickly and on time—its core competence was, and is, managing logistics. Other delivery companies manage logistics, but FedEx does it better. Nordstrom is widely known for its high levels of service. Apple is known for innovation. You don't have to be a big brand, though, to have a core competency. Consider your business and the products or services it offers. What things do you do better than anybody else that are central to the products or services you provide? These are your core competencies.

Perhaps you really can't identify anything you do that sets you apart. You're about as good as the competition. That discovery could be an indication that the long-term sustainability of your business is at risk, and it may represent an important input for the strategic planning process. On the other hand, your analysis may identify a significant strength you have that would be difficult for competitors to replicate—a strength that reflects something that customers highly value. This is a core competency that you can leverage to your benefit and is, again, an important input to the strategic planning process.

Core competencies are core in that they represent the fundamental purpose of your business. When companies consider elements of their business that could be outsourced, core competencies do not fall on that list. These are the things that only you can do and that represent your competitive advantage. A home builder, for instance, might outsource—or subcontract—the electrical work or the plumbing, but the actual construction of the house is core to the business.

Importantly, core competencies need to reflect the *most important* attributes you have—not *all* attributes. "Every part of the organization doesn't have to be great," says one product manager. "It's important for companies to figure out where their greatest strengths are. You can have a very successful and very profitable organization without being good at everything."

Financial Position

Your company's financial position involves consideration of the viability, sustainability, and profitability of your business. Careful review of this information can yield some startling results, as one woman found out through her own strategic planning process.

When analyzing financials and direction, says one small-business owner and consultant, she looked at nine years worth of data focusing on revenue trends and percent and amount of revenue. She had a feeling that one company in particular—a public seminar company—was having a negative effect on her business development. She created some simple *control charts* to look at what was happening over time and discovered she was right. "Over the nine years, the public seminar company had become an increasing part of my business and, as it did, overall revenue declined while the percentage from this company increased." The analysis helped her to make a business decision about increasing the diversity of revenue sources—and a decision to continue her strategic planning efforts.

DEFINITION

A **control chart** is a tool that is used in statistical process control. It shows data points over time and how these data points vary from the mean (or average). The variation gives an indication of whether a change is statistically significant or just a random occurrence. The control chart was developed by Walter Shewhart, an American physicist, engineer, and statistician, in the early 1920s.

Looking at data over time provides an indication of trends as well as levels of performance. Reviewing information in this way—over time—helps avoid drawing inaccurate conclusions. For example, a company that suddenly sees a drop in sales for a particular product in March might decide to make changes to that product in terms of production or promotion if looking only at that one month's data. But, when plotting activity over time on a control chart, the company can see whether the decrease was part of a statistically significant trend which would warrant some attention or if it was just a random downturn that should not be cause for concern.

Looking at Trends and Levels

Companies that don't consider trends as well as levels of performance can become their own worst enemy. Consider, for instance, a catalog company that promotes its service through direct mail. Catalogs are mailed out one month and the results of that particular effort are not realized until one to two months later. If the cataloguer makes changes based on a particular month's activities—changing catalog format, copy, design, mailing lists, etc.—it can start a vicious cycle where the business never really knows what efforts are leading to good or bad sales. If, on the other hand, the cataloguer keeps activities stable over several months and monitors trends, he will have a better idea of when changes might be necessary.

MISSTEPS

Be cautious about jumping to conclusions over a single data point. What you're seeing may represent a single, chance event, rather than a trend that warrants action.

Several areas may represent strengths or weaknesses for your company from a financial standpoint:

- Ability to raise short- and long-term capital
- Tax considerations
- Price/earnings ratio
- The availability of and access to working capital
- The relative size of your organization in terms of revenue and annual budget
- The ability to control or reduce costs

Three Key Areas of Financial Analysis

Three key areas that you will evaluate to help paint a picture of your financial position are:

- Profit or loss
- Cash flow
- The balance sheet

You should be looking at each of these on a regular basis—generally monthly—so the information should be readily available to you as you enter the strategic planning process.

Your profit or loss is determined through the following formulas:

Revenue – Cost of Goods Sold = Gross Profit

Gross Profit – Overhead Expenses = Net Profit

Cash flow is the cash you have on hand to deal with the ongoing obligations of doing business—payroll, supply expenses, etc. It is possible for businesses to show a profit and yet have a negative cash flow. How? If the profit is based on revenue not yet collected, for example. Your cash flow is a reflection of cash you are actually receiving and doesn't include any payments that are forthcoming. So while you may have many customer commitments for sales, until you actually have the money—from a cash flow perspective—it doesn't count. The formula for calculating cash flow is:

Beginning Cash Balance + (Cash Coming In – Cash Going Out) = Ending Cash Balance

The balance sheet provides a snapshot in time of the financial position for your company, showing your assets, liabilities, and owner's equity. Owner's equity provides an indication of the value of the company.

Assets – liabilities = owner's equity.

In preparation for the strategic planning process, you will be doing a historical view of your financial data. This will include a review of revenue by product or service and perhaps by location (physical and online). Which products are selling well? Which are not? This information can help you determine areas where you may wish to eliminate products and services, as well as areas where you may wish to invest more effort into improving and promoting products and services.

Your type of business will also impact the type of financial information you gather and which information you look at most closely. A medical practice, for instance, will be most interested in the numbers of encounters or patient visits. A manufacturing company would be most interested in shipping and inventory levels. In thinking about the type of financial information that is most meaningful to you, consider the numbers that you look at almost automatically to give you an indication of how your business is doing—those numbers are likely to be a good starting point.

Your financial data will also come into play as you use the strategic planning process to help you move forward. You will rely on the information you have to help predict how successful new product introductions may be, for instance, or to provide information needed for budgeting purposes.

BEST PRACTICES

When it comes to using financial information effectively, don't hesitate to call upon outside resources if you, or other members of your staff, don't have strong expertise in this area. A good accountant can provide a great deal of value in terms of helping you analyze this very important piece of internal intelligence.

Employee/Staffing Issues

Your employees drive the development, delivery, and support for your products and services, whatever it is that you produce. Knowledgeable, committed, loyal, and satisfied employees are critical elements for the success of a business, particularly in service industries. Consequently, employee data will be an important input to the strategic planning process. You will want to consider such things as:

- **Staffing levels and trends.** What are the primary positions in the company? Which positions are vacant, and how long, on average, do these positions stay vacant before being filled? How long do people stay in one position? How difficult is it to fill certain positions?

- **Turnover rates.** What is the rate at which employees are leaving your company on both a voluntary and involuntary basis? Is turnover higher in certain areas or during certain times of the year?

- **Employee satisfaction.** How satisfied are employees with their jobs, their supervisors, their co-workers, their opportunities to develop and advance?

- **Succession planning.** In what areas might you be at risk for losing key employees?

Let's take a closer look at each of these areas.

Staffing Levels and Trends

For most companies, staffing costs represent a significant part of their operating expenses. In considering staffing levels and trends, you will want to consider the following questions:

- How many employees do you currently have?

- How have these numbers changed over time?

- What is the ratio of employee staffing costs to revenue, and is this number increasing, decreasing, or staying about the same?

If you are paying more for staff but producing less, that is an issue that needs to be addressed. You should strike a delicate balance when it comes to staffing. Having too many staff can lead to unnecessary costs. Not having enough staff, on the other hand, can lead to poor quality and service—which can have a negative impact on customers and, ultimately, the bottom line.

There are two primary ways in which companies can reduce staffing levels: technology and outsourcing. Businesses should continually be looking for opportunities to increase efficiency through new technology and should also consider tasks that could be more effectively done by others. Many small companies, for instance, outsource the HR function (or a good portion of it) to Professional Employer Organizations (PEOs). Those activities that are not core to your business are the activities that could most readily be outsourced.

The monitoring and adjustment of staffing levels must be considered in concert with customer satisfaction and quality data. For instance, if both employee numbers and customer satisfaction are declining, it could indicate a problem and may suggest that existing employees are not able to adequately meet customer demands.

Turnover Rates

Staff turnover has an impact on your company in terms of costs to rehire and train new staff as well as the impact on operations; when productive staff leave, new staff members must be brought up to speed.

Turnover should be reviewed for both voluntary and involuntary departures. Voluntary departures may occur when employees take another job (perhaps with a competitor!), move, or retire. Involuntary departures are related to terminations or layoffs. Both numbers give you an indication of issues that may exist relating to hiring, training, and management effectiveness. High rates of voluntary turnover, for instance, may indicate that the jobs are not meeting expectations of employees and that the information they were given during the hiring process did not reflect reality. High rates of involuntary turnover may suggest that employees are being hired without the important skills necessary to succeed on the job—both in terms of job-related abilities and cultural fit. High turnover may also point toward issues related to employee satisfaction.

Employee Satisfaction

Employee satisfaction surveys, conducted on a regular basis, can give you insights into areas of opportunity for improvement. These surveys, which can be quite simple, indicate not only levels of satisfaction but also trends over time. A simple rating scale of 1–5, with 1 being very dissatisfied and 5 being very satisfied, can be used. Common questions related to satisfaction include: "How satisfied are you with …":

- Your job?

- Your access to the tools to help you do your job effectively?

- The support you receive from your supervisor or manager?

- Your relationships with peers?

- The communication you receive about the company?

- Your ability to influence factors that affect your job?

- How well your supervisor or manager listens to you?

- Access to training you need to do your job well?

- The opportunity for personal development?

- The recognition you receive for the work you do?

- Your ability to balance work and personal responsibilities?

Surveys are not the only way to gather information about levels of employee satisfaction, though. Focus groups and even casual, everyday interactions with employees can provide you with an indication of the levels of employee satisfaction and morale for your organization.

BEST PRACTICES

A great question to ask employees that is highly correlated with job satisfaction is: "Would you recommend this company as a place to work?" The more employees who say yes, the higher their levels of job satisfaction.

Reviewing your workforce as an input to strategic planning should also involve consideration of where you may be vulnerable to losing key employees. Small companies in particular are at risk when even one key employee leaves. Identifying those key spots and taking steps to minimize risk should be an ongoing practice.

Succession Planning

It's important to consider the skills mix of employees and any gaps that may exist to satisfy both current needs and projected future needs. Succession planning is a way to proactively protect against the risk of losing important *intellectual capital* and ensuring a smooth transition when key people leave the organization. Succession planning considers areas where the company may be at risk for turnover—through retirement, through the loss of employees to other jobs, etc. Succession planning also involves looking to the future to determine what new skills and competencies will be necessary to meet business challenges. Basically, it involves making decisions today about the type of talent you will need in the future.

> **DEFINITION**
>
> **Intellectual capital** is the collective value of the knowledge resources that your business has, generally represented through what people know. In a heavy service economy, intellectual capital can be as valuable as—if not more valuable than—financial capital.

The skills and knowledge that your employees bring to your business represent value to your organization. There is also the potential for risk if that value is lost through turnover. While intellectual capital is often considered to be residing in people's heads, companies can and should take steps to capture that knowledge so it is retained and can be passed on when employees leave.

When considering succession planning, there are a number of steps to take:

1. Identify skill and competency needs.

2. Identify positions that may be at risk—this may be due to an impending retirement or to the critical nature of the job.

3. Identify potential internal successors—who are the individuals within your company who may be able to move into at-risk positions if they become vacant?

4. Identify skill and knowledge gaps and work to fill them.

Being aware of these areas of potential risk can provide an important input to the strategic planning process. Potential impacts include both HR needs (need to hire, train, etc.) and potential impacts on product and service quality and delivery that could be at risk if those in key positions leave.

What's Working and What Isn't?

In preparation for strategic planning, you should also consider your internal systems and processes. What processes are working well? Where are there areas of inefficiency or weak performance? The ability to process orders quickly and cost-effectively is a strength. A high number of product returns may represent a weakness in terms of quality or product claims that are not consistent with customer experiences.

When considering internal systems and processes, businesses basically need to be asking themselves: "What's working and what's not?" Those answers may revolve around a number of areas that include:

- The cost and availability of supplies
- Inventory control and turnover
- Ability and capacity to meet customer demand
- Equipment efficiency
- Technological competencies
- New product development

Value Chain Analysis

Depending on your business and the factors that are most critical to your success, you may not review all of these factors, or you may review additional factors. As with other areas of review, you will examine current performance, compare it to past performance, and compare yourself to other firms in and outside of your industry (based upon your access to information and the cost of obtaining that information). Much of this information you may have already identified during the competitive analysis process (see Chapter 9).

A *value chain analysis* can be a good way to gain an overall perspective on the efficiencies in your organization in terms of primary activities (operations, marketing, and service) as well as critical support functions (finance, HR, and technology).

DEFINITION

Value chain analysis is a term that was popularized in 1985 by Michael Porter in his book *Competitive Advantage: Creating and Sustaining Supervisor Performance* (see Appendix B). It is the process of looking at the series of steps that lead to the delivery of a product or service and identifying areas where there may be weak links in the chain that might represent opportunities for process improvement.

Value chain analysis begins with the identification of the key primary and support activities for the company. Next, you would consider the value of each of these activities to the customer(s) for that activity. These customers may be internal or external. For instance, the customers of the HR department are internal. They may value prompt responses to their questions and accurate, reliable information. The customers for the sales department would be external. They may value accurate descriptions of products and services, knowledgeable answers to questions, and prompt delivery and follow-up service.

The process of reviewing the value chain based on customer needs will likely generate plenty of opportunities for ways to increase value. These, of course, serve as important inputs to the strategic planning process.

Making Sense of It All

The internal analysis encompasses a lot of areas. Once complete, the small business owner may be scratching his or her head trying to figure out how to make sense of it all. A process for gaining meaning from the data can be helpful:

1. Identify the key internal factors that drive success.

2. Evaluate performance on these factors by considering current performance compared to past performance.

3. Look for sources of comparison to give a sense of whether your performance is high, low, or in the middle of the pack.

4. Identify those factors that represent basic must-haves, key advantages, and potential areas of vulnerability.

The key internal factors that drive success may be based on your analysis of your core competencies and value chain but may also extend beyond these to include other factors that you believe are important to your business. For instance, one web-based publishing firm had a significant source of capital available through a family-run foundation. This was a very important factor for the company that didn't reflect a core competency.

A comparison of current to past performance is important to determine trends that should be monitored and, potentially, addressed. It is important not to jump to conclusions here. As the consultant who found that one of her clients was representing too large a portion of her business noted, the use of control charts can be helpful. In her case, it was possible that her concern was just a reflection of recent activity and not typical of results over time. But looking at performance over time, using a statistical tool like a run chart, indicated that the change was, indeed, significant—and important enough to require an action of some kind.

In addition to comparing your current performance levels to your results over time, it's important to have some indication of whether your results are good, bad, or mediocre. How do you know, for instance, whether a 3.5 on a 5.0 scale of employee satisfaction is cause for concern? That's where external benchmark information about the results that other companies are attaining can come into play.

BEST PRACTICES

Involvement in trade and professional organizations that represent your business or industry can provide you with access to data and information to help you benchmark your performance against others.

Finally, you will consider the impact of the information you've gathered in terms of the level of risk—or potential opportunity—it may present. This will occur more formally during the SWOT analysis, discussed in Chapter 12.

The Least You Need to Know

- Your business success factors—your core competencies—are unique and driven by what your customers value.
- Your financial position can be measured in a variety of ways; looking at trends can add important perspectives.
- Evaluating staffing levels and turnover can help identify potential areas of risk.
- Reviewing internal systems and processes can identify areas for potential process improvements, which can lead to increased employee and customer satisfaction.

The Planning Process

This part of the book represents the meat of the strategic plan. You'll learn about the core elements of the strategic plan—goals, objectives, strategies, and tactics—and how to develop them appropriately. You'll discover the importance of clear alignment between these plan elements and how to focus on those things that matter most in achieving success. You'll also learn about the foundation for effective strategic planning—the SWOT analysis, an important tool that you'll come to love.

We'll cover the difference between objectives and strategies, and how to put these tools to use to create plans that generate focused action. Finally, you'll learn how all of the material you gathered and the SWOT analysis you conducted help provide focus as you develop the actual plan.

Mission, Vision, and Values

In This Chapter

- Your mission statement
- Your vision statement
- Defining your core values
- Letting employees know what you expect
- Revisiting your mission, vision, and values regularly

Your company's mission, vision, and values lay the foundation for any planning effort. That is, of course, if you have them! Not all companies do, at least not in a documented format—especially small companies. Most companies do, however, have some sense of what their mission, vision, and values are, even if they're not explicitly stated.

Mission, vision, and values statements don't just apply to companies. Divisions, departments, or even roles within a business can also have mission, vision, or values statements. If they do, though, these individual statements must be supportive of and aligned with the mission, vision, and values of the overall business.

Much could be written on how to develop mission, vision, and values statements. That is not our purpose here, though. These statements play an important role in strategic planning, but the strategic planning process should not be focused on rewriting or recreating the mission, vision, and values. Instead, these statements should be reviewed to ensure that they accurately reflect what the business is and wishes to be—and how it interacts with others. Once this is confirmed, these statements serve as a guide that can be used to consider the appropriateness of goals, objectives, strategies, and tactics, which must all be aligned with the company's mission, vision, and values.

In this chapter, we'll take a look at the role of the mission, vision, and values in relation to the strategic planning process.

A Clear Organizational Mission

Which comes first, the mission or the vision? That's a debate that rages in far too many boardrooms across the country. Sometimes you'll see the mission listed first in a diagram that aligns mission, vision, and values. And when we see the words used in business books and journals, they're often written in that order; however, this probably has more to do with how the phrase sounds than the actual order of the terms. In fact, the vision is the highest level of these statements, the mission comes next, and the values support the ability of the organization to achieve both.

But we'll start with mission here as well because it is the statement that reflects the reality of what your business does and whom it serves. Unlike vision statements, which describe what the organization desires to become in the future, *mission statements* describe the primary work of the business today.

DEFINITION

A **mission statement** is a statement of the reason your business exists and reflects both who you wish to serve (a definition of your customers) and the value that you hope to provide them with.

Your mission statement should be a brief statement about the purpose of the existence of your business. Your mission should provide guidance on a day-to-day basis for your staff when they have decisions to make. The mission statement is, in essence, what you stand for. But keep in mind that mission statements should be designed to provide focus and direction. You can't stand for everything or be everything to all people. The process of developing and regularly reviewing your mission statement should help you maintain focus on what your core business is and whom you serve.

Here are some classic examples of mission statements:

- Mayo Clinic: "Mayo Clinic will provide the best care to every patient every day through integrated clinical practice, education, and research."

- The Coca-Cola Company: "To refresh the world…To inspire moments of optimism and happiness…To create value and make a difference."

- Starbucks: "To inspire and nurture the human spirit—one person, one cup, and one neighborhood at a time."

- Walmart: "To give ordinary folk the chance to buy the same thing as rich people."

Importantly, the mission statement should reflect reality—many don't. A lofty mission statement that is not an accurate reflection of what your business really stands for has no value. And employees—and other *stakeholders*—can see right through that.

DEFINITION

Stakeholders are individuals or groups that are impacted or affected by the activities of your organization and its ability to fulfill its mission and vision.

Some companies struggle to achieve their mission and some fall off the path of supporting their mission. Toyota's mission statement, for instance, is: "To attract and attain customers with high-valued products and services and the most satisfying ownership experience in America." Massive recalls of Toyotas in 2010 certainly challenged the credibility of that mission statement. However, hopefully you can see how that mission could serve as a starting point for Toyota's strategic planning efforts for the future.

What the Mission Statement Does for You

You may not be the Mayo Clinic, Coca-Cola, Starbucks, Walmart, or Toyota, but it doesn't matter. You still have a mission. Why are you in business? What is your overall purpose? For example, suppose you opened a restaurant because you wanted to serve locally grown and personally prepared food for residents of your community. That, in essence, is your mission! It is why you are in business.

Every business has a mission—often living inside the head of the founder. Your challenge is to get that mission out of somebody's head and down on paper where it can serve as a guide to your organization. The simple act of stating your mission does something powerful for your company. It provides a focus. In the previous example, the mission of serving locally grown and personally prepared food for residents of your community would help you respond to the following opportunities or ideas:

- Your restaurant is located in Illinois and a customer suggests that you serve key lime pie; however, key limes aren't grown in Illinois. Easy answer: "No." Reason: "We serve locally grown food."

- An employee suggests that you could save a lot of money if you began to use prepared sauces available through a vendor in a neighboring community. Easy answer: "No." Reason: "We serve personally prepared food."

That is how a mission statement should work to help guide your decisions. Again, an important point is that the mission reflects reality. It is easy for you—and your employees—to determine whether or not it does reflect reality based on the decisions you make. If you did begin serving key lime pie, or buying prepared food to serve in your restaurant, the credibility of your mission would be challenged.

MISSTEPS

"A mission and vision are good to have, but they can become a distraction," says an employee with an energy firm. "You can spend a whole day just trying to define a mission, and some people like to engage in that kind of argument. At the end of the day, they just want to see their words incorporated into the statement." Mission and vision statements can be helpful, he says, but adds: "They're a lot like semicolons—they're good to have if you know how to use them, but if you don't know how to use them, don't put them in."

One woman who worked with a start-up company based in London on its strategic marketing planning process says that when she went into the project, she had the view of mission statements being primarily a manifesto but soon changed her opinion. Rewriting and refocusing the mission and vision to align with the target market, she says, is critical. It can make the company's market proposition much more targeted and can even open up entirely new areas of marketing opportunity. Taking the time to do this review and revision, she says, resulted in a list of solid and focused recommendations and a strong marketing strategy. "To tell the truth, I was quite surprised," she admits.

Developing the Mission Statement

If you don't already have a stated mission statement, it is important to define one. But don't make this simply a writing exercise. Too often more time is spent on word-smithing than on coming up with a mission that provides direction and focus for the organization. In fact, the process of developing mission statements has become such a joke among many businesspeople that Scott Adams, the creator of the *Dilbert* cartoon, created a mission statement generator that pokes fun at the general, "one-size-fits-all" tone of many mission statements.

DID YOU KNOW?

Personal mission statements have become popularized by various self-help gurus. In fact, Nightingale Conant, a producer of personal development material, whose authors and speakers include such luminaries as Earl Nightingale, Tony Robbins, and Brian Tracy, offers an online personal mission statement generator at www.nightingale.com/mission that is intended to be a legitimate starting point for people working on their own personal mission statements.

But while mission statements are the butt of many management-related jokes and automatic mission-generating tools, a carefully crafted mission statement that accurately reflects reality can help to guide your company, division, or department—and your strategic planning efforts.

As you develop your mission statement, keep in mind it should provide an answer to three questions:

1. What do we do?

2. How do we do it?

3. Who do we do it for?

Your mission can be whatever you would like it to be—it just needs to be real. So your mission could be "to provide the best value to budget-stretched diners by searching nationally for unique food at bargain prices" or it could be "to make everything from scratch for discerning diners." It's entirely up to you!

A good mission statement will serve many needs for an organization, including providing overall direction for employees and for decisions made on an ongoing basis. From a strategic planning perspective, the mission also provides important direction. It lays the foundation for the process and serves as an important reminder to all involved about why the business exists, what it does, and whom it serves. It establishes boundaries that can be helpful when going through the process of coming up with new ideas for strategic direction. Not every good idea will support the mission. That doesn't mean it's not a good idea, it just means that it's not a good idea for you.

A Compelling Organizational Vision

In addition to a mission, organizations have a vision. There is often confusion between the mission statement and the *vision statement*. While the mission statement is designed to be a simple reflection of what the purpose of your business is, your vision statement is a forward-looking statement of what you aspire to. The mission statement answers the question "What do we do?" The vision statement describes "what we would like to be."

DEFINITION

The **vision statement** is a far-reaching statement that provides an indication of what the company hopes to be or achieve over the long-term.

Vision statements should be clear and challenging enough to stand the test of time and guide the organization for many years. Jim Collins and Jerry Porras are authors of *Built to Last* (HarperBusiness, 2004), an enduring book about how great companies stand the test of time. They talk about the vision as the organization's core purpose or reason for being. They say the vision "… captures the soul of the organization." Good vision statements do exactly that.

A very successful hospital's CEO had long been opposed to developing a formal vision statement because he felt the organization's mission was so strong and such a driving factor for employees that a vision statement was unnecessary and might actually distract employees. After some conversation with him, though, the consultant working with the hospital on a strategic planning initiative discovered that the hospital used a statement frequently in its written materials, on its website, and in company meetings. The statement was: "Simply the Best." "That's it," said the consultant. "That's your vision." And it was.

Vision statements describe what you are trying to become to meet the needs and expectations of those you serve—your stakeholders. They are usually broad and inspiring and should present a challenge to your business: "To be the top provider of pet care services in the region (or state—or even nation!)." Not: "To be the average provider of pet care services in the XYZ neighborhood." Your vision may never be attained but should always reflect something you are aspiring to and that you believe could be attained through your focused, strategic effort.

A welding business that serves the local community would probably not have this vision: "To be the superior welding business in the nation." Ford Motor Company, however, can and does have this vision: "To become the world's leading consumer company for automotive products and services." The vision should reflect something for the business to aspire to—a stretch of a goal, but not an impossible feat. While vision statements are intended to be forward-looking and inspiring—a compelling look at what the business owners would ultimately like it to achieve—they should not describe an end state that nobody believes is possible. Just as with the company mission, the vision should reflect reality and should be meaningful and real to employees.

BEST PRACTICES

Reviewing mission and vision statements is probably the least-enjoyed part of any strategic planning process. Make this important step more meaningful for participants by focusing specifically on how these statements will help to guide the development of the plan.

Here are some examples of vision statements that provide a clear and compelling sense of the desired future of each business:

- "I Love Rewards' vision is to be the most successful web-based Rewards & Recognition company in the world." (iloverewards.com)

- "Our vision for the future is to be the customer's first and best choice in the products and services we provide." (State Farm)

- "Space Adventures' vision is to open spaceflight and the space frontier to private citizens." (Space Adventures)

- "Our aim is to become the leading manufacturer and marketer of hydrocarbon products in the Americas." (SABIC Americas)

Some of these are from companies you've probably heard of before; some aren't. Some are quite lofty yet inspiring. Will these companies realize their visions? Who knows? What is important, though, is that these visions provide the direction for their strategic planning processes so that the strategies they choose to work on move them toward their visions of success.

As with the mission statement, if you don't already have a formal vision statement that is written down somewhere and communicated to employees, you should spend some time to identify and document one. Chances are, like the hospital CEO, you already have one, although you may not know it.

Your Core Values

Values statements describe the core behaviors that guide the work your business does and the actions that employees take. They define how all members of your business will act, consistent with your mission in pursuit of your vision.

Values serve as guiding principles for your business and define what you believe is right and wrong, providing direction for employees' day-to-day activities as well as a benchmark against which to evaluate elements of your strategic plan.

Whole Foods Market, for instance, has its core values prominently posted on its website, where it says: "These core values are the soul of our company." The core values are:

- Selling the highest-quality natural and organic products available
- Satisfying and delighting our customers
- Supporting team member happiness and excellence
- Creating wealth through profits and growth
- Caring about our communities and our environment
- Creating ongoing win-win partnerships with our suppliers
- Promoting the health of our stakeholders through healthy eating education

The Body Shop, a company that produces natural skin care products, says that its values are: "The way we do business, the way we make products, the way we source ingredients, and the way we use our voice; we're different because of our Values." These values are:

- Activate self-esteem
- Against animal testing
- Support community trade
- Protect our planet
- Defend human rights

It's easy to see how these core values can help to guide the behaviors of employees on a day-to-day basis—when purchasing products to sell to customers, when interacting with customers, when considering opportunities to support the community, or when dealing with suppliers. That is what values statements are intended to do—they send a message to all members of the company about what the company is and is not supportive of, in favor of, or committed to. And, again, these statements absolutely must reflect reality. Too many don't. When they don't, everyone knows—so what's the point?

MISSTEPS

Don't create values statements that you're not prepared to hold employees accountable for. Employees learn more from their leaders' actions than their words. A company that was ramping up its customer service efforts spent a significant amount of time developing a list of service values that employees would be held accountable for. But when it was time to communicate those statements, one of the team members asked, "What will we do if someone doesn't live up to one or more of these values?" Because the group could never agree on what level of accountability, if any, employees would be held to, the statements were never used.

Making Values Explicit

As a business owner, you probably have a good idea of what you expect from your employees. But have you made those expectations explicit? If not, you should—not only for strategic planning, but also for the purpose of ensuring that employees know what you expect of them. Doing so can make a big difference.

One manager in a small advertising firm was often frustrated that employees just didn't seem to have the commitment she expected. Driving home from work one night, she had a big aha moment. "I've never actually told them what I expect of them," she mused. "Maybe they don't know." She found it hard to believe that this could be the case—she thought her expectations were pretty basic and straightforward. But she acknowledged to herself that she might be taking too much for granted. She decided to document, explicitly, her expectations of her employees. But instead of just declaring these expectations from on high, she decided to engage employees in the process—to have them also come up with expectations for her and for each other. The result was, in essence, a series of values statements that the group shared and agreed to follow. It made a difference and reduced frustration for all involved. It seems simple, and, to a certain degree, it was. But that's the process—and it's a process that can, and does, work.

While values statements may not seem to have as much pertinence to the strategic planning process as the mission and vision, they do still provide direction in terms of actions that may or may not be supported. It's a good idea to go through the process of revisiting and reviewing them so that all members of the planning team are aware of what they are. Again, the idea here is not to rewrite, eliminate, or add to these statements. The idea is simply to confirm that they are an accurate reflection of the company's expectations of its members.

Achieving Alignment

The strategic planning process will include a review—and sometimes revision—of the mission, vision, and values of your business. This is an important first step for a couple of reasons:

- It reminds everyone of what the mission, vision, and values are. Let's be realistic—few employees, or even business owners for that matter, can accurately recite these statements!

- It establishes the foundation for the focus of the planning session: "This is who we are, who we serve, and who we aspire to be. These are the values that direct our actions."

Once the group has reviewed and verified that these statements are still an accurate reflection for the company, they can be used with confidence as a barometer with which to evaluate the goals, objectives, strategies, and tactics that you will ultimately come up with through the planning process.

Company missions and visions can, and do, change. Values also change. In fact, they *should* change over the course of a company's life span as the company responds to changes in the business environment and changing customer needs. Consider how the mission of many traditional brick-and-mortar companies changed as it became more and more common to use the Internet to do business. Consider, too, how businesses like Blockbuster can (or should) review and change their mission to deal with technology changes that can threaten their success.

The process of reviewing the mission, vision, and values statements generally occurs at the beginning of a strategic planning session. It is done both to remind the group of what they are (it is not unlikely that some won't have them memorized!) and to confirm that they are still accurate. If the mission is still an accurate reflection of what the business is, what it does, and whom it serves, you can simply move on—this is not the time to wordsmith and change language simply because someone thinks another way of phrasing the statement might sound better.

For smaller companies, the process can be a bit less time-intensive and contentious since the business owner likely has a good idea of what the business should do and whom the business will serve. Similarly, the business owner probably has a good idea of where the business is headed in the future. If you are the business owner, and you're driving the strategic planning process, don't be afraid to be firm in your statement of your mission and vision. It is, after all, *your* mission and vision.

What you are attempting to do at this step in the strategic planning process is to familiarize and remind all of those involved what your business mission and vision is. You are not looking for opinions or debate. You simply want to focus the attention of the planning group on the business mission and vision as the starting point for a discussion of the strategies needed to help it achieve its mission and vision. It's important to listen to input from team members about whether or not they feel the mission or vision is supported by actions of the business and, if not, to consider making appropriate changes; however, the debate should not be over what the mission or vision should be.

Importantly, agreement or consensus on the mission statement should focus not so much on the words used, their placement, or how nice they sound together, but more on whether the statement provides an accurate sense of the purpose of the business.

BEST PRACTICES

A good way to test the validity of your mission statement is to ask a few employees: "What do we do and whom do we serve?" See how closely what they say matches the stated mission—not in terms of actual words used, but in terms of the meaning behind those words.

When there is not alignment between the mission, vision, and values or between the formal statements and your business reality, they should be changed.

The Least You Need to Know

- A mission statement defines what a company is.
- A vision statement describes what a company would like to be.

- Values statements provide direction to all members of the business to guide daily decisions and actions.

- Expectations should be clearly communicated to employees so they understand the role they play in helping to achieve the mission and vision and supporting the company's values.

- For the purpose of strategic planning, the review of the mission, vision, and values is not intended to be a rewriting exercise but confirmation that the statements reflect reality.

The SWOT Analysis

In This Chapter

- The value of a SWOT analysis
- Participants in a SWOT analysis
- Understanding the four elements of SWOT
- Is it a strength or a weakness?
- Steps to get started
- How to prioritize the input

One of the most—if not *the* most—important tools in the strategic planning process is the SWOT analysis. It is an exercise that you can use to help lay the foundation for the development of your strategies and tactics—and it is an excellent starting point for the strategic planning team, as you'll soon see.

The inputs to the SWOT analysis will be all of the information gathered during the situation analysis. The output of the SWOT analysis will drive decisions related to the development of the actual plan and will be the basis for deciding where the business will focus over the next planning period.

How a SWOT Analysis Works

Basically, the *SWOT analysis* is a brainstorming session. There are no right or wrong opinions, suggestions, or ideas—except from the standpoint that these inputs need to be based on facts and evidence gathered through the situation analysis.

DEFINITION

A **SWOT analysis** is a review of an organization's *strengths, weaknesses, opportunities,* and *threats,* often used as an early step in a strategic planning process.

The SWOT analysis relies on all of the information you gathered during your situation analysis (see Chapter 6). This data serves as the factual base of knowledge you and your team will use to identify the strengths and opportunities you will leverage—and the weaknesses and threats you will attempt to avoid.

The SWOT analysis creates a common understanding among all participants of the problems and opportunities the business faces. It helps to generate discussion that might not otherwise have taken place by creating an environment where team members can focus on key business issues, and it aids in the identification of priorities for the future.

Inputs may range from the very basic ("The color of the walls in the break room is great!") to the broad and much more complex ("Cultural and political issues in Country X are challenging the ability to continue trade with this area"). But all inputs are valuable and all should be captured.

DID YOU KNOW?

While the origins of the SWOT analysis are unclear, with its inception being credited to a variety of sources over a wide range of years, the process is believed to have originally used the acronym SOFT, standing for Satisfactory, Opportunity, Fault, and Threat.

Benefits and Potential Risks

There are a number of benefits to conducting a SWOT analysis. It provides an opportunity to initiate discussion about the issues most critical to your organization, and to achieve consensus on those issues. It can help identify ideas and opportunities that might otherwise go unnoticed. The biggest benefit of the SWOT analysis, though, is its output—a list of the top factors impacting your organization that you can either leverage (strengths and opportunities) or take steps to overcome, avoid, or minimize (weaknesses and threats).

There is risk to the SWOT analysis, as well, and that risk relates to the cultural or political issues that may impact team members' comfort levels with sharing their opinions. This is where an outside facilitator can bring significant value to the discussion through his or her understanding of group dynamics and ability to manage overbearing or hesitant team members. (See Chapter 4 for more on bringing in outside help.)

Who Participates?

The participants in the SWOT process may or may not be the same as the members of your strategic planning team. Participants may represent a subgroup, the actual team, or the team in addition to other members. The result of the SWOT analysis will be used by the strategic planning team as they continue their work.

Even people from outside your company can have useful perspectives that you should incorporate—especially when it comes to considering opportunities and threats that are external to your organization. Seeking input from a variety of perspectives—internal and external—can provide a valuable insight and help avoid blind spots.

If you have a very small business or a solo operation, feel free to reach out to members of your network, customers, and others who are familiar with your business and can share inputs and opinions. For instance, start by considering the business advisors you may already be working with—your attorney, accountant, marketing professionals, etc. These individuals have knowledge of your business, but their perspective is different than those on the inside. That knowledge and unique perspective can be invaluable to the SWOT process.

Another source of useful input can be your current or former customers and clients. Because they are familiar with your business and its products and services, they are likely to have very valuable opinions.

The Elements of SWOT

There are four standard elements involved in the SWOT analysis. During the SWOT session, participants will go through each of these elements, in order, using a brainstorming process. Their observations will be captured by the recorder but not debated.

Organizational Strengths

The first phase of the SWOT analysis involves focusing on organizational strengths. Strengths are distinctive and positive things about your company and its products and services that set you apart from the competition. Strengths can represent something unique about your company that no competitor can claim, or they can be some key business result or process that is performing exceptionally well.

Strengths are internal. They can relate to your product, your service, your location, your staff—virtually anything about your business that represents something positive that you can emphasize to your advantage. For example, a coffee shop might exhibit these strengths:

- A proprietary secret recipe makes its brewed coffee stand out from the rest.

- Its location is easily accessible for both car and pedestrian traffic.

- The staff is loyal, self-motivated, and efficient.

- It offers earlier hours of operation than the competition to capture the key customer base: morning commuters.

Such things as location and hours of operation are straightforward and factual. Other strengths—like customer satisfaction or employee dedication—may be more difficult to confirm, but they can be verified through data gathered during the situation analysis.

MISSTEPS

Be careful that an identified strength doesn't unintentionally lead to a weakness. For instance, if you note a strength of low staffing costs, you may want to make sure that your employee satisfaction levels aren't declining or that turnover isn't increasing.

Organizational Weaknesses

Weaknesses represent problem areas that could get in the way of your success. A weakness is a deficiency or problem that exists related to the potential success of your business. Weaknesses are often known, but not necessarily by those in leadership positions. The SWOT process can help bring these weaknesses to light—but only if your company's business leaders, the team leader, and the facilitator allow open and candid input during the discussion.

While the strengths portion of the SWOT can be invigorating and fun, the weakness portion can be a bit discouraging and may even generate defensiveness on the part of some team members. Here are some examples of weaknesses that might emerge for the coffee shop I introduced earlier:

- The equipment is too old to keep up with the demand.

- The owner is the only one who knows the proprietary recipe, which limits expansion and hampers the day-to-day operations.

- There is limited access to additional capital to grow the business.

These are all issues that are internal to your organization—and all issues that could hold you back. Again, each should be based on fact or supported through data.

Opportunities for the Organization

An opportunity is something favorable to your business in the world outside of your business that you can leverage to your benefit. It is something that you have not yet taken advantage of but that, if explored, could have the potential to improve your business in some way. This portion of the SWOT analysis really represents a place where the creativity of your team comes into play and, like the strengths section, will invigorate the group again.

Opportunities may be short- or long-range. The time frame will be driven by the type of plan and the period that it covers. The important thing is to encourage participants to think broadly, creatively, and outside the box. For our coffee shop, for example, some opportunities might include:

- A major medical study was recently released, suggesting that drinking coffee counterbalances the ill effects of cholesterol.

- A new business is locating near you that will employ hundreds of people.

- A major bakery chain in the area has approached you about forming some type of partnership.

Hopefully you can see the many different directions this portion of the process can lead you and how valuable the information you generate can be. Remember, the power of brainstorming is to be creative—accept all ideas and think big!

Threats to the Organization

Threats are those things that could have a negative impact on your business. Threats may emerge from competitors, the economy, government regulations, or environmental conditions.

As with opportunities, you should encourage your team to think big and broad—you want to uncover as many potential threats as you can, because ultimately, you will be taking steps to avoid those threats that you consider to be most likely and of the greatest potential impact. Again, let's return to our coffee shop for some examples of threats:

- A drought in the country that supplies your beans has limited supplies and driven up prices.

- The county board recently announced plans for a major bypass that will impact the level of traffic that drives past your store.

- A major coffee chain is coming to town.

The value in identifying these threats, just as in identifying internal weaknesses, is getting them out in the open. Ultimately, you will prioritize and focus on those threats that pose the most risk for your organization and take steps during the strategic planning process to minimize them.

Flexibility Is Key

Even though the operational definitions for each of the SWOT categories are distinct, there are certain situations in which an item might appear under more than one category. This may be related to the varying perspectives of members of the group—what one might consider a strength, another may consider a weakness.

An optometry practice that was developing a strategic marketing plan identified as a weakness the fact that there was limited capacity to meet demands—sometimes patients had to be turned away or couldn't get appointments when they wanted them. This same factor was also pointed to by another member of the team as a strength because this difficulty in gaining access created a sense of scarcity that could actually boost demand. A bit of a stretch, perhaps—but every holiday season there is at least one hot item that is in scarce supply, and demand for that product continues to escalate.

The point here is that the team leader and facilitator should be open to the potential for items to appear on more than one list. Again, don't spend time debating or challenging the perspectives of group members—just write down the items. Those that are extraneous or that represent a minority opinion will fall to the bottom of the list during the ranking and prioritization process.

Some Steps to Get You Started

Conducting a SWOT analysis is a very straightforward activity that you can easily accomplish with a minimum of time and effort. Following are some recommended steps to plan for and begin your SWOT analysis.

Select a SWOT Facilitator and Recorder

The role of the facilitator will be to gather input from the group, to make sure everyone has a chance to participate, and to keep the group on track. The facilitator is not someone who will actually contribute to the discussion but someone who will help to keep the process moving forward. While the SWOT facilitator may or may not be the same as the facilitator for your strategic planning process, it is usually more effective if he or she is not part of the larger team. This will ensure a fresh perspective and new, valid inputs to the general process.

MISSTEPS

Your SWOT analysis session can deteriorate quickly if participants begin critiquing the inputs as they are offered. It is critical that the facilitator is comfortable moving the group forward.

You will also want to assign the responsibility of taking notes. The recorder's role will be to capture the inputs during the SWOT session and for use after the session. The recorder's task is different from capturing inputs on a flip chart during the discussion, which I discuss later in this chapter.

During one SWOT process, a vice president at the organization attempted to facilitate the process with a group of his direct reports. While he was a skilled facilitator, in this case he was too close to the issue being discussed and had a hard time resisting the urge to subtly, or not so subtly, support those inputs he agreed with and challenge or resist writing down those he disagreed with. This became frustrating for the team members, who became hesitant to share—this was their boss, after all! Fortunately, he had the self-awareness to recognize the problem and relinquish the facilitator role to an administrator in another department not so closely tied to the issue.

BEST PRACTICES

If you can afford it, consider a skilled outsider as a SWOT facilitator. Business coaches and consultants can serve this function. Facilitators are also available through local educational institutions—colleges, technical schools, or small-business outreach programs. See Chapter 4 to learn more.

Share Collected Data

During the situation analysis, you gathered and synthesized a great deal of information: external data that provided you with perspectives on your industry, your target market, and your competitors as well as your own internal data about your business, customers, sales, and operations. This analysis serves as the foundation for discussions during the SWOT analysis and should be provided to all team members to the extent that you feel comfortable doing so.

The background information you've gathered can be helpful to outside participants but you will, of course, want to be judicious in sharing information that may be proprietary or confidential. Others, though (your attorney or accountant, for instance), may appropriately receive all such information. You might provide summaries, rather than complete details, in some cases. For example, the executive summary of a customer survey might be provided rather than a copy of the entire survey.

BEST PRACTICES

SWOT participants generally like to have hard copies to refer to during the session. A binder of information provided to all participants can be a great way to group inputs by category in an easy-to-access format that can also be used for note-taking by participants.

Find a Time and Place to Meet

The meeting time for your SWOT analysis may or may not coincide with the meeting times you've established for your overall strategic planning initiative, particularly if there will be different participants involved. Find a time for the group to gather in a quiet place where there will be no interruptions and where you have access to flip charts, whiteboards, a computer that can access internal or external information as needed, and a lot of room for people to spread out materials and relax. (Oh, and food always helps, too!)

Two to four hours is a good time frame and should be sufficient to work through the process. Your facilitator can help move the discussion along to stay within your selected time frame. Because it is likely that you will need to refer to the ground rules during the discussion, it's a good idea to have them posted prominently someplace in the room. Even if you have ground rules in place for your strategic planning sessions, it's a good idea to establish a fresh list based on input from your SWOT participants to get their explicit agreement to follow these ground rules.

Capture the Inputs

The value of the SWOT analysis is the discussion that ensues and the broad range of inputs that are received. It's important to capture these inputs so that they can be referred to during the SWOT analysis; that way, they can potentially be shared with others who were not part of the process. They can also serve as a documented record of the process for use in subsequent planning sessions.

Flip charts work well for the SWOT discussion. They allow you to write large enough for everyone to see—and look back on—the points that have been raised.

The facilitator can be a good person to write the points on the flip chart for two reasons:

- The facilitator should be just that—a facilitator—and should not attempt to influence the process or the points raised.

- If another volunteer from the group is asked to capture the points in writing, he or she is distracted from the more important role of contributing to the process.

Note that the task of writing the comments received on flip chart paper is different from the recording process for the meeting as a whole.

MISSTEPS

When capturing inputs, make sure that they accurately reflect the spirit and intent of the comment. Participants should feel free to ask for a correction if the recorder doesn't capture their input correctly, and the recorder should ask for clarification of any input that is not clear.

The facilitator will first capture all of the strengths until the group has no more ideas, then the weaknesses, then opportunities, and, finally, threats. Additional items for previous categories may come up as you proceed, and that is fine—they can simply be added to the appropriate list.

An Alternative Process

While SWOT sessions are generally conducted in a live group setting, you can also use an online process. One small accounting firm gathered input for its SWOT analysis by distributing a series of questions to all employees:

- What do you see as the ten best improvements the company could make?

- Think like a little kid—no limits, no obstacles—and answer this question: "Wouldn't it be neat if our company…"

- As we look to create our strategic plan, what are those things that are no longer acceptable in our company?

- What are the major opportunities that we should seize?

- What are the major strengths we have that could be maximized?

- What are the five compelling reasons to use our company?

The questions were sent out through an online survey tool so the answers could be automatically compiled. This process can work well for gathering input from people who are not strategic planning team participants, and it can also work well in situations where the planning team itself may be based in different locations.

For this company, based on its industry, size, and culture, gathering information from the entire company in a format that didn't require the entire company to meet as a group worked well. It may not work for all, but it demonstrates that there are other options for conducting the SWOT.

Prioritizing the Inputs

Once you've gone through the process of developing these lists, you're likely to feel both a sense of accomplishment and somewhat overwhelmed. Now what are you supposed to do? The final step in the SWOT process is to prioritize the inputs you've received to trim the list down to make it manageable and, ultimately, actionable.

The SWOT process is designed to be a democratic method of gathering and organizing inputs. Ultimately, the process should result in an abbreviated list of items in each category which the group, collectively, feels are most important. What is determined to be most important in each category is based on the combined input of individual participants based on their frame of reference, background and experience, and, to a great degree, their personal opinions. These collective inputs will be provided to the strategic planning committee. The SWOT team should understand that the ultimate decision about which key factors to focus on will be made by the strategic planning team. However, during this process, each member of the SWOT team—and any others who have been asked to provide input—should be instructed to pick the items in each category that they, individually, feel are most important.

Nominal Group Technique

Nominal group technique is a method that can be used to prioritize a long list of items or concepts. It is a process that allows every team member—or even a broader group of people if you choose—to have an equal voice in selecting the list of top-priority items. It is a democratic process whereby those items receiving the most votes rise to the top of the list.

There are a number of options you might use to create this prioritized list:

- Members can list the items they consider to be most important on a sheet of paper and turn the list in to someone to tally the response.

- Each member is given a certain number of stickers that they place next to the items on the flip charts in each category that they feel are the most important. The items with the highest numbers of dots become the top priorities.

- Computer-based survey tools (like SurveyMonkey or Zoomerang) can be used to calculate results automatically.

After the overall list is narrowed in this way, the process can continue to be used to narrow the list even further. Ultimately, a list of three to five items from each category is a good, manageable list to work from.

Gathering Broader Input

Just as you did with the SWOT session, you may wish to involve a broader group in the prioritization process. Large companies can extend the input process company-wide. One example of a company that did this is a privately held educational firm that had a culture of inclusiveness and wanted all of its employees to have the opportunity to review and rank the SWOT inputs generated in the formal SWOT session. The team leader used an online survey tool that listed all of the SWOT items and asked employees to rate the items on a scale of 1 to 5 in terms of their perception of the importance of each item. The survey tool automatically calculated the results, allowing for a rank-order list that provided a high-level look at priorities based on input from all.

BEST PRACTICES

Since employees will eventually be called upon to help implement or support the plan, it's a good idea to offer them an opportunity for involvement at some point in the process. Giving them a chance to review and vote on the long list of items can be one way to do this.

Once the final list of top items in each category has been generated, through whatever means the team chooses to use, the planning team will review the items and reach consensus on the list. These items then become an important input to the next step in the strategic planning process—developing goals, objectives, strategies, and tactics (GOST), covered in the next four chapters.

The Least You Need to Know

- The SWOT analysis involves a brainstorming session that identifies the organization's strengths, weaknesses, opportunities, and threats.
- Involve a broad variety of people in the discussion to ensure you are capturing multiple perspectives.
- Be flexible in the process of generating the SWOT analysis and open to different perspectives; what one considers a strength another may consider a weakness.
- Be sure to use the inputs you gathered during the situation analysis process to support points raised during the SWOT.
- Prioritizing the SWOT list provides a critical input to the development of the actual strategic plan.

In This Chapter

- The importance of goals in strategic planning
- Tying goals to strategic advantages and challenges
- Tying goals to mission and vision
- Establishing your goals
- Using strategic planning tools to achieve consensus
- The attributes of effective goals

There is a lot of confusion when it comes to the definitions of four important terms in the strategic planning process—goals, objectives, strategies, and tactics. The definitions are important, but wasting significant time arguing about them is not. While we'll explore the traditional definitions here and in the next few chapters, in practice what you should be most concerned about is having shared definitions among your planning team and that, whatever you call them, there is alignment between your goals, objectives, strategies, and tactics. Ultimately, tactics should represent the final step in the process of developing your plan to achieve your highest-level goals.

One helpful way to remember the correct order of these terms is through the acronym GOST, which stands for goals, objectives, strategies, and tactics. It all starts with the goal. Objectives (discussed in Chapter 14) tie back to the goal. Strategies (Chapter 15) are developed to support the objectives and, finally, tactics (Chapter 16) are created to achieve the strategies. Ultimately, action plans may also be developed by employees to outline a plan for achieving the tactics assigned to them.

The alignment is important and ensures the appropriate focus on the overall achievement of the plan. If all is aligned, and all of the elements are well developed, your chances of success are enhanced.

In this chapter, we'll take a look at goals—what they are, the importance of tying goals to the mission and vision, and some specific attributes of effective goals.

What Is a Goal?

The children's book *Alice in Wonderland* can give us some insight into the purpose of *goals*. When Alice asks the Cheshire cat for some help in deciding which route to take, the cat asks where she would like to go. Not an unreasonable question. Alice says she doesn't know, and the cat points out that, in that case, it doesn't really matter which route they take. And so it goes with strategic planning. Without a goal, how can you possibly determine how to get where you'd like to go? And that, in essence, defines what a goal is—it is simply a statement of where you're like to go, the end point that will be your measure of success. A goal can be thought of as a desired end state.

DEFINITION

Goals are general statements that describe what an organization, a department, or an individual wishes to accomplish.

Here are some examples of goals:

- Grow the business.

- Improve website performance, customer interface, and overall value.

- Improve customer satisfaction and loyalty.

- Improve availability of data and information.

- Improve quality in key areas.

Notice that all of these statements are broad and, while they indicate a sense of general direction through words like *grow* or *improve*, the statements are not specifically measurable. They're not supposed to be. They're goals!

The Difference Between Goals and Objectives

When it comes to defining the difference between goals and objectives, confusion reigns—even in business circles and among academics.

Since these terms are often used interchangeably and inconsistently, then, we will define them here and suggest that readers use these definitions to help guide them through the process—and the disagreements!

BEST PRACTICES

When we're setting personal or professional goals, we are often counseled to make sure these goals are measurable. In strategic planning, however, goals are broad. Don't get hung up on the confusion—just go with the GOST flow!

Here's a definition that will help guide our discussion. It's from a comment posted on a social media site in response to the question, "What is the difference between goals and objectives?"

> The difference between a goal and objective is the ability to quantify and measure. Goals and objectives are confusing because many see them as interchangeable; they're not. In my mind, objectives are clear, measurable and obtainable. They are steps that one takes to obtain the goal.

That is exactly right!

The reason that goals and objectives are so often confused and interchanged may relate to the fact that they work closely together. Goals can be compared and contrasted to objectives, which I'll talk about in the next chapter. Understanding how they relate to each other can help:

- Goals are broad—objectives are narrow.
- Goals are general—objectives are specific.
- Goals are abstract—objectives are concrete.
- Goals cannot be specifically measured—objectives can and should be.

The main difference between these two terms is their level of concreteness. Objectives follow some specific criteria that make it possible for two independent people to agree on whether or not they have been met. Goals, on the other hand, are more subjective. They tend to be broad and often very lofty statements. Here are some examples:

- Strengthen the child welfare system to achieve better outcomes for children and youth.

- Increase membership and member services.

- Create a safe environment for patients and staff.

- Deliver exemplary competency-based education that meets the diverse needs of students and the community.

As you can see with these statements, there are no specific criteria that can be used to determine whether or not the goal has actually been achieved. That's where the objectives come in.

Goals Set the Stage for Measurable Objectives

A goal is something to be aimed for—a general view of where the company, department, or function would like to be. Objectives support the goal and provide measurable insights into whether or not they were achieved. While you can't measure the goal of "create a safe environment for patients and staff," you could attach multiple objectives to this goal that could be measured.

> **DID YOU KNOW?**
>
> The U.S. Constitution originally outlined six goals for the new government: to establish a more perfect union, to establish justice, to ensure domestic tranquility, to provide for the common defense, to promote the general welfare, and to secure the blessings of liberty to ourselves and our posterity.

A non-business example may help to illustrate. Let's consider New Year's resolutions, which have probably been made by all of us at some point in time. Sometimes these resolutions are stated as goals, and sometimes as objectives:

- "I want to lose weight" is a goal.

- "I want to lose 15 pounds by June 1" is an objective.

- "I want to read more" is a goal.

- "I want to read three business books by March 1" is an objective.

The difference is measurability. Does it matter? It depends. In our personal lives, it will matter if we only state a goal that is broad and non-measurable like "I want to lose weight." It doesn't really matter, though, if we make a New Year's resolution of "I want to lose 15 pounds by June 1," and call it a goal, even though it's really an objective. In the business world, there is definitely value in using these important terms appropriately during the strategic planning process. However, what you don't want to happen is to generate debates over terminology instead of focusing on important business discussions. What matters the most is that there be some measurable elements of your plan, as we'll see in the next chapter.

Ensuring Goal Alignment

The debate over terminology is just the tip of the iceberg. The next important challenge you will need to successfully address is achieving agreement among your planning team over what the goal (or goals) should be. Yes, your strategic plan can have more than one goal, and many plans do. Let's take a look at how your strategic advantages (strengths and opportunities) and your strategic challenges (weaknesses and threats)—identified during the SWOT analysis—can serve as a springboard for the goals you will focus on.

Alignment with Strategic Advantages and Challenges

As you consider the following example of a health-care company, think about whether or not each of the goals presented fits in terms of either capitalizing on an advantage or overcoming a challenge—or both.

Strategic advantages: customer service, relationships, performance excellence

Strategic challenges: growing competition in industry, rising health-care costs

Goals:

- Implement disease and lifestyle-management programs.
- Develop partnership relationships with key customers.
- Invest in technology.

In this case, the first and second goals fit. The first could be tied back to customer service (providing services that benefit patients) and addresses a challenge (rising health-care costs). If we can help patients better manage their health, they will need fewer health-care services. The second also capitalizes on the relationship advantage and addresses the challenge of growing competition. The third, however, doesn't seem to have any direct ties to the identified advantages or challenges. What this should illustrate is the importance of being thorough and thoughtful in the development of the SWOT analysis. It should ultimately be an accurate reflection of the impacts on your business that will help drive the development of your plan.

But suppose you got to this point and someone on the planning team insisted that investing in technology was a must and should be a high-level strategic goal. What should you do? Well, in this case, the team leader and facilitator have a couple of different options, and their decisions about which direction to take will depend on the dynamics of the group, the understanding of the process, and leadership abilities. They could:

- Assert the authority of the team leader to say, "No, this is not a fit."

- Pull out the SWOT analysis to determine whether there is a potential fit and, if not, point out the disconnect between this recommended goal and the SWOT analysis, reminding the group of the purpose of the SWOT analysis.

- Add the item to the list and see how it plays out through the planning process.

What's the right choice? It really depends on the group. Any of these choices can be—and are—made all of the time during strategic planning processes. The greatest risk, of course, is that the wrong choice consumes resources (time and money) and diverts attention away from the right choices. Sometimes this will become clear as the planning process proceeds, and ultimately, the misfit goal will be abandoned. But sometimes the goal will remain, and time and attention will be diverted in support of it.

DID YOU KNOW?

When Bill Gates was asked to explain the success of his company, Microsoft, his immediate response was "Our vision, which has not changed since the day the company was founded."

Alignment with Vision and Mission

Let's consider another example of a travel company.

Vision: To be the premier worldwide provider of luxury travel and hospitality products and services.

Mission: Product and profit dominance.

Goals:

- Increase profits by 50 percent.

- Extend luxury line into Europe.

- Expand into rural market areas with bargain pricing options.

In considering alignment of these proposed goals with the mission and vision, it's clear that the first and second fit, but the third does not. The introduction of bargain pricing is not consistent with the organization's stated vision, and this would be an issue to be addressed. In this case, the team leader or facilitator could rightly point out that this proposed goal is inconsistent with the organization's vision, which was (hopefully) reviewed and reaffirmed earlier in the planning process. Unless the team wishes to reconsider and potentially revise the vision, this proposed goal should be rejected.

This same process of ensuring alignment would occur with the development of functional plans (such as a human resources strategic plan or a marketing plan) or department plans. Regardless of the level of the plan, alignment with the organization's mission, vision, and values and the identified strategic challenges and advantages will help to ensure that everybody in the organization is pulling in the same direction. Obviously, clarity on these items—mission, vision, values, and strategic advantages and challenges—is very important.

Establishing Goals

The more goals you have, the more complex your plan will become. It is best to focus on a single goal or a few goals that are most critical to the success of your business.

In addition, your goals should be lofty enough that they stretch your organization and represent a significant challenge. These goals are sometimes called *BHAGs*. A commonly used example of a BHAG is President Kennedy's pledge to send a man to the moon. Clearly that was a lofty goal at the time! Challenging goals can be good; the trouble, though, is that if these goals are regularly unmet, it can be disheartening to the organization and the planning team. It's important to find a balance; ideally, the goal should represent a challenge to those pursuing it, yet not so much of a challenge that it is impossible to achieve.

DEFINITION

The acronym **BHAG** (pronounced *bee-hag*) stands for Big Hairy Audacious Goal. A BHAG is an extremely challenging goal that pushes the organization beyond its comfort zone.

Here are some additional examples of BHAGs set by well-known companies:

- Twitter: "To be the pulse of the planet."

- Microsoft: "A computer on every desk and in every home."

- Ford: "To democratize the automobile."

- Goodyear: "To reach $23 billion in sales in 5 years."

- General Electric: "Become number one or number two in every market we serve and revolutionize this company to have the speed and agility of a small enterprise."

Clearly these are not easy tasks, but these companies have arguably accomplished their BHAGs. Only you can know what represents a stretch goal for you or whether or not your company, division, or department could benefit from a BHAG. But again, an important input into your decision-making process is the SWOT analysis you did earlier.

Using the SWOT

The SWOT analysis, as we discussed in Chapter 12, is an important input to the establishment of goals, opportunities, strategies, and tactics. The list that your team has developed will suggest areas of strength and opportunity that you might leverage, and areas of weakness and threat that you might minimize or overcome. The broad statements that indicate your desire to leverage a strength or overcome a weakness become your goals, as shown in the following table.

Strengths	GOAL
Proprietary technology	Increase market share
High customer satisfaction	Expand into new market areas
Access to capital	Open new facilities
Weaknesses	
Need more salespeople	Recruit experienced sales staff
High turnover	Improve employee satisfaction and retention
Opportunities	
Local competitor closing	Increase local market share
Global demand for product	Expand globally

Threats

Impending legislation	Expand lobbying activities
New competitor in market	Maintain market share

The SWOT provides a good frame of reference for the development of goals and can also be used as a tool to evaluate goals that don't seem to be tied to any identified business need or opportunity. This can happen during the planning process when, for instance, some individual has a pet project or idea they wish to put forward. The best way to respond in this instance is to ask the person to identify through the SWOT analysis or the information gathered during the situation analysis the evidence that supports this proposal. It is sometimes also necessary to review the process of developing and prioritizing the SWOT, which was designed to provide an indication of the issues most important to the organization.

Achieving Consensus and Moving Forward

While the primary purpose of the SWOT analysis is to provide input to the goal-setting process of strategic planning, based on good facts and data gathered through the situation analysis, this level of rigor is not always used. In a small business environment, it is possible that the business owner says, "Our goal is to have the greatest market share in our industry," and with no discussion or debate, this becomes the goal. Or a particular function within the company may have identified an opportunity or threat and convened a team to create a plan to address it.

BEST PRACTICES

While a business owner who is leading a strategic planning effort could just say, "This is our goal," having a group discussion and reaching consensus on the goal(s) to drive the process can be an important part of team building. If you involve your team in establishing goals, they will be more invested in achieving them.

An HR department, for instance, may be concerned about the increasing length of time to hire new employees in a competitive industry and may bring a team together with the intent to develop a plan with a goal of shortening hiring time. However, even in these apparently clear-cut situations, it is not uncommon to have disagreement, debate, or varying opinions and ideas about what goal(s) to focus on.

No business can do everything. Decisions must be made about the most important goals to pursue during the particular time frame you are dealing with. This doesn't mean that a goal might not be addressed at some later time, but it may mean that the goal will not be addressed now.

This type of debate occurred in a health-care organization that was developing its annual strategic plan. One of the vice presidents for the organization felt strongly that a goal of "support the community" be included; others felt this goal was reflected in the organization's mission and did not need to be included for the purpose of driving the strategic planning activities. Several other vice presidents objected to removing the goal of "provide exceptional customer service," but the CEO felt that results from the previous year indicated that the goal had been accomplished and could be sustained through ongoing activities that did not need to be reflected in the overall plan.

There are no easy answers to these debates. Fortunately, there are some tools you can use to help you decide which goals to include and how they should be prioritized:

- The **SWOT analysis** provides an objective framework for decisions about where to focus efforts. Still, the list of areas of potential focus may be long and too much to tackle at one point in time. The mission, vision, and values can then serve as a means of helping to narrow and prioritize the list of options.

- The **mission** serves as a reminder of what the business does and whom it serves. A proposed goal that would suggest expanding into an entirely new area of business or serving a different population, therefore, would be a goal that would need to be challenged or that might prompt a revision of the mission.

- The **vision** provides an indication of what the company strives to be. If the vision suggests that the company wishes to be the premier provider of food products in the Midwest, a goal of reducing operational costs through the purchase of lower-quality raw products should be questioned.

BEST PRACTICES

Holding the planning team accountable to the SWOT, mission, vision, and values can help to ensure focus at the very beginning of the planning process.

The identification of goals is where it all begins, and all of the other elements of the plan will be based on these goals. If you get it wrong here, the entire plan is likely to fail as you move forward. Or, worse yet, the plan may have a negative impact on the business if not aligned with its identified purpose and vision.

Elements of Effective Goals

While goals are not measurable in the same manner as objectives, effective goals have some key elements. Goals should be ...

- Aligned with mission, vision, and values.

- Long-term. Goals are something businesses strive toward over time; objectives are shorter-term statements that help to support the goal.

- Realistic. Some might debate this in favor of BHAGs (Big Hairy Audacious Goals), but ultimately, you do want to be able to achieve success.

- Few. Sometimes just one overarching goal will drive the strategic planning process.

- Agreed upon.

Goals represent the starting point for the development of your strategic plan. They will drive the creation of objectives, strategies, and tactics. Because of this, it is important that your planning team achieve consensus on the goals and agree that they reflect the direction the organization, department, or work group wishes to take.

The question of how many goals you should have is also one that your planning team will need to decide on. Sometimes strategic plans are guided by a single, overarching goal; sometimes strategic plans have several goals. While there is no magic answer, the key is to not focus on so many goals that your resources are stretched too thin.

The Least You Need to Know

- Goals are big and broad and provide general direction for the work of the planning team.
- Goals drive the development of objectives, which are measurable.
- The appropriateness of selected goals can be evaluated by referring to the SWOT, mission, vision, and values.
- Achieving consensus among the planning team on the selected goals is critical.
- Effective goals are aligned with an organization's mission, vision, and values.

Establishing Objectives

In This Chapter

- Objectives as part of strategic planning
- SMART: the elements of effective objectives
- Process and outcome objectives
- Aligning objectives with goals
- Making objectives measurable

In strategic planning, goals are broad and general. They set the stage for the long-range view of what the strategic planning team hopes to accomplish and provide a focus for planning efforts. Whereas goals set the stage for high-level performance, objectives get us down to a more measurable level. Since goals aren't measurable, objectives must be! Otherwise, how would we be able to evaluate our success? Objectives are really the foundation of a strategic plan. When expressed correctly, they tell us exactly where we want to go and what we want to do. Most importantly, they give us the information we need to determine whether or not we are making progress. Remember the value of strategic planning is not the planning—the value lies in the doing!

In this chapter, we'll take a look at the attributes of effective objectives and how they can be created, evaluated, and implemented to help drive the success of your strategic planning efforts.

What Is an Objective?

Objectives answer the questions of "How much?" and "By when?" Goals (see Chapter 13), strategies (Chapter 15), and tactics (Chapter 16) are more qualitative. Objectives tell us, broadly, where we want to go and give us a sense of how we will get there, but they are absent any quantitative, number-based, specific, measurable criteria that will help us determine how well we performed these actions. That's what objectives are for.

> **DEFINITION**
>
> An **objective** is a measurable and time-based action that will be necessary to achieve a goal. Objectives are the only truly quantifiable element of the strategic plan.

To illustrate the difference between goals and objectives as used in the strategic planning process, recall the example from Chapter 13: New Year's resolutions can be stated as either goals or objectives. "I want to lose weight" is a goal. "I want to lose 15 pounds by June 1" is an objective. The first statement gives us a sense of general direction. The second statement clarifies the first and gives us a specific, measurable goal. "I want to quit smoking" is a goal. "I want to quit smoking by the end of January" is an objective. Here, the distinction may at first seem subtle, so let's take a closer look. The first statement gives us a sense of general direction, yet more specific than "I want to lose weight." Quitting smoking is an either/or sort of goal—either you do or you don't. So why isn't this an objective? Because it doesn't give us an end point. When will we quit smoking? This year? Next year? When we're 80?

Objectives represent a very important step in the development of a strategic plan. Getting them right is important, not only because having a measurable target helps you know when you're successful, but also because your objectives will provide important guidance for the development of strategies and tactics, as you'll see in later chapters.

Attributes of Effective Objectives

There are some specific criteria that we can use to evaluate whether or not the objectives we create are appropriate. The acronym used to describe these criteria is SMART. While you'll find some variation in the terms used in this acronym, it generally stands for Specific, Measurable, Attainable, Relevant, and Time-bound. Each of these elements must be present for an objective to be effective. Let's take a look at each of these criteria and how they can be used to evaluate the effectiveness of your objectives.

DID YOU KNOW?

Perhaps as a counter to the SMART acronym, there is a lesser-used acronym, DUMB, which stands for Doable, Understandable, Manageable, and Beneficial.

As you consider each of these elements, keep in mind that they are cumulative. The examples I show will build to ultimately incorporate all of the elements, which should be your goal in creating and evaluating objectives.

Is It Specific?

A specific objective is one that is clear and explicit. It includes distinct items or details. "Be the best that we can be," is not specific. "Score in the top 10 percentile" is. "Lose weight" is not specific. "Lose 15 pounds" is. To be specific, an objective must be stated in such a way that we will be able to tell whether we have achieved it. We can't tell if we're the "best" unless we include some specific indication of what "best" is. Here are some examples. Which ones do you feel are specific?

- Reduce absenteeism by 15 percent.

- Improve customer satisfaction by 35 percent.

- Increase partnerships by 20 percent.

Okay, this is a trick. While each of the above statements is somewhat specific, each could be more specific to represent a better objective. Remember that we want to be clear and explicit. That means we want to be as precise as possible when stating our objectives so that there will be no disagreement at the end of the evaluation period when we attempt to determine whether or not we achieved our objective.

The first statement is okay, but do we mean absenteeism of all employees, or are there specific employee segments where we want to achieve a 15 percent reduction and other segments where some other measure might be more appropriate? While we might assume that this statement reflects a measure of all employees, not explicitly stating that can lead to confusion later. So we might more appropriately state this as "Reduce absenteeism among all employees by 15 percent."

The second statement is similar. While it is somewhat specific, it would be a better objective if we were explicitly clear about which customer segments we wished to improve customer satisfaction in. All customers? New customers? Long-term customers? Customers who have purchased certain products?

The third statement is far too general. What types of partnerships are we talking about? Partnerships with community groups? With customers? With certain types of customers? With competitive firms? In this case, a more specific objective might be "Increase supplier partnerships by 20 percent in areas representing more than 10 percent of total supply costs." This gives us more specific detail and direction both to know what it is we're going to do and to determine later whether we did it!

Is It Measurable?

Measurable objectives are simply objectives that can be measured in some way. "Tell people about my business" is not a measurable objective. "Build an e-mail subscription list of 500" is.

In addition to determining if an objective is measurable, strategic planners need to consider whether the objective can be measured. An objective of "slow global warming" is measurable, but probably cannot actually be measured—at least not in a way that proves that an organization's activities were directly responsible for the outcome. Determining whether a measure is *measurable* is related to whether or not it can be quantified in some way. Determining whether it *can* be measured is a practical consideration related to whether you can actually gather the information necessary to quantify the results.

In considering whether objectives are measurable, it's important to also consider whether it can be measured in a cost-effective way. Having to establish new processes or even hire new people to measure whether or not you're achieving your objectives is not where you want to be. Your objectives should be tied to criteria that are important enough to your company that you are already measuring results to gain important business knowledge—or you should be. As you establish objectives, think about what is need-to-know information versus just nice-to-know.

A restaurant, for instance, was considering an objective related to how quickly food was served to diners after the waiter took the order. Measuring this would require waiters to note the time they took the order and the time they delivered the meal, and they would need to keep track of this information in some way. So for busy waiters, it would require a couple of new process steps that would need to become part of their routine. Then, somebody would need to collect all of that information, summarize it, and present the information. (As an aside, the validity of the information would be suspect if the person doing the data collection was part of the process.) A better solution would be to measure customer perception of the timeliness of meal delivery. After all, what is a short time for one customer might be a long time for another.

What the restaurant was most concerned about was customer satisfaction with the time, not the specific time. So in this case, a better objective might be "Achieve a 90% satisfaction rate among customers with the timeliness of their food service." Satisfaction could be measured through a simple survey delivered with the bill.

Is It Attainable?

Sometimes you will see the term *achievable* used instead of attainable. It doesn't matter—they both mean the same thing. Our objectives need to represent things that we can actually do. The concept of attainability is closely tied to our discussion of BHAGs in the last chapter, so this is a good place to provide some additional clarification. BHAGs—big, hairy, audacious goals—are embraced by some companies as stretch goals that represent an end point they'd like to attain at some point in the future, with the recognition that they are lofty, difficult, and, perhaps, unattainable. Goals can be lofty because objectives are designed to help get us there. So while we might have a BHAG of "To become the most widely used operating system in the world," our objectives will be designed to help us move toward this goal over time. Initially, we might have an objective of "To be the most widely used operating system in the United States."

DID YOU KNOW?

Twitter's BHAG is "To become 'the pulse of the planet." In January 2010, they had reached 75 million users, so they appear to be well on their way!

Consider how this might work on a personal level. A woman who weighs 150 pounds will probably not be able to attain a 60-pound weight loss—it's not attainable. But 20 pounds might be. Of course, what is attainable is subject to interpretation and some debate. While organizations should not avoid setting objectives that are challenging, they should focus on being realistic as they establish these objectives. "Can we achieve this?" is a fair question and one to consider as objectives are established. Remember, these are not goals, which can be lofty and aspirational—these are objectives, which are designed to be accomplished!

The issue of whether or not objectives are attainable is one that should be discussed by the planning team, often with input from others in the organization. It is important for the group to consider the resources that would be required to achieve the objective in terms of time, money, and staff and whether those resources are, or could be, available.

Is It Relevant?

Objectives represent building blocks that are established to meet identified goals. Therefore, each objective needs to be directly related—relevant—to the established goals. Let's take a look at a few examples.

Goal: "To improve customer satisfaction levels."

Proposed Objective: "Improve employee satisfaction by 10% over the next six-month period." (While some might argue—and perhaps persuasively—that employee satisfaction is ultimately related to customer satisfaction, this is not directly relevant to this specific goal.)

Proposed Objective: "Conduct a customer survey of 30 percent of the customer base to determine current satisfaction levels by March 30." (Yes, determining satisfaction is directly related to the goal of improving satisfaction.)

Proposed Objective: "Reduce complaints by 10 percent over the three-month period from March 1 through May 30." (Yes, reducing complaints would also be related to improving satisfaction.)

Just as goals need to be tied to mission, vision, values, and strategic challenges and opportunities, objectives need to be tied to goals. They need to be relevant.

Is It Time-Bound?

Time-bound simply means that there is some indication of when the objective is expected to be accomplished. While the statement "Lose 15 pounds" is specific and measurable, and we'll assume it's attainable and relevant, it is not time-bound. There is no indication of "by when" we will lose 15 pounds. As you can imagine, this is an important element of an effective objective. So we could add this element and restate the objective as "Lose 15 pounds by September 1." This would give us an objective that meets all of the criteria. This short sentence effectively meets all of the SMART criteria and represents an appropriately stated objective. On September 1, two independent observers could measure your weight, compare it to your weight now, and calculate whether or not you had lost 15 pounds. And that, in a nutshell, reflects the purpose of objectives and the importance of making them SMART.

The Final Analysis

In addition to reviewing each objective and holding it up to the SMART criteria, your planning team should consider the collection of objectives that fall under each goal and ask the following questions:

- Are we confident that these objectives will be sufficient to achieve our identified goal?

- Are we confident that we have the resources required to accomplish these objectives?

- Are we confident that these objectives can be achieved during the identified time frames?

- Are there any objectives here that may be subject to internal concerns or resistance? If so, what will we need to do to overcome that resistance?

BEST PRACTICES

Objectives may support more than one goal. An objective of "Increase customer satisfaction by 15 percent by year's end" could support the goals of "Grow market share" and "Become the provider of choice." It's okay to have this kind of duplication in your plan—it reflects synergy.

Again, remember that each of the SMART criteria must be met in order for the objective to be effective. While "Lose weight" is measurable—we can tell if someone has lost weight because the numbers on the scale will go down—it is not specific. "Lose 15 pounds" is both measurable and specific, but it is not time-bound. All of your objectives should meet all of the SMART criteria.

Process vs. Outcome Objectives

There are two different types of objectives that you might develop. A *process objective* deals with the development or improvement of some type of process—doing something. An *outcome objective* specifies desired results. Let's look at an example. Suppose we have a goal of "Increase customer satisfaction." A related process objective might be "Conduct a customer survey of 30 percent of the customer base to determine current satisfaction levels by March 30." A related outcome objective might be "Achieve a 10 percent increase in customer satisfaction by March 30 of next year."

DEFINITION

A process objective indicates what you are doing and how you will do it and describes the participants, interactions, and activities involved; for example, "Train 10 customer service reps to use the customer relationship management system by June 1." An **outcome objective** identifies a specific outcome or result; for example, "Achieve a 100 percent pass rate on the customer relationship management system efficiency exam by June 1."

Consider the different impact that these two objectives would have for a goal of generating new customers:

- Introduce Product XYZ in March.

- Generate 250 requests for sales demonstrations of Product XYZ during the first three months of product introduction.

Both of these statements represent objectives, although one is more numbers-based. The first is a process objective; the second is an outcome objective. Could two independent observers, in each case, determine whether or not the objective had been met? Yes. They are both specific, measurable, attainable (we'll assume), relevant (based on the goal), and time-bound.

While process objectives can be used, generally outcome objectives will provide you with the best means of setting yourself up for success. Process objectives can be helpful to describe the types of activities that must take place to achieve a goal. Outcome objectives describe the measurable results that will indicate that goals are being achieved.

Avoiding Wishy-Washy Objectives

Measurability is key. Objectives should be stated in such a way that, at the end of the planning period, two independent observers could look at the objective and the results and agree on whether or not the objective has been achieved. That is the acid test.

It's not enough to say, "I want to lose weight," or "I want to quit smoking." Those statements are too wishy-washy for objectives. How much weight do you want to lose? By when? When will you stop smoking? The problem with wishy-washy objectives is that they leave the door open for disagreement and dissent down the road. Let's take a look at a business-related example.

Keep It Measurable

An accounting firm has been growing rapidly and the HR department is concerned about employee satisfaction and retention. The director embarks on a strategic planning process. A goal of "Improve employee satisfaction and retention" is developed. In support of that goal, the planning team establishes an objective of "Support staff and improve internal efficiency." Do you see anything wrong with that objective? Actually, there is a lot wrong with it. It's certainly a noble objective. Who wouldn't agree with the importance of supporting staff and improving internal efficiency?

The problem is that each of these elements is wide open to interpretation. What does "support staff" mean? Does it mean allowing staff to work when they'd like to work? Does it mean providing them with training? Does it mean paying them more? What does "improve internal efficiency" mean? Chances are, if we were to ask each member of the planning team these questions, they would come up with a range of different responses—and that's the problem. Effective objectives need to be clear, concrete, and measurable. Just as with the personal examples of losing weight or quitting smoking, we need to have some way of knowing if and when we've achieved success.

Use Quantitative Objectives

Here's another example that is somewhat more specific but still doesn't pass the test. A law firm is developing a strategic marketing plan and, to support a goal of "Increase market share," establishes an objective to "Grow the client base."

"Grow the client base" seems like a measurable objective. All involved in the development of the plan believe they will be able to measure whether or not they grew the client base. They don't really think they need to establish a time frame because the plan is designed to run from January through December of their fiscal year. So off to the races they go in pursuit of their objective. At the end of March, the planning group convenes to take a look at results. The firm has gained two new clients since the first of the year. Can they claim success and consider the plan complete?

Clearly, most people will say, "Of course not." Yet, at what point will they have achieved success? How do we know? How might individual members of the planning team have different expectations of what success looks like? And that's the point.

BEST PRACTICES

Hold your objectives up to careful scrutiny as they are developed. A SMART checklist can help. Objectives must represent measurable expectations that help you determine whether or not you are being successful as you implement your plan.

At least the objective of "Grow the client base" had some measurable basis. To grow is quantitative, unlike "Support staff." Yet it is not measurable enough. An objective should be specific enough that all of the individual members of your team—and the members of your organization as a whole—can agree, at the end of the planning cycle, whether or not the objective has been achieved. This seems like such a simple concept, yet it is far too often overlooked at many organizations.

Evaluating Objectives

Here are some examples of actual objective statements from various strategic plans:

- To expand the business aggressively and offer above-average returns to shareholders.

- Greater responsiveness to community needs through programs offered, the establishment of college areas of particular strength, and area workforce development.

Let's take a look at these examples based on the SMART criteria. We'll evaluate whether they meet the criteria, and then, where they don't, we'll restate them so they do. This is the same process that you would use in evaluating whether or not what you have developed is truly an objective (and not a goal or strategy—more about this in the next chapter).

Original: "To expand the business aggressively and offer above-average returns to shareholders."

SPECIFIC	Maybe
MEASURABLE	Not enough to be objectively agreed upon
ATTAINABLE	Perhaps
RELEVANT	Yes, we'll assume so
TIME-BOUND	No

The problem with the way this objective is stated is that the terms used are subjective. What does "aggressively" mean? What are "above-average" returns? Clearly, the use of these terms could lead to disagreement at some point when those reviewing the results have different perspectives. That's why it's very important to use quantifiable terms in your objectives.

Restated: "To grow the business by 50% over the next 12 months and offer returns to shareholders that are at least 10% higher than the industry average." As restated, this objective now gives us some specific measures that we will use to evaluate our performance and a specific time frame to achieve those measures.

Let's take a look at another one.

Original: "Greater responsiveness to community needs through programs offered, the establishment of college areas of particular strength, and area workforce development."

SPECIFIC	No, what does *greater* mean?
MEASURABLE	Not enough to be objectively agreed upon
ATTAINABLE	Perhaps
RELEVANT	Yes, we'll assume so
TIME-BOUND	No

This objective actually incorporates elements that could be strategies. To restate this as an appropriate objective, we could say "Increase responsiveness to community needs, as measured through the annual community survey, by 25% by year's end."

As these examples illustrate, one of the traps that many businesses fall into when developing objectives is attempting to be too lofty. Establishing objectives isn't about saving the world in the vast majority of cases. Establishing objectives is simply about defining a mutually agreed-upon and measurable end point.

MISSTEPS

"Slow global warming" is an actual objective that is included in a strategic plan for a governmental nonprofit agency. It's a worthy objective, to be sure, but one that will certainly be difficult to quantify. When developing objectives, make sure you evaluate them to ensure that they are SMART objectives.

Even without specifically considering each element of the SMART acronym, agreeing whether or not an objective is specific and measurable is fairly straightforward. Contemplate the objective and ask yourself, "At the end of this planning period, will each member of my planning team be able to independently determine, and collectively agree, whether or not the objective has been reached?" Following this guideline should ensure that the objectives you set are not wishy-washy.

The Least You Need to Know

- Objectives differ from goals in that they are more specific and are measurable.
- SMART (Specific, Measurable, Attainable, Relevant, and Time-bound) is an easy-to-remember way to ensure that objectives are developed appropriately.
- While objectives may be either process- or outcome-based, outcome objectives are preferred.
- Objectives must relate directly back to specific goals and will drive the development of strategies and tactics.

Creating Strategies

In This Chapter

- The concept of strategy
- What it means to be strategic
- How to develop your strategies
- Choosing the right strategies
- How to rate the effectiveness of your strategies

Your goals outline the broad direction that you are headed in. Your objectives help to clarify that broad direction by defining specific and measurable outcomes you will achieve along the way to accomplishing your overall goals. So now you know, quite specifically, what it is you want to do. The next obvious question is "How will we do it?" The answers to that question represent your strategies.

As with other elements of the strategic plan, there is often confusion about what a strategy is and how a strategy differs from a tactic. While the two are closely aligned (just like goals and objectives, discussed in the previous two chapters), they are not the same.

In this chapter, we will take a look at what strategies are and how they impact your plan. We'll also explore how your strategies can benefit from a look back at your SWOT analysis to help you leverage your strengths and opportunities and minimize the weaknesses and threats that you previously identified.

What Are Strategies?

The concept of *strategy* is widely used by the military—generals come up with strategies for conquering new territory or defeating enemies, for instance.

> **DEFINITION**
>
> A s**trategy** is a statement that indicates, generally, how you will approach meeting your objectives. Strategies are directly related to leveraging the strengths and opportunities and overcoming the weaknesses and threats you identified during the SWOT analysis.

Here are some common examples:

- Kill or capture insurgent leaders.
- Divide and conquer.

Strategies are also very common in sports and games. Those playing a sport or game have a number of options to choose from that will presumably help them win (the goal). These options represent strategies. When playing Monopoly, for instance, a player may have a strategy of buying as many properties as possible, focusing only on the high-end properties (like Boardwalk and Park Place), or not buying properties at all and attempting to build cash reserves (probably not the best strategy!). An objective in this case might be to end the game with hotels on the blue, green, yellow, and orange properties and $5,000 in cash. Or it might be to have no properties but not be the first person to leave the game. In sports, games, and other situations, our objectives will lead to the strategies we select to help us achieve those objectives.

What Does It Mean to Be Strategic?

Businesses, the military, sports teams, and other groups often say that they value good strategic thinkers. But what does it mean to think strategically, and how can those involved in strategic planning processes for their organizations develop effective strategies? What does it take? That question was posed on a social media site frequented by small business people and the responses were interesting—and varied:

- Strategic thinking is about process. If you are consistent and stick to it, strategic thinking will just happen naturally over time.
- [It takes] an iterative process to create a vision for the future and a clear, concise blueprint for realizing that vision. It can be logical or creative.

- Look five steps ahead instead of just now, including tomorrow, next week, next month, etc. Practice visualizing what is far ahead in everything.

- No doubt it's about thinking … but it's about thinking systemically.

> **DID YOU KNOW?**
>
> Chinese general Sun Tzu's *The Art of War* was written in the sixth century B.C. It is an exploration of military strategy and is still used in many business courses as a textbook on how to develop effective strategies.

Thinking strategically can be a difficult concept to wrap our heads around. It's one of those "We'll know it when we see it" concepts. We can probably all think of people we've worked with or business leaders we've known who are strategic thinkers. They just seem to be able to come up with the perfect solutions to whatever issues they face. They take advantage of opportunities that others have not yet even identified. They overcome obstacles that others did not even know existed. They seem to be thinking far into the future and often seem somewhat prescient—as if they can predict the future!

Strategic thinking involves looking ahead to what might be and then considering how what might be could be influenced by what you do. Hockey player Wayne Gretzky illustrated this well in his now-famous quote: "A good hockey player plays where the puck is. A great hockey player plays where the puck is going to be." That is strategic thinking—what it requires is a thorough understanding of the game (or business or industry) and the ability to predict how the players in the game (collaborators as well as competitors) may react. And then, of course, it requires developing strategies to impact the outcome in a way that is most favorable to you.

Developing Your Strategies

As you consider the strategies that you will use to help meet your objectives, think broadly about the approach you will take. Your strategies are, in essence, a description of how you will accomplish your objectives. Strategies describe a general approach, rather than specific actions or tactics, which are discussed in the next chapter.

Suppose you have established a goal of growing your business and a related objective tied to that goal of increasing market share by 20 percent over the next year. The next step is to determine how you will increase market share. This list of potential *hows* represent strategies. For instance:

- Introduce a new product.

- Expand into a new geographic market area.

- Expand production capacity.

- Grow relationships with current customers to expand their purchases.

- Develop an online presence to expand sales nationally or internationally.

All of these ways that you might increase your market share represent strategies—the answer to how you are going to do it. Like goals, they are broad statements. Strategies represent an important turning point in the development of your strategic plan. While your goals and objectives provide an indication of what you want to accomplish, your strategies and tactics need to indicate how you're going to accomplish those goals and objectives. This is the part of the strategic planning process that begins to get creative juices flowing. It is, in fact, the part that many people anxiously look forward to—and try to jump to—earlier in the process. But strategies aren't just plucked out of the air. They really depend upon all of the work that you have done so far.

Where Strategies Come From

Hopefully you are beginning to see how the GOST (goals, objectives, strategies, and tactics) process works by providing a clear line of sight from the organization's mission and vision through the development of goals, objectives, and—now—strategies to support that mission and vision. Your strategies will represent the direction you want to go to achieve an advantage or overcome obstacles and to meet the needs of your customers and other important stakeholders.

In considering strategies that might be appropriate for you, there are a number of questions you should ask:

- What are we trying to do in the long term? (Your mission and vision can give you good direction here.)

- What markets do we want to compete in?

- In what ways could we perform better than our competitors?

- What resources do we need to be successful?

- What factors in our external environment represent either opportunities that could be leveraged or challenges that need to be overcome?

Strategies can exist at the corporate, division, department, or individual level and will vary based on the type of strategic plan being developed. A corporate strategy might relate to expansion into a new market area or the development of a new product line. A department strategy might relate to the development or training needs of employees or the improvement of specific departmental processes.

Thinking Strategically

While great strategic thinkers often seem larger than life and sometimes even somewhat mystical, the truth of it is that they are simply (whether they realize it or not) following a logical process that improves their chances of success.

Effective strategic thinkers certainly are creative, but they are creative within boundaries. The strategies they develop aren't just picked out of thin air but are based on the following:

- Solid foundational information—the SWOT analysis
- An identified goal
- Specific objectives

Strategies are aligned and supportive of the other elements of the strategic plan. Our SWOT analysis provides us with important information about the industry we're in, our competitors, and our own strengths and weaknesses. Our goals give us direction and tell us where we want to be headed. Our objectives narrow our focus and give us measurable targets that we hope to achieve.

BEST PRACTICES

Thinking strategically really just involves considering all of the things you have going for and against you, deciding where you hope to go, and then coming up with ideas for how to get there.

In working with a planning team to develop strategies, it's important to keep them focused on the goals and objectives that are driving the strategies. In addition, they must think about the strengths and opportunities that can be leveraged or used to their advantage in achieving the identified objectives, as well as the weaknesses and threats that need to be considered and, sometimes, overcome.

Aligning Strategies with Objectives

While it's not uncommon for businesses to start at the point of strategy—"We're going to introduce a new product!"—doing so without the benefit of clearly defined goals and objectives makes it more likely that the implementation of the strategy will not yield positive results. Objectives lead to strategies by providing businesses with a prioritized list of things they would like to achieve. Not just things—but the most important things! Once a business knows what it most wants to achieve, it can develop and prioritize strategies for how to do it.

Just as we did with the relationship between goals, mission, and vision and the relationship between objectives and goals, let's take a look at the relationship between strategies and objectives. Given an objective of "Grow business in the primary market area by 30 percent over the next two years)," your team will have a discussion about how they are going to do this. There are many possibilities:

- Advertise more aggressively in this area.

- Purchase or merge with a competitor in the area.

- Introduce new products.

- Expand into a new demographic market (for example, reach out to the retiree market).

- Open new stores in the area.

- Reduce product prices to drive up sales.

- Increase product prices to drive up revenue.

Could each of these strategies serve to meet the objective of growing business? Sure, it's possible. But while an initial brainstorming session can be a good starting point to get your team thinking strategically, not all ideas will be good ideas.

Selecting the Right Strategies

Your strategies will reflect your plans to achieve your identified outcomes. Strategies are ideas that are proposed as possible ways of achieving your objectives. As you might imagine, there are many, many ideas that could be generated. Fortunately, there are some tools we can use to help gain the focus required to ensure that our ideas are truly strategic.

As with the other elements of your plan, the process of identifying strategies can draw upon the SWOT analysis you developed in Chapter 12.

Timing and Scope Provide Guidance

The timing and scope of our objectives will impact the strategies we develop. For instance, consider how these two objectives, established November 1, would impact your choice of strategy:

- Decrease average time to hire by 30 percent by December 1 (of the same year).

- Decrease average time to hire by 30 percent by December 1 (of the following year).

Just a simple change—the addition of 12 months—will clearly have an impact on the types of strategies you might select. A longer time frame reduces the pressure to achieve the objective and gives you some leeway in terms of how you might utilize your resources. The same would be true if your target dates remained the same but you changed "Decrease by 30 percent" to "Maintain." At least that might be what we would assume. We'll soon see, though, how the information gathered through your SWOT analysis can provide additional important information to help guide your decision-making.

Leveraging Strengths and Opportunities

Once again, the SWOT analysis you developed at the beginning of your strategic planning process will serve as a very important point of reference as you come up with strategies designed to help you achieve your objectives and, ultimately, your goals.

While coming up with strategies does involve brainstorming, it is focused brainstorming. Thinking about the strengths and opportunities that you can take advantage of to help you achieve your objectives helps you remain focused on the resources you have that can help lead to success. Thinking back to the hiring example we just looked at, let's assume your objective is "Maintain average time to hire at its current level—one month—through the end of the next year." And let's say that your SWOT analysis indicated that …

- One of your strengths is a competent HR department with expertise in staffing.

- One of your opportunities is a tight local economy and some plant closings that have resulted in a steady stream of potential employees for your business.

Recognizing these strengths and opportunities provides you with direction and focus in terms of the strategies you develop. The strategies are based on a solid understanding of both where you want to go (specifically!) and insights into some advantages you can leverage to get there.

This part of the strategy-setting process would involve these steps:

1. Reflect on the overall goal.

2. Reflect on the specific objective.

3. Consider the strengths and opportunities from the SWOT analysis that could positively impact the ability to achieve the objective.

Some questions you might ask yourself are:

- How can we use our strengths to take advantage of our opportunities?

- How can we take advantage of our strengths to avoid potential threats?

Of course, in addition to considering your strengths and opportunities and how they might help you achieve your objectives through the development of appropriate strategies, you must consider the impact of your weaknesses and threats.

The following table shows how a list of strengths and opportunities developed during the SWOT analysis can be used to generate ideas for potential strategies created during an HR strategic planning process focused on a goal of "Attracting and retaining high-quality employees" and an objective of "Reducing turnover by 20 percent by the end of the calendar year."

Strengths/Opportunities	Strategy
Strong corporate culture	Promote work environment
Limited bureaucracy	Promote work environment
Strong management team	Use management team as recruiters
Open to new ideas	Promote work environment
Access to local graduates	Develop partnerships with schools

Minimizing Weaknesses and Threats

Let's use the same example of the hiring objective of "Maintain average time to hire at its current level—one month—through the end of the next year." And let's say that your SWOT analysis indicated that ...

- One of your weaknesses is that you do not have an automated system in place for processing applications.

- One of your threats is the entry of a large company in your market area, which will employ the same type of skilled staff you employ.

MISSTEPS

As the team looks back at the SWOT analysis, there can be a tendency to revisit past discussions and debate, again, whether a weakness is really a weakness, for instance. The facilitator has an important role to play here in keeping the team on track and focused—reminding everyone that the SWOT has already been created and approved.

These impacts would represent an entirely different situation than the one discussed previously. In considering how this information would impact our development of strategies, you would want to consider ...

- How significant your risks were in terms of these identified weaknesses and threats.

- If, and how, you could minimize your weaknesses and threats.

The responses to these questions would point to potential strategies that you could use to achieve your objective despite the weaknesses and threats you face.

Based on the weaknesses and threats you identified during the SWOT analysis, what ideas do you have for how to overcome or minimize these weaknesses or threats? These become potential strategies.

Weaknesses/Threats	Strategy
Low awareness of company	Create awareness campaign
New employer competitor	Focus on competitive strengths
Low employee satisfaction	Focus on work/life balance
	Become known as one of the best places to work in the area

Evaluation Tools

While you can't, of course, be 100 percent sure that the strategies you pick will be the right ones, there are some tools you can use to help choose from among the various strategies you are considering. These tools can help you evaluate and prioritize the various strategies that you're considering to meet your stated objectives.

A simple *matrix*, based on criteria you select and weighted to help provide you with a relative measure of potential success for each strategy, is one way to consider which strategies have the most potential for you. Let's look at an example. Suppose you were considering various strategies to help meet an objective of "Expand market share by 30 percent by the end of the calendar year." Your planning team has brainstormed various strategies and has come up with a number of great ideas—too many, in fact, to be able to pursue all of them.

DEFINITION

A **matrix** is a grid that allows planners to consider the relative value of various items based on identified criteria.

You know that your resources are limited and that you can't possibly pursue all of these strategies at the same time. You need to narrow the list to choose those that hold the most potential. To do this, you would first develop a list of criteria to help you make a decision. These criteria might include the following:

- Likelihood of success

- Availability of resources

- Potential risk

- Support by staff

Your next step would be to determine how critical each of these factors is on some numerical scale to help you calculate a comparative ranking of the strategies you're considering. So in this case, let's assume that, based on a total of 100 points, you assign weights as follows:

- Likelihood of success—20

- Availability of resources—35

- Potential risk—20

- Support by staff—25

Next you would create a table like the one shown below and assign a rating to each of the strategies you are considering. In this example, we'll rate the strategies on a scale of 1 to 5, with 1 being the lowest priority and 5 being the highest, for each of the criteria. Each strategy would be ranked, and then that ranking would be multiplied by the value assigned to the criteria (as shown in parentheses in the table).

When considering the "success" criteria, the ratings might reflect the following:

1 = Very low chance of success

2 = Somewhat low chance of success

3 = Chance of success is unclear

4 = Likely chance of success

5 = Success is virtually guaranteed

Criteria	Value	Strat 1	Strat 2	Strat 3	Strat 4
Success	20	3(60)	4(80)	2(40)	4(80)
Resources	35	4(140)	2(70)	3(105)	4(140)
Risk	20	2(40)	3(60)	4(80)	1(20)
Staff	25	3(75)	3(75)	2(50)	4(100)
TOTALS		315	285	275	340

Based on this evaluation, strategies 1 and 4 scored highest. The team might then decide that these are the two strategies they would move forward with at this time. The key to making this process work effectively—and achieving a good, quantitative indication of relative value for each strategy—is identifying the criteria that are most important to you; assigning an objective, relative value that the group agrees upon (before rating each of the strategies); and then reaching agreement on ratings for each of the strategies based on the selected criteria. This is one way to consider which strategies represent the best opportunity for you.

Another method is to use a simple survey format, asking team members to rate each strategy based on the criteria you selected along a continuum. The ratings scale might include 3, 5, or even 7 ratings points—the number selected is not critical, but designed to give a sense of the relative ranking of each factor based on the input for the group. An even number of ratings points could also be used—it forces those rating the categories to choose either a favorable (the upper half of the numbers) or unfavorable (the lower half) response instead of choosing a middle or neutral response.

Strategy 1								
Low Success	1	2	3	4	5	6	7	High Success
Few Resources	1	2	3	4	5	6	7	Many Resources
High Risk	1	2	3	4	5	6	7	Low Risk
Low Support	1	2	3	4	5	6	7	High Support

The criteria you select and the ratings you give to both the criteria and the rankings for each strategy are still subjective to a certain degree. But using a rating method like the examples given here can be a good way to help provide a more objective basis for the team's decisions about which strategies to pursue.

The Least You Need to Know

- Strategies indicate how you will leverage strengths and opportunities and minimize weaknesses and threats to achieve your objectives.
- Encourage team members to think strategically by taking a forward-looking approach based on the possible implications of the SWOT analysis.
- The SWOT analysis is an important input when developing strategies.
- A rating process of some sort can help prioritize, and even eliminate, strategies.

Developing Tactics

In This Chapter

- How tactics work with a plan's strategies, objectives, and goals
- Elements of effective tactics
- Involving your team
- Developing an action plan

Finally—the tactics. It's not uncommon for organizations and individuals faced with a strategic issue to jump immediately to solutions, or tactics. Somehow we seem to be wired that way! The truth of the matter is that when you start with tactics, you're really taking a huge leap of faith that those tactics are going to be related to some strategy that supports some objective that drives some high-level goal you hope to achieve. You might have some general idea ("We want to increase sales"), but as you've hopefully seen in the previous chapters, the more specificity you can put around this general idea, the more clearly focused you can become and the better choices you can make.

All businesses, regardless of size or level of success, have limited resources. There are only so many people to do the work, only so much money to fund the work, only so much time in a day. Given these limitations, businesses hope to get the most bang for their buck. The process I've been describing is designed to help them do just that.

In this chapter, we'll take a look at the final step in the GOST process—the tactics or operational plans that outline how the plan's strategies, objectives, and goals will be realized.

Creating Tactics

The operational steps that you identify are your *tactics*. While strategies give a general indication of how you will approach the accomplishment of an identified objective, tactics outline specifically what you will do. In fact, a good way to determine whether a strategy is really an objective is to ask yourself whether it is a *how* statement or a *what* statement. "Divide and conquer" is a *how* statement. "Deploy troops to infiltrate base camps" is a *what* statement, indicating what you will do to "Divide and conquer."

DEFINITION

Tactics are specific to-do items that are designed in support of strategies.

Most of us are pretty good at coming up with tactics—at least, we think we are. In fact, we do it all the time. Every day we make decisions about what we're going to do. The trouble is that the things we do are not always well aligned with the strategies, objectives, and goals that we are ultimately working toward. We want to avoid that in the development of our strategic plans, so we take steps to ensure that this final step is designed to support all of the work that has gone before.

Generally, coming up with tactics is relatively straightforward. There are some challenges you will face, however:

- Making sure that tactics are directly tied to other elements of the plan—this isn't the time to generate new ideas that come out of the blue!

- Ensuring that you have the resources available—or that you can afford to develop the resources—to accomplish the tactics.

- Making sure that the people who need to be involved to make the tactics happen have been, or can become, engaged in the process.

- Developing the right mix of tactics designed to achieve the strategies at the lowest possible cost in terms of times and effort expended.

Just as with the other elements of the strategic plan, there are some specific things you can look for to determine whether your tactics are correctly stated and appropriate.

Making Sure There Is Alignment

Hopefully it has become abundantly clear by now how important alignment is throughout the strategic plan. From the situation analysis, to the SWOT analysis, to the review of mission, vision, and values, to the development of goals, objectives, strategies, and tactics, alignment will help to ensure the appropriateness of your plan and increase the odds that your plan will be a success. Tactics are the final step (well, very close to the final step) in ensuring that this alignment occurs. Tactics do not exist in a vacuum. They should not be created independently without being tied to strategies, objectives, and goals. In fact, your tactics will stem directly from and will support the strategies that you developed in support of your objectives.

Let's take a look at an example of how this might work. Suppose we have the following goal, objective, and strategy developed:

- Goal: To become the industry's employer of choice.

- Objective: To reduce the percent of open positions by 25 percent by year's end.

- Strategy: Leverage social media to promote what's great about working at XYZ Company.

Here are two tactics under consideration:

- Develop a Twitter account to build followers and direct them to the Internet site.

- Update XYZ company's application form.

While the second tactic might be something that the organization wants to do, it doesn't fit here. It is not directly aligned with the strategy of leveraging social media to promote what's great about working at the company. Developing a Twitter account with the intent of driving more traffic to the Internet site is related to leveraging social media to promote what's great about the company. Importantly, if this tactic had been stated only as "Develop a Twitter account," it would not have been quite so clear whether it was, indeed, aligned with the strategy. Even with tactics, it's important to be specific!

Are the Tactics Really Tactics?

In addition to making sure that tactics are directly aligned with the strategies that have been developed, and therefore likely to help achieve the stated objectives, it's important to make sure that the tactics really *are* tactics. Let's review some examples of actual strategies and tactics to see if they are appropriately stated:

Strategy: Increase percentage of alumni supporting the development fund.

Tactics:

1. Increase the sense of alumni ownership of the fund.

2. Ensure 100 percent participation of the board.

In this case, the strategy is okay. It is an indication of how we might achieve an objective that we will assume is SMART (see Chapter 14). The tactics, however, are not tactics. What are they? Well, the first is currently stated as a strategy but could be easily rewritten as an objective: "Increase the percentage of alumni who indicate they feel a sense of ownership of the fund (as measured through our annual survey) by 25 percent by the end of the year." The second tactic could also be a strategy or, with the addition of a time frame, could meet the criteria for an objective. But neither of these are tactics. Why? Because tactics should tell us what we are going to do to achieve our strategy. What will we do, in this case, to increase the sense of alumni ownership? To ensure 100 percent participation of the board? We need specific operational items that we will literally assign to someone to accomplish. So in this case, to achieve our strategy of increasing the percentage of alumni supporting the development fund, some specific things we might do could include …

- Developing a direct mail campaign to be sent to all alumni asking for their support of the development fund.

- Holding a fundraising event for alumni and their families.

- Developing a telephone campaign to call alumni and personally ask for support of the development fund.

It is not uncommon for tactics to be initially stated more like strategies. One of the challenges teams face is that, after spending a significant amount of time at fairly lofty levels in terms of contemplating goals, objectives, and strategies, the focus of the planning effort suddenly changes to become more operational. Instead of talking about outcomes or things they would like to accomplish, they now need to talk about what they will do—specifically—to accomplish those outcomes.

BEST PRACTICES

Don't dampen the enthusiasm of those creating tactics by critiquing them the minute they come out of their mouths. Instead, write them down, make sure you capture all of the good ideas, and then go back to evaluate whether they are aligned and stated as to-dos versus strategies.

Are Tactics Realistic and Reasonable?

We're not done with our evaluation yet! In addition to making sure that our tactics are clearly stated as tactics, we need to evaluate whether the list of tactics we have developed to support each strategy is realistic and reasonable. Let's consider an example using our previous scenario of leveraging social media to raise awareness of your company as a great place to work. Specific tactics might include:

- Establishing a Facebook fan page.

- Growing followers on Twitter by running a contest.

- Creating a blog.

All of these things could certainly raise awareness of your company. As you consider this list of tactics, though, you need to look back at the objective the strategy supports to determine what level of awareness you are hoping to attain. Are the tactics you identified sufficient to reach this level of awareness?

Next you need to determine whether you have the resources and people available to accomplish the tactics. In this case, you might ask your team the following questions:

- Do we have anyone on staff who knows about social media or blogs?

- If not, what resources (time and money) would be required to train somebody on staff so they would have this knowledge? What trade-offs or risks might there be in terms of the time it would take to accomplish this tactic and the quality of the implementation?

- If we decide to not do this internally, are there resources available externally we could hire? What would be required to find, select, and work with these resources (time and money)?

There is, admittedly, a certain level of subjectivity involved here. You and your team are charged with giving your best effort to identify the right mix of elements (tactics) to support your strategies and achieve the related objectives in support of your overall goal or goals.

Tactics are operational. They indicate the things that must be accomplished to ultimately accomplish the goals your strategic plan was developed to achieve. In creating tactics, you will also consider questions related to who will be assigned to accomplish the task, by when, and at what cost. These elements will not necessarily be included in your statement of the tactic, but they will be key items to include in the plan to make sure that you have the resources to make it happen.

DID YOU KNOW?

The great military theorist Carl von Clausewitz said, "Tactics is the art of using troops in battle; strategy is the art of using battles to win the war."

The goal when developing tactics is not to simply develop a laundry list of things that you could do but to create a list of those things that would be best to do given your stated strategies, objectives, and goals. *Best* can be further defined as those things that would cost the least (in terms of time, effort, and money) to achieve the most (consistent with your objectives). Overkill represents wasted resources. Underkill represents lost opportunity.

There are, unfortunately, no right or wrong answers when developing tactics (or any part of the strategic plan, for that matter)—there are just some answers that may be better than others, depending, of course, on the other elements of the plan.

Involving Subject Matter Experts

It's quite possible that your team has no idea what you might do to accomplish this strategy. That suggests that this would be a good time to pull in other members of your staff who might or to turn the plan over to the operational departments, teams, or individuals in your organization to have them recommend appropriate tactics. In the earlier example about the university hoping to grow alumni support, for instance, the university planning team might turn to their development department to ask for a list of proposed tactics to support this strategy: "Increase the percentage of alumni who indicate they feel a sense of ownership of the fund (as measured through the annual survey) by 25 percent by the end of the year." The development department would then consider the things they could do to support this strategy and achieve the objective, and they would come back to the planning team with a list of proposed tactics to review.

MISSTEPS

Don't be too specific when developing tactics. Tactics are operational, but they should not represent extremely detailed steps of a broader process. "Hold a press conference" is an appropriate tactic. Breaking that down into "Develop list of media contacts," "Write e-mail invitation," and "Send e-mail invitation" would be a level of detail that might show up on an individual employee's action plan but would be too specific for strategic plan tactics.

Keep in mind that, when identifying or approving tactics, you want to ...

- Select those things that are most likely to support your strategy with the least amount of time, effort, and cost. Less is more. There are many, many things that you could do, but that doesn't necessarily mean that you should!

- Consider the consistency and appropriateness of the tactics to your business mission, vision, and goals.

- Consider available resources—staff, time frame, access to external expertise, etc.

- Be sure to involve the appropriate people in the development of the tactics— those closest to where and how the work is actually done.

It's not a bad thing to reach a point in your planning process where your team members do not have the background, information, or skills to identify appropriate tactics. In fact, that can be a very good thing, because it provides an opportunity to further engage those in your company who will actually be doing the work to accomplish the plan.

Often, the formal strategic plan includes elements up through the strategies. Strategies are then assigned to specific departments, teams, or individuals who are charged with creating the tactics—to make the strategies happen.

One organization, for instance, involved its top- and mid-level leadership team in the development and biannual revision of the strategic plans through a review of the goals, objectives, and strategies—with updates as necessary. Leaders were assigned to strategies and charged with working with their teams to develop plans for achieving the strategies, which were then reviewed again by the team and prioritized for action. This can be a useful way to manage the process, because when you get to the point when you're thinking about what needs to be done to accomplish the plan, you need to hear from those on the front lines. You need concrete, operational input about what needs to be done, who will do it, and what resources will need to be provided (time, money, and expertise) to make the plan a reality.

The list of actions identified by those who need to put the plan in motion will need to be reviewed and prioritized—and may, in some cases, impact the plan itself.

Timing and Personnel

This is the point in the strategic planning process when the rubber meets the road—the point at which you begin considering the operational implications of your plan. Who is going to actually make things happen, and do they have the time and resources they will need to be successful? It is at this point that you will also recognize the importance of involving those who will be doing the work in designing the tactical elements of the plan.

Those being tapped to participate in the implementation of the plan, or who will likely be assigned to various tactics, should be involved in the development of those tactics or—at a minimum—be aware of them before the plan is communicated to the company at large. As one woman who has watched strategic plan implementation fail notes, "The best results come from plans developed inclusively, getting feedback and input from all levels within the company. Mandates seldom result in solutions without input from those that will be charged with making everything happen."

A strategic planning consultant who works primarily with non-profit organizations agrees and says this is an area that he sees as one of the biggest barriers to successful strategic plan implementation. Having a plan that is presented as a done deal and dropping it in the laps of staff members who have no frame of reference for its development, and who had no input into the tasks they've been assigned, can be a recipe for disaster. Instead, he recommends taking a break between the development of goals, objectives, and strategies and the development of tactics. "If you take a break, or you physically wait for a week or two before moving forward with tactics, the team's mindset is different," he says. In fact, he doesn't even tie this portion of the planning process to the rest of it. He calls it *developing the plan of action*.

Another woman who has worked with various organizations on the development of their strategic plans says, "I don't think they get down and dirty enough. They need to get to the point of 'I need you to do this,' 'I need you to do that,' 'I need you to do this,' and 'I need you to do it by ...' Oh, and 'This is how we'll know if we've been effective.'"

To be effective in executing their strategic plans, companies need to break the plan down into tactics, either through the planning team or through individual department or functional assignments. Those tactics must be assigned to individuals who are held accountable to achieve measurable outcomes. And, equally importantly, the company needs to ensure that these individuals have the resources they need to get the job done.

MISSTEPS

When strategies are turned over to departments or individuals to develop tactics outside the scope of the team's work, there can be the potential for tactics to stem from new ideas or opinions that do not represent the team. Be sure to develop some process for following up and reviewing the tactics developed to ensure that they are appropriate and reflective of the team's intentions.

Involving Staff

The staff members tapped to do the work necessary to achieve the plan will need to provide the planning team with ...

- The list of tactics (or activities) that they feel will achieve the strategy.

- Estimated time and cost for completing those activities.

- An indication of whether resources currently exist to achieve the tactics.

Staff members will need to consider whether ...

- The tactics necessary to achieve the strategies will take the place of something currently being done.

- The tactics necessary to achieve the strategies are new. If so, is there capacity to accomplish those tactics?

- There isn't additional time available to accomplish the new tactics. In that case, additional hours or additional staff will be needed.

- There is additional time available but no internal expertise to accomplish the task.

In addition, those assigned to accomplish the tactics are often asked to create action plans that provide step-by-step details on how the tactics will be accomplished. These action plans guide the employee's activities and provide a framework for achieving the tactics in support of the strategies.

A small manufacturing firm follows this process: "As tactics are assigned to staff members, they are asked to develop (or update) steps, time lines, resources, costs, and measures of success. These plans are entered into a database for review and tracking. A final balancing meeting is held to review the plan as a whole and make needed adjustments to the timing of plans and financial and human resource requirements."

The Approval Process

Timing and coordination are everything when the strategic planning process gets down to the tactical level. For organization-wide plans, this is the point where supporting plans (such as marketing plans) will be developed. All of the supporting plans must be developed and in place before the company budget can be developed and approved. And since the budget will need to be approved before activities can begin taking place, it is important that the time frame required for the approval process be built into the plan initially.

One small company learned this the hard way when it started its first organizational strategic planning process in October. By the end of December, the team was ready to turn the plan over to departments for the development of tactics and action plans, but January, the beginning of their fiscal year, was literally right around the corner! There was no time for the important steps of approving the tactics and developing and approving the budget to support the plan. Make sure that you have built in steps—and enough time—to allow tactics, supporting plans, and actions to be developed and a budget to be approved.

Developing Action Plans

The last formal step in the strategic planning process that will take place at the department or individual level is the development of *action plans*. Once your plan has been turned over to staff to implement, the development of action plans can be a good way, on an individual or department level, to ensure that things happen and that tactics, strategies, objectives, and goals are met.

DEFINITION

An **action plan** is a step-by-step, specific to-do list of the actions that need to be carried out to accomplish a tactic.

Action plans outline for the department or individual doing the work exactly what needs to be accomplished, by when, to ensure that things get done. They help to provide an indication of the steps, the people involved, and the resources needed. In short, they indicate who is going to do what by when.

At the point where you are determining precisely what needs to be done, you can begin identifying …

- The human resources you need—internal or external—in terms of both time and expertise.

- The financial resources you need—to hire people, to train people, to cover expenses required to implement tactics.

- The capital resources you need.

You may have a great plan, but if you don't put enough resources forward to accomplish the plan, it's not likely to happen.

As action plans are developed, they may point to barriers or obstacles that the planning team didn't consider. This is not unusual, but is more likely to happen if the team failed to involve the right people at the right times during the planning process. Getting input from those on the front lines is important all along the way. But sometimes things are overlooked—when you reach the action-planning stage, you may find that the additional resources required are not within your means at this time, and you may, therefore, need to remove or change some of your strategies or tactics.

Planning is an *iterative* process, which means that it is repetitive and we learn as we move forward. Strategic planning done correctly is never truly done. Each iteration provides input into the next cycle of planning—whether it is the formal planning cycle or a course correction that needs to be made along the way (more about this in Chapter 21).

DEFINITION

Iterative is an adjective used to describe a cycle of activity that is ongoing and that changes from cycle to cycle as new information is gained. An iteration reflects one cycle in the process.

The Least You Need to Know

- Tactics represent the to-do list that needs to be accomplished to make the plan happen.
- Consideration of tactics includes consideration of the resources—people and money—needed to get things done.
- Tactics should be evaluated for their likelihood of achieving the strategies and should be both realistic and reasonable.
- Tactics are often developed by people in the departments or divisions that will be doing the work.
- Time needs to be built into the plan to develop supporting plans, as necessary, and to develop and approve budgets.
- Action plans provide specific detail about the steps, individuals, and resources required to accomplish tactics.

Pulling It All Together

In This Chapter

- Making sure all parts of your plan are aligned
- Is the goal supported by clear and specific objectives?
- Are strategies appropriate to achieve objectives?
- Are identified tactics sufficient to accomplish strategies?
- Aligning plans internally

Your planning team has gone through a lot of work to this point, but there is still a bit more to do before you begin the actual process of implementing your plan. At this point—once you have gone through the process of developing goals, objectives, strategies, and tactics—you need to take a look back at the plan to determine whether you have the right mix of activities in place to meet your goals. Is anything missing? Are all of the elements aligned or tied together appropriately? Is anything out of place? Are there any key strengths or significant weaknesses that you have overlooked? Are your plan elements achievable based on the resources you have available? Are time lines realistic? Are any of your plan elements potentially working at cross-purposes?

In this chapter, we'll explore the final steps you need to take to evaluate your draft plan to determine if you're ready to move forward with implementation.

Evaluating Plan Elements

Once all of the elements of your plan have been developed, the first step you should take is to ensure that each plan element is properly defined. This should have been done on an ongoing basis as you developed your goals, objectives, strategies, and tactics in the previous four chapters, but a double check at the end is a good idea. Let's take a look at an example based on the strategic plan for a small medical clinic to see how this process might work:

- Goal: Become the provider of choice

- Objective: Increase employer presence

- Strategy: Develop relationships with local employers

- Tactic(s): Visit employers, join Chamber of Commerce, form business advisory committee

You will look at each and ask:—is the goal a goal, the objective an objective, the strategy a strategy, and the tactics, tactics? In this case, they are, except that the objective is not stated in SMART terms—it needs a measurable element and a time frame. In fact, the way it is currently stated, it is more of a strategy than an objective. So it might be better stated as "Increase the number of networking relationships with benefits administrators at area employers by 20 percent by the end of the fiscal year." This provides a measurable objective that is related to the goal. It is, then, supported by the strategy of developing relationships and some specific methods (tactics) that can be used to develop those relationships.

Here's another example, from a restaurant's strategic plan, where the elements really aren't quite right:

- Goal: Add 4 new locations by the end of the fiscal year.

- Objective: Grow business by 25 percent.

- Strategy: Add new locations.

- Tactic(s): Research site locations, decide whether to buy or lease, select Realtor.

Oh boy—where to begin with this one? Let's first start with determining whether the goal is a goal, the objective is an objective, the strategy is a strategy, and the tactics are tactics:

- "Add 4 new locations by the end of the fiscal year" is an objective, not a goal. How do we know this? Because it is specific and measurable. Goals are broad and general.

- "Grow business by 25 percent" is close to being an objective, but it still needs a time frame. That's easy enough to fix. We'll restate as "Grow business by 25 percent by the end of the fiscal year."

- "Add new locations" could be a strategy. It would be related to the objective of growing the business, and as we already saw, it was the basis for the incorrectly stated goal.

- The tactics are a bit problematic. Yes, technically, they are tactics. They are things we would do. But they are at a level of detail that is far too task-related for the purposes of a strategic plan. They might appear on the task list of an employee assigned to a tactic of "Open a restaurant in City X," but they would not be outlined at this level of detail in the overall plan.

BEST PRACTICES

When reviewing plan elements, it can be helpful to revisit the definitions of GOST and even to distribute a "cheat sheet" that offers these definitions, along with some specific examples.

Going through this process has shown us that the goal is not really a goal. We could have stopped right there to ask, "What is our goal?" It's okay that we continued through the process of verifying the appropriateness of the other plan elements. But at this point, we really need to take a step back to consider whether we need this particular objective, strategy, and related tactics. Do they actually support one of our business goals? In this case, the answer would be yes if a business goal was to "Grow the business." And that's okay. We can work this backward. But what if that wasn't a goal of the restaurant? Then none of these items would be appropriate and should be eliminated.

While this process may seem somewhat tedious, it's important—and it can also be very helpful to involve the planning team. The team leader could do this process outside of the planning meetings and bring a final plan back to the group. However, depending on the group, the purpose of the plan, and the group's experience with strategic planning, there are two reasons you may choose not to do this:

1. The group may question or challenge why the team leader chose to remove or change a plan element.

2. The group would not benefit from the value of the discussion about the plan elements, which can provide a great learning experience about both the important attributes of each of the GOST elements and their relationship to each other.

If you do decide to do this work outside of the team meetings, be sure that the person doing the review understands that he or she needs to be focused on whether the plan elements are correctly stated, and not the content or intent of the plan elements.

Aligning the GOST

The goals, objectives, strategies, and tactics that you created during your strategic planning process do not exist independently. They should be integrally and directly linked to each other. In fact, this is a good example of a situation where the whole is truly greater than the sum of its parts. You should be able to look at each tactic and ask, "Does this tactic support the overall goal(s) for the plan?" If the answer is no, or if you're not sure, it may not be the best tactic. The same is true of all of the other elements of the plan.

In addition, your strategic plan should be supportive of your organization's mission and vision. You clarified the validity of the mission and vision at the beginning of the planning process, and it's a good idea to do another check at the end of the planning process to ensure that all of the elements of the plan are still supportive and aligned with your stated mission and vision. Here's an example of how this might work.

A travel agency has just completed a strategic marketing planning process and is evaluating the plan to ensure that all of the elements are aligned. The agency's mission is "To provide the highest level of service and professionalism to ensure that clients achieve their travel goals."

- Goal: To increase the number of clients.
- Objective: To add 125 new clients this fiscal year.
- Strategy: Focus on fewer, more personal connections with prospects.
- Tactic: Hold a summer picnic event for prospects who respond to an online promotion.

In evaluating whether there is alignment between these elements, the travel agency planning team would consider such questions as …

- Is the tactic of holding a summer picnic in conflict with our organization's mission? No.
- Does the tactic of holding a summer picnic for prospects support our goal of increasing the number of clients we have? Yes.

- Will the tactic of holding a summer picnic potentially lead to the addition of new clients? Yes.

- Is the tactic of holding a summer picnic consistent with a strategy of focusing on fewer, more personal connections with prospects? Yes.

In this case, this tactic is aligned with each of the other elements of the GOST. But let's take a look at another potential tactic: "Run television ads in the metro market area."

- Is the tactic of running television ads in conflict with our organization's mission? No.

- Does the tactic of running television ads support our goal of increasing the number of clients we have? Yes.

- Will the tactic of running television ads potentially lead to the addition of new clients? Yes.

- Is the tactic of running television ads consistent with a strategy of focusing on fewer, more personal connections with prospects? No.

In this case, while the tactic is supportive of the mission, goal, and objective, it is not aligned with the strategy of focusing on fewer, more personal connections with prospects.

MISSTEPS

Avoid the tendency to put too much into your plan—too many goals, too many objectives, too many strategies, and too many tactics. Start small; you can always build as you move forward. Focus on those things that you believe can actually be accomplished.

It's important to note that this doesn't mean this is not a good tactic. It simply is a tactic that is not aligned with this particular goal. The travel agency may, in fact, have another strategy of "Create a national advertising campaign" that would be consistent with this tactic—or it may not. The point is that, as you review the elements of your plan, make sure everything fits—that there aren't items just thrown in that may represent what someone thought was a great idea but, when held up to the scrutiny of the plan, just doesn't have a place. It's a good idea in any planning setting—even informal planning—to examine tactics (or ideas) in light of their consistency with organizational strategy, objectives, and goals.

Here's an example. A new employee in the development office for a community hospital was an avid runner. She recommended to the development manager that a running event might be a great way to raise funds in support of the hospital. The development director agreed. "That's a great idea!" she enthused. And perhaps it was. But where did it fit? Was it tied to the hospital's mission? Was it supportive of a hospital goal? Did it support an objective? Was it related to some strategy? In this case, the answers were "kind of," "somewhat," "maybe," and "not really." But the event was held and resources—staff and money—were put toward it. It did raise some money for the organization, which was a development goal. The important question for the organization, though, was: would some other tactic have been more clearly aligned with the organization's stated mission, vision, goals, objectives, and strategies and therefore a more appropriate use of resources? And the answer was yes.

For businesses, this is really the key consideration when evaluating the elements of a strategic plan. Does the plan represent the best use of organizational resources given the organization's stated mission, vision, goals, objectives, and strategies?

There are a lot of things that any business could do. The important question, though, is whether it *should*. A well-developed strategic plan can help to answer that question and ensure that resources are being used wisely to achieve the most with the least.

To streamline this process, the team leader should first remind the team of the mission and vision of the company, division, department, or team (just as a reminder, not as an opportunity for discussion or debate!), and then move through the following review process.

Do Goals Reflect the Desired Outcome?

Review all of the goals in the plan. It's okay if you just have one goal. But assuming you have more than one, are they appropriately stated? Do they relate back to and support the mission and vision of the organization? Are they the appropriate goals at this point in time? Will they, working together, accomplish the overall objective of the planning activity? Is anything missing?

Do Objectives Drive Toward the Goal?

Starting with the first goal, review the related objectives. Are they appropriately stated? Do they contain all of the SMART elements? Are they directly related to and supportive of the goal? Is anything missing? Will these objectives, working together, accomplish the goal? Do this with each of the goals and related objectives.

Are Strategies Aligned with Objectives?

Starting with the first objective, review the related strategies. Are strategies supportive of the objective? Do they serve to either leverage a strength or opportunity, or to minimize or overcome a weakness or threat? Are they appropriate and realistic?

Are Tactics Linked to Strategies?

Starting with the first strategy, review the related tactics. Are the tactics directly related to the strategy? Do the tactics reflect a specific task to be accomplished? Do you have—or can you obtain—the resources necessary to achieve the tactic? Will these tactics, working together, be sufficient to achieve the strategy?

Internal Alignment

As I've mentioned, there are a variety of different types of strategic plans that may exist in any company. In a perfect world, the overall strategic plan for the business would set the stage for the development of supportive plans that become progressively more operational. The overall strategic plan might guide the development of a marketing strategic plan, which might lead to the development of a marketing communications plan, advertising plan, and media plan. All of these plans would, ultimately, support the plan above it and the overall strategic plan. They would be aligned. This is the perfect state, but it does not always exist.

It's not uncommon for companies—and particularly large companies—to have divisions, departments, or individuals working at cross-purposes. They may each have a plan, and those plans may be well developed and consistent with good strategic planning principles, but if each plan is not supportive and aligned with other plans, company resources may be misspent.

BEST PRACTICES

Companies with multiple strategic plans should create a process and time line for ensuring that all plans are tied back to support the overall organizational plan.

This type of misalignment happens in companies with and without formal strategic plans. In a company without a strategic plan, it's easy to see how this lack of alignment might occur if managers are acting independently to set goals for their areas of responsibility. The manager of production may be taking steps to improve quality (which adds costs and lengthens the production process), while the manager of finance is working to decrease expenses. The manager of HR is focused on the implementation of a new HRIS (Human Resource Information Management) system, while the CEO is concerned about a number of upcoming retirements in key positions that may leave the company vulnerable. The call center manager is attempting to increase productivity by reducing the length of time spent on individual calls, while the marketing manager is concerned about customer service.

A strategic plan should—theoretically—provide the basis for identifying some of the types of activities that might otherwise occur and work against the company's best interests, despite the good intentions of employees. But this is only possible if each of the plan elements is reviewed to determine potential unintended impacts on other elements of the plan.

The *Balanced Scorecard* (BSC) approach to strategic planning is used by many organizations, some more rigidly than others. (See Chapter 19 for more information, and see Appendix B for details on books that more fully explain this approach.) One of the primary benefits of the approach is a focus on balancing the various elements of the plan to ensure that they are not working at cross-purposes. It is not impossible to have goals of increasing customer service levels and reducing costs of providing service—however, discussing how the objectives and strategies that would support these goals could be developed and implemented without working at cross-purposes is an important part of the alignment discussion.

 DEFINITION

The **Balanced Scorecard** (BSC) is a strategic planning management tool developed in the late 1990s by authors Robert S. Kaplan and David P. Norton as part of an overall organizational process designed to help businesses align and manage all of their critical functions. The BSC tracks business performance across four broad categories: financial performance, internal business processes, learning and growth, and customer satisfaction.

Coordination and consistency are critical. Ideally, the strategic planning process should start at the top of the organization. Then divisions, departments, and individuals should develop plans that support the overall plan. In this manner, alignment can be ensured and economies of scale can be achieved by avoiding duplication of effort and maintaining focus on the critical tasks that must be accomplished in support of the overall direction of the organization.

Many planning teams breathe a long sigh of relief when they get to this point in the process, and rightly so. Strategic planning can be an intense process. The good news is that you've successfully created a plan designed to achieve measurable results. But your work is far from over. In fact, the really important work begins now—implementing the plan.

The Least You Need to Know

- Each element of the plan needs to support the elements it is tied to.
- A final check by the planning team of the appropriateness, accuracy, and alignment of all plan efforts is important.
- Individual strategic plans also need to be aligned with other strategic plans.
- While you've accomplished a lot, your work is far from over at this point!

Implementing and Updating the Plan

While much of the work seems to go into the development of the plan—and that's an achievement certainly worthy of celebration—your real work is just beginning at this point. Your planning goal should be about getting results, not the creation of a plan!

In this part, we'll take a look at how you can ensure that your plan is effectively implemented, from considerations about format, distribution, and communication to tracking results and making course corrections along the way. Here you'll learn also about the most important part of planning—execution—and steps you can take to ensure that your plan won't just sit on a shelf gathering dust but will really generate measurable results.

Implementing the Plan

In This Chapter

- Getting internal and external feedback
- What to include in the final plan
- How to structure and distribute the plan
- Getting buy-in from key stakeholders
- Paving the way for successful execution of the plan

Once the strategic plan is created, it needs to be committed to some type of tangible format so that it can be shared, referred to, and updated as the plan is implemented. In the old days, this meant a written document, and it still may mean that in some cases. Technology, though, has made it possible to create strategic plans that can be living documents that are accessible online by any member of the planning team or the entire organization.

Communicating the contents of the plan effectively involves much more than simply giving everyone a copy, though. Those not involved in the planning process need to be educated about the plan so they can understand why it was developed, what it means to the company (and to them), and why they should get behind the plan to help in its successful implementation. That is no small feat. While those who have labored long and hard to produce the plan will hopefully be strong supporters and cheerleaders (and you'll want to make sure you call upon them to do just that!), those not involved may be harder to engage. Yet engage them you must if you want your plan to be a success. Even those employees not directly involved in the implementation of the plan need to understand what it is, what it contains, and why their co-workers are so thoroughly involved in its implementation.

It is human nature to resist change—especially when we haven't been part of designing that change. One of the reasons that strategic planning efforts can fail is that not enough time and energy is put into the very important process of implementation—and the communication associated with that implementation.

In this chapter, we'll take a look at the critical issues related to creating and distributing the plan, ensuring buy-in, and paving the way for successful plan execution.

Getting Feedback

Once the plan has been finalized by the planning team, an interim step before formally producing and publishing the plan can be a review by key internal and external audiences. This review can serve as an opportunity for some final feedback to make sure that nothing critical has been missed. It can also serve as an important political step, particularly with key external people—board members, important customers, regulators, etc.

> **MISSTEPS**
>
> It may seem like a small point, but make sure to proofread the plan document carefully before it is distributed. Even small errors can call into question the credibility and professionalism of the group creating the document.

Distributing a draft plan for comments is not a step that all organizations will take (or one that must be taken), but it is a potential step along the way toward a final completed plan. If you intend to take it, here are some tips that can help ensure a smooth process—and avoid the potential to have to go back to the drawing board or retrace your steps:

- Label the document, whether online or in hardcopy format, as the final draft. This sends a subtle signal that, while you are inviting input, you are looking for general input, not a critique or revision of the individual plan elements.

- Include a cover letter or e-mail note that not-so-subtly indicates the purpose of this final review. It could be something as simple as "Our plan is complete and we wanted you to be one of the first to see it."

- Include an overview of the process steps used (including the sources of information for your situation analysis) and the people involved. This can be helpful in managing expectations of those you send the plan to so that they can see that you covered all of the bases!

- Let these earlier reviewers know when the plan will be more widely distributed. "We'll be formally releasing the plan to all of our employees and (whatever additional audiences) on (date)." Give a date a week or so after you send the final draft. This gives you a date after which you can legitimately expect no additional comments.

- Consider any input you do receive seriously. It is quite possible that you have missed something or misstated something, so you don't want to discount any feedback you may receive. On the other hand, you don't want the feedback you receive to unnecessarily send you backward in the process.

- Have a plan in place for how—and who—will respond to any unsolicited suggestions for changes in the plan. The team leader can be a good choice, but if the team leader needs to be isolated from certain recipients (board members, for instance), select someone else from the planning team.

- Move on and move forward. There will always be input to be received. There will always be new ideas to consider. These ideas can become fodder for the next formal review of your plan!

Creating the Final Plan

An important consideration for you in producing your final, formal strategic plan will be the format you will present the plan in—hard copy or online? Brief and to the point or long and voluminous? Complete with appendixes that share all of the critical inputs that went into the plan or streamlined to just cover the high points? There are many decisions to make when it comes to actually writing the plan document. Fortunately, technology makes many of these decisions less burdensome than in the past. In fact, it's easy for the answer to be "all of the above" when it comes to deciding what to include.

We're going to take a look at what the typical strategic plan format looks like and the parts that are often included. Then we're going to take a look at a recommended approach for small businesses that want to use the plan to make things happen (which I hope is all small businesses). A combination of both of these approaches may be what you select, but keep in mind that, when it comes to strategic plan implementation, simple is best and a focus on execution is critical.

Elements of a Strategic Plan Document

If you went online to search for strategic plans, you would find a lot of examples, primarily from government agencies, educational institutions, and not-for-profit agencies. These plans primarily reflect these groups for a couple of reasons:

- These are the groups that tend to engage in strategic planning frequently.

- Because these groups serve public audiences, they view it as important to share information broadly with the public.

- Unlike privately held businesses, these groups don't feel the same competitive pressures that would hold them back from sharing this information.

As you look at these plans, you'll probably notice a number of similarities. One commonality is that many of these plans are professionally produced in high-quality formats that make use of graphic design elements, photography, and professional layouts. Again, this is often because of the external-facing audience that the organizations that create these plans have. While you certainly could produce your strategic plan in such a format, it's not necessary. In fact, your plan can be produced in a simple one-page format designed to let you quickly see everything you need in one place—and in a format that can easily be brought to meetings for review and updating.

> **BEST PRACTICES**
>
> One effective way to keep the plan alive is to use it as the basis for meeting agendas at every level of the organization. This is a good way to continually reinforce that the plan is directing the activities of the organization and is not just a writing exercise.

Another thing you'll notice as you review these plans is the wide discrepancy between the ways that goals, objectives, and strategies are presented. And as I've discussed in Part 3, you'll definitely see examples to illustrate the confusion that exists about how these terms are defined.

You'll also begin to see a fairly standard pattern in the way that these documents are organized. The standard strategic plan includes the following elements:

- **An executive summary.** A brief overview of what the plan document contains, often including the overall goals and key strategies designed to achieve those goals.

- **A list of the planning team members.** Included either as part of the executive summary or in a separate document, this is generally a list of those involved in the creation of the strategic plan.

- **Background.** A brief description of the organization, its history and current state, and the purpose for the plan.

- **Mission, vision, and values statements.** A reiteration of your company's mission, vision, and values statements.

- **The goals, objectives, strategies, and (sometimes) tactics.** These are often presented in narrative format, although as we'll see in a bit, a table format can be most helpful when communicating the plan elements.

- **Appendixes.** Plans often include appendixes that contain the background materials, or summaries of the background materials, used in the development of the plan. This might include elements of the situation analysis, the SWOT analysis, or meeting minutes.

Reviewing these formal plans can be instructive perhaps most importantly from the standpoint of what you *don't* have to do. You don't have to create a masterpiece. In fact, my recommendation is that you don't. The purpose of your plan should not be the creation of the plan. The purpose of your plan should be to achieve some measurable results and outcomes.

Keep It Simple!

A simple one-sheet format can be used to show the alignment between GOST and keep track of progress. "I think an Excel spreadsheet works well—you can add columns, sort it, mark it when it's done, and it's easy to update. You can print it off and post it," says one business manager. The headings you choose can be simple:

Strategic Plan: XYX Company

Goal: _____

Objective	Strategy	Tactic	Assigned To	Status	Comments

One woman who has led strategic planning activities for both large and small companies notes that, when a plan is produced in a high-quality, expensively designed format, there is a sense among those in the company that the plan is carved in stone. That can be a barrier to making the plan part of the ongoing operations of the company. She believes that the simpler, more brief, and more flexible plan documents are, the greater the likelihood that they will actually be used.

Finding a Compromise

In some cases, depending on your organization and its stakeholders (for example, if you're a not-for-profit that serves the community), you may feel compelled to produce an official strategic plan document. In most cases, though, a simple one-sheet document is all you will really need—or you could take an approach that's somewhere in the middle.

> **DID YOU KNOW?**
>
> Today's technology makes it easy for you to set up a folder on a shared drive or a home page on an intranet site where you post all of the pertinent background information, data, and details that you feel your audience might be interested in.

Even if you distribute a hard copy to certain audiences, having your plan accessible online can allow ready access to everyone who needs to reference the plan and make the updating process fairly straightforward. In addition, all of the supporting materials—situation analysis, SWOT, meeting minutes—can be available online for those who want more detail or as background resources for future planning efforts. Then, as you work your plan, you can rely on a simple spreadsheet format to help you communicate and update the plan (see Chapters 20 and 21). In writing the plan, your focus should not be on the plan but on what needs to be communicated to ensure that the plan is implemented. It's all about execution!

Distributing the Plan

Regardless of the format you choose to use to document your plan, you will need to make decisions about who you will share the plan with and what portions of the plan will be shared. Everyone will not need the same level of detail.

Certain people may get complete copies (or access to complete information about the plan)—the planning team, for instance, or your board members and management team. Many companies, especially small companies, choose to make the plan available to all employees. There may be others outside your organization with whom you want to share the plan (or portions of the plan)—key advisors such as your accountant and attorney, key customers, or key community partners, for instance. There are two primary considerations involved in determining who should have access to the plan:

1. **Who needs to know?** Who will you be counting on to help make sure the plan actually happens and results are achieved? These individuals should certainly have access to the plan—initially and on an ongoing basis as changes are made.

2. **Who do you want to know?** For relationship, business development, and PR reasons, there may be certain groups or individuals with whom you want to share the plan to inform them about your business and its goals and plans.

In addition to determining who to distribute a print copy of the plan to, you may also need to consider who to give electronic access to. If you plan to put the plan online in a shared file or if you're using a software program to help you track and update the plan, you must determine who should have access only to view the document and who can actually modify the plan elements.

Alternatives to distributing a full copy of the plan in a printed version to targeted audiences may include the following:

- Developing a summary plan document that can be printed on 1 or 2 sides of an 8.5 × 11 sheet

- Excerpting key elements of the plan for inclusion in internal or external newsletters and other communication materials

- Providing internal and external access to portions of your plan—or all of your plan—on your website

Whatever the decisions you make about distributing your plan, it's important to realize that your task is far from over. You are at a critical juncture in the strategic planning process—the point at which things start to happen!

Getting Buy-In and Approval

Once your plan has been completed and committed to some tangible format, your team's concern becomes the implementation of the plan. How do you ensure that, once your plan has been completed, you can get buy-in? Much depends on how well you did at the very beginning of the planning process in terms of involving the right people and communicating with those not involved. Much also depends on the effectiveness of your company's senior leader (if he or she is not the planning team leader) and the visible commitment of the strategic planning team's leader.

MISSTEPS

Team cohesiveness and support is critical in gaining buy-in for the final plan. Be sure to fully address any areas of disagreement or concern before moving forward with broad distribution of the plan to avoid problems later.

Let's assume that your planning team has already bought in to the plan and that its approval signifies their commitment to supporting the plan and helping to make sure it is actually implemented. But, despite the team's commitment and backing, it's possible that you will need buy-in and support from others in the organization before the plan can become a reality.

From Senior Leaders

The commitment and support of senior leaders is critical. Those senior leaders not on the planning team, but who may be involved in implementation or who may have employees who will be needed to help make the plan a reality, need to be supportive of the plan. Ultimately, the responsibility for the overall success of the plan lies with the team leader or owner of the plan. With organizational plans, this individual will be the business owner or CEO. It is critical that this individual is visibly supportive of the plan—in fact, that this person be an energetic and enthusiastic cheerleader for the plan. "You can put all the structure you want in place, but if the top leader isn't enforcing the use of the plan, monitoring its success, holding people accountable, and communicating about progress, you're destined to fail," says one business leader.

From Others Impacted

In addition to the team leader, all members of the planning team have a role to play in supporting and promoting the plan once it is complete and throughout implementation of the strategies and tactics. Team members can also assist in communicating with and educating those not involved in the plan development.

Getting buy-in from everyone you need to make the plan happen can be challenging. And those who have done this say it can be especially challenging if you refer to the process as *strategic planning* or to the plan as the *strategic plan*. Those terms tend to cause employees' eyes to glaze over! What to call it instead? One woman who has led a number of strategic planning efforts says, "I'd call it 'the most important things we need to get done'—I'm serious. There's no reason to complicate things with employees by using business terms."

It's a good point. Buy-in from your employees will occur when they understand why they need to do what you're asking them to do and how it ties in to the big picture. You need to explain to employees the why, what, and how of the plan. And, importantly, you need to explain to them what you need them to do to support the plan. The role of the team leader and the employee's direct manager are critical here. Both must be verbally and visibly committed to the plan.

Employees can quickly tell when managers are just giving lip service to the plan because they're following orders. That's why it's so important that you first get buy-in from the leaders in your company—real buy-in, not just lip service.

BEST PRACTICES

Buy-in from employees can be supported by incorporating the identified strategic plan activities and tasks into their job descriptions and their evaluation process. Implementing the plan then becomes part of what they do—not an add-on.

Attaining buy-in for the plan is not a one-time activity. There needs to be ongoing support and communication of the plan and its importance to the entire company. Everyone needs to be aware of and involved with the plan's implementation, even if their involvement is simply as part of a department team.

From the Organization at Large

Ongoing communication about the plan with updates on progress and celebrations of success can help to engage employees in the process. This can help them see that the plan is really guiding how work is done and is not just an exercise in creating a document that sits on the shelf.

One woman tells how this was done at her organization by creating a color-coded scheme to tie the strategic (green) initiatives to departmental (blue) and individual (red) tasks. The color-coding was used to demystify the process and avoid using the scary *strategic* word. All employees really needed to understand was that green work was very high level and drove blue work that was departmental and, ultimately, red work that was individual. The best indication of buy-in is when you hear employees talking about the plan—not in "business speak" but in everyday conversation related to how they do their work. "At our company, people didn't refer to the strategic plan—they referred to the green arrows—that was pretty powerful. If you asked them what their department's green arrows were, they knew," she says.

The step of getting approval and buy-in is a critical one. In fact, one strategic planning consultant says, "Only about one in five organizations are successful in reaching their goals, and where they tend to fall apart is when trying to gain buy-in. People are willing to establish the goals, willing to say 'Yeah, let's do it,' but haven't bought in to the work that needs to be done. They either don't agree with the tasks or don't believe it's their job."

One way to establish buy-in and commitment is to build the implementation of the plan into the expectations you have of employees. "It has to be personal—they have to see how it relates to their work. It can't just be something hanging in a frame on the wall," the consultant says. This can mean something as simple, yet powerful, as building elements of the plan's execution into performance management expectations at the senior, middle, and front-line levels of the organization. This helps to ensure that the plan doesn't become something extra that the company is working on but part of the day-to-day operations of the company as reflected through performance expectations.

Establishing Responsibility and Accountability

Establishing responsibility and accountability for the execution of the plan should be specific and straightforward, but it often isn't. Those involved in strategic planning efforts note that by spending so much time on the development of the plan, the focus tends to become the plan itself rather than implementation of the plan. This is an important misstep to avoid.

BEST PRACTICES

Companies that focus on explicitly assigning responsibility for elements of the plan, developing measures to track performance, and requiring regular reporting on progress are those that see results.

Establishing accountability for the accomplishment of the plan can't be left to chance. It won't just happen despite what the behaviors of many planning teams seem to suggest. The implementation of the plan will be most effective if it is formally built into the way the company does business.

Here's an example of a process used by a school system:

> Each of the district's 17 objectives is assigned an owner that attends weekly team leader meetings. These owners are ultimately responsible for the action plans to support the tactics and address the objective from the district strategic plan. The action plans are developed within the owner's department. The owner monitors the action plans quarterly—or more often if the data indicates the need—and reports quarterly to team leaders on the progress of these actions and the results of the key measures of performance.

Here's a process used by a manufacturing firm that illustrates how the various strategic plans in the organization can be tied together:

> We use a layered approach to time horizons. The visionary strategy is for 10 years into the future, product innovation and consumer strategy is for 5 to 10 years, the customer strategy is for 3 to 5 years, the industry restructuring strategy is for 1 to 3 years, and operational excellence tactical plans are for 1 year. Cross-functional strategy teams are formed for each of these areas and charged with ensuring the plan is implemented down through line staff. They are responsible for monitoring measures, gathering feedback, and updating the plans on an annual basis.

Once the plan has been implemented and communicated, the real work continues. The next step for companies involved in strategic planning is to make sure that they have established specific ways to measure—and report on—progress.

The Least You Need to Know

- Providing a final draft review can help to pave the way for the introduction of the plan.
- A simple and concise plan is most likely to be read and used—readers will tune out anything that is too long or complicated.
- Buy-in starts with the planning team and cascades from the top to the bottom of the organization.
- Building accountability for accomplishing plan tactics into staff expectations is a good way to ensure execution.

Evaluating the Plan

In This Chapter

- Identifying measures of success
- Choosing a format to report progress
- Methods for monitoring performance
- What to do when expectations aren't met

As the plan is implemented, measures need to be put into place to monitor performance. Measures may be related to the achievement of specific milestones or activities or may be stated in terms of levels of performance to be attained.

There are various reporting formats that can be used, but the important thing is to keep it simple. You should not put more time and effort into developing and tracking metrics than you put into implementing the plan!

In this chapter, we'll look at some ways you can keep track of progress to determine whether your plan is achieving the results you want and what to do if it isn't.

Measuring Your Success

When you created your strategic plan, your objectives provided you with some overall measurable outcomes that you were attempting to achieve. As your plan is implemented, you will want to track progress toward these objectives to determine whether your efforts are working. There are two primary types of measures—*process measures* and *outcome measures*. Process measures are measures that tell you whether something has been done—for instance, "Send thank-you cards to every new customer."

Outcome measures tell you the impact or outcome of your efforts—for instance, "Increase new customer satisfaction by 25 percent."

DEFINITION

Process measures tell you about steps along the way to some final outcome; **outcome measures** reflect the final outcome. The number of news releases sent is a process measure. The number of stories run by the media is an outcome measure.

Leading and Lagging Measures

Measures may also be either leading or lagging. Leading measures provide an indication of some future outcome. So for instance, the number of people who ask for more information about a new product could be a leading indicator of future sales. The number of customer complaints could be a leading indicator of lost customers. A lagging measure is a measure of a result that it is too late to impact. For example, sales is a lagging measure because the sales have already been made. Employee satisfaction results are lagging because they have already formed their opinions. By identifying and managing leading measures, organizations can impact lagging measures.

The same measure may be both leading and lagging, relative to other measures. Following are some additional examples:

Leading Measures	Lagging Measures
Customer satisfaction	Product sales
Product sales	Market share

As you consider the implementation of your strategic plan, you will want to be able to monitor progress. To do this, you will come up with measures that will help you determine whether you are on track to meet the objectives that you have established. Your objectives represent high-level measures. You will also likely have additional, lower-level measures related to your strategies that provide direction for staff members establishing tactics and action plans.

The objectives that you established during the development of your plan will serve as your starting point. Let's take a look at an example to illustrate this. Consider a strategic HR plan with an overall goal of "Increasing the efficiency and effectiveness of HR processes." Some of the objectives related to this goal include:

- Reduce turnover by 25 percent

- Reduce average time to hire by 7 days

Based on these objectives, the HR department will implement strategies and tactics designed to achieve these results, and the measures of success will be based on their achievement. But both of these objectives represent lagging indicators. They are the end result of a series of activities that may have measures of their own. So, at the HR department level, there may be additional measures that are monitored:

Lagging Measures	Leading Measures
Turnover	Employee satisfaction
	Salary levels
	Management competencies
Time to hire	Requisition approval time frame
	Reference checking time frame

Measuring Strategy Effectiveness

The measures you develop are designed to give you an indication of whether or not you're being successful at meeting your plan objectives. Measures can tie back to your tactics (generally based on process objectives—yes, we did this, or no, we didn't), strategies, and objectives, and will ultimately tell you whether you're realizing your goals. The objectives you established should give you important clues about the measures you will ultimately use!

Here's an example based on actual strategies for a not-for-profit and the measures established at the department level to achieve these strategies. Note how the measures reflect possible objectives that may have been stated in the plan:

Strategy	Measures
Chapters and national office are organized and staffed	Reduce turnover by 33 percent for success
	Reduce turnover by 20 percent
	Core competencies created for all
	Updated job descriptions for all
Volunteer management structure supports board members	100 percent of chapters have job descriptions for chapter fundraising

You'll notice that some of these measures are process measures (job descriptions in place) and some are outcome measures (turnover levels). As I mentioned, both of these types of measures may be reflected in your objectives. The key is that you are choosing measures that really give you an indication of success. Don't pick measures just to say you have measures. You need to make sure that they're meaningful.

For example, suppose you have an objective of "Increasing national market share for the business by 10 percent over the next year." One of the strategies you developed to do this is to "Leverage social media to raise awareness of our company." You develop the following measures to judge your progress:

- Set up social media profiles on LinkedIn, Facebook, and Twitter.

- Generate 400 Facebook fans.

- Generate 400 Twitter followers.

What's wrong with these measures? They're meaningless. If your stated strategy is designed to increase awareness, then your measures need to be designed to tell you whether or not you've increased awareness. These measures don't do that. The following measures would be more meaningful:

- Increase consumer awareness measure on annual survey from 15 to 35 percent within the next 18 months.

- Increase percentage of customers who are aware of our advertising campaign by 25 percent by the end of the year.

Think carefully about the measures you select to make certain that they are really giving you information to help you determine whether or not you are being successful.

DID YOU KNOW?

Joseph Juran, a renowned quality guru and management consultant who lived for more than 100 years (1904–2008), said, "If you don't measure it, you can't manage it." Think about that.

The creation of your strategic plan will provide you with guidance about the types of things that should be monitored and measured to give you an indication of whether you're on track to meet your plan objectives and, ultimately, your overall plan goals.

Monitoring these measures can give you early indications of when changes need to be made in tactics or strategies and will serve as important inputs back to the planning team. This monitoring occurs at all levels of the organization, and as we'll see in Chapter 21, the more closely measures can be aligned to individual job expectations and performance management, the more the plan will become a living document that helps to guide the activities of the organization.

As you identify the measures that you will monitor, it will be important to assign responsibility for monitoring and reporting on progress. Some of these activities may occur at the individual or department level; others may occur at the planning team level as individual measures are aggregated. It doesn't really matter where or who does the reporting, although it makes sense for reporting to occur as close as possible to where the information is attained. What matters most, though, is that you know who is going to be held accountable to track the measures that let you know how you're doing.

Reporting Formats

It's important that collecting and reporting your measures doesn't consume the majority of your time. You want the majority of your time to be spent focusing on the implementation of your plan! Communicating performance is best done simply, and there are some commonly used reporting formats that can help you do just that. Two methods of reporting are dashboards and scorecards.

Dashboards

Many companies use dashboards to help them monitor progress. A dashboard is a very simple method of communicating progress on measures that uses a color-coded approach based on the familiar traffic light signals:

- **Green**—Target was met or measure is exceeding expectations.
- **Yellow**—Target was met or measure is meeting expectations, but trend has been negative and there is cause for concern about future performance; this is a measure to watch.
- **Red**—Trend is negative and targets are not being met.

One small business owner says, "What I have used that worked very well was to create a tool that we call a dashboard. We created our dashboard report by looking at our strategic planning process and determining which indicators in our company (revenue; COGS—cost of goods sold; EBITDA—earnings before interest, taxes, depreciation, and amortization; days sales outstanding; inventory turns; etc.) would allow us to know if our tactical activities were actually moving us toward realizing our strategic vision. By looking at weekly, monthly, and quarterly trends, we were able to make reasonable internal adjustments to put ourselves back on track. It seems rather simplistic, but in a small company environment it seemed to have kept us moving in the right direction with becoming paralyzed by too much analysis and planning."

Here's an example of a dashboard report used by a department of transportation to report on progress. Note the simplicity of the report:

Performance Measure	Performance	Comments
Traffic fatality rates	[Yellow]	
Injury crash trends	[Yellow]	
Percentage of highway miles in good condition	[Red]	
Mowing vs. herbicide costs	[Green]	

The Performance column would be completed by the person responsible for the measure as a report on progress. A simple color-coding method using familiar stoplight indicators is used to indicate good (green), average (yellow), or poor (red) performance. (Normally, these would be indicated by ovals shaded red, yellow, and green. Here, we've chosen to spell them out.) The Comments column would be used by the person making the report to note anything pertinent to the performance results—explanation for performance, recommendations for future actions, etc. For instance, a comment related to the red indicator for percentage of highway miles in good condition might be "There has been a decrease of major highway miles in good or better condition over the last three years."

You can see how such a report would provide a quick and easy way of conveying information about performance. Looking at an entire dashboard with many measures, department and company leaders and the planning team can quickly see areas that need attention, areas that are at risk, and areas that are performing well, which allows them to allocate their time accordingly. Dashboards can also be set up to track activities over time so that trends can easily be identified as indicated in the following table:

Performance Measure	Jan	Feb	Mar	Apr	May
Traffic fatality rates	[Yellow]	[Yellow]	[Red]	[Yellow]	[Green]
Injury crash trends	[Yellow]	[Yellow]	[Yellow]	[Green]	[Green]
Percentage of highway miles in good condition	[Red]	[Red]	[Yellow]	[Green]	[Green]
Mowing vs. herbicide costs	[Green]	[Green]	[Yellow]	[Green]	[Green]

As you can see, reporting on performance in this manner allows you to quickly assess how things are going. In this case, by the end of May all of these measures were performing at the green level, indicating strong performance toward meeting the strategic plan objectives.

When tracking performance over time, don't jump to conclusions about why shifts are occurring—many of these shifts are random. So, for instance, if sales go up one month it may or may not reflect a positive trend. How can you be sure? You can use *statistical process control* (SPC) methods to help determine whether trends are real or random. A complete discussion of SPC is beyond the scope of this book, but it is important to know that this is another method for measuring performance over time.

DEFINITION

Statistical process control (SPC) is a method of tracking measures over time to determine whether change is random or due to some statistically significant change.

Note that, in addition to this report, those responsible for tracking these performance levels would have detailed information that would be available for review if the department, company, or planning team wanted to drill down into more detail. This format is simply a method used to provide quick updates at regularly scheduled meetings (more on this in Chapter 20).

Scorecards

Another format that is commonly used is a scorecard format, popularized by Robert S. Kaplan and David P. Norton in their now-classic book *The Balanced Scorecard* (see Appendix B). Full use of the balanced scorecard approach can be quite complex. I won't get into the details here, but the concept of using scorecards in a much simplified way can be helpful for small businesses even without a thorough understanding of balanced scorecard techniques.

In essence, the concept of the Balanced Scorecard (BSC) approach is based on the idea that businesses need to balance performance across four key areas of operations:

- Financial performance
- Internal business processes
- Learning and growth
- Customer satisfaction

The organization is viewed from these four perspectives and metrics are developed, collected, and analyzed for each. The goal is balance. A company does not, for instance, want to achieve exceptional financial performance at the expense of customer satisfaction.

In many organizations, scorecards look very much like dashboards. The primary difference is that performance across these four key areas is reported.

As one small business owner notes, "When it comes to small businesses, there are probably two aspects of strategic planning that are typical—setting a few key metrics (most likely revolving around sales and operations) and setting a tactical plan to get there. While there is nothing inherently complicated about the Balanced Scorecard, it does require a level of business complexity and overhead resources to track that aren't typical of a small business. I would utilize a much simpler tracking mechanism to remain focused on what are likely to be a few key initiatives and metrics."

Using a format such as this one can be a simple way to visually track performance across a wide range of measures. Progress can easily be shared with employees and other key stakeholders who can also quickly understand the "red, yellow, green" coding system. Even very large businesses use this approach as a simple way of communicating what might otherwise be very complex information.

Monitoring Performance

"I take a contrarian view to the tracking question," says one business owner. "I believe that too many companies obsess about their tracking tools instead of selecting the right metrics."

That's a good point. But what are the right metrics? The answer will vary by company and can be driven to a large degree by the strategic plan objectives (assuming the objectives have been developed effectively). Key organizational measures are often referred to as *key performance indicators* or KPIs. They are the set of measures that tell an organization how it is doing. Monitoring these measures will allow a company to know when all is well, when signs are pointing to impending trouble, and when all you-know-what is breaking loose. Tracking these measures regularly over time can help to make sure that all you-know-what doesn't break loose. That's the idea.

 DEFINITION

Key performance indicators (KPIs) are measures used to monitor what a company determines are its most important indicators of success.

Here are the KPIs that a print shop has developed to evaluate every step of its production process:

Production Process	Key Measures
Sales, Estimating, Scheduling	Number of complaints
Design and Preflight	Number of complaints
	Percentage chargeable time
Prepress	Number of complaints
	Percentage chargeable time
	Pages preflighted
	Cost per plate
Press	Number of complaints
	Percentage chargeable time
	Make-ready and run speeds
Bindery	Number of complaints
	Percentage chargeable time
Fulfillment	Number of complaints

It's not enough to have measures in place and to look at performance measures on a regular basis. Businesses need to take action based on the performance they see. Oddly enough, some don't. In the department of transportation example described earlier, for instance, the comment that "There has been a decrease of major highway miles in good or better condition over the past three years" is a sign that despite poor performance, nothing is being done. That's a problem. Monitoring performance should be about identifying both areas of exceptional performance and areas of declining or poor performance, and then doing something about the latter!

Areas of exceptional performance can signal the opportunity to document best practices or to share best practices with other parts of your company. For instance, suppose you have five restaurant locations and each is tracking employee turnover. One of the five locations is consistently in the green. That reflects an opportunity to find out what that location is doing differently and share those best practices with the other locations. Areas of yellow performance suggest the need to be watchful of the measures over future reporting periods. Areas of red performance should send off alerts, and steps should be taken to get performance back on track.

Course Correction

When performance is not meeting expectations, you need to take steps to determine why and to make course corrections. Sometimes the reason expectations are not being met is because targets were set at unreasonable levels. Sometimes it's because those responsible for achieving the results don't have the resources—staff, time, money—they need to be successful. Sometimes it's because the plan is simply not being followed (yes, that can happen!).

If the strategic planning process described here has been followed, when a measure indicates that an objective is at risk of not being met, the next step needs to be gathering the right people together to determine why. This can be done by tracking back through the process from action plans (the specific, nitty-gritty things being done by some individual in support of tactics), to tactics, to strategies to identify where changes need to be made.

BEST PRACTICES

Using statistical process control (SPC) charts can help establish thresholds for action based on performance over time. An SPC chart is a way of tracking performance across time, using standard deviation calculations to indicate when variation in performance is simply due to random variation as opposed to a change that is significant. Sales may fluctuate up and down from month to month with no cause for concern. A sudden shift up or down may represent random variation—or may be a statistically significant shift. SPC charts can be used to determine which is the case.

Establishing a Process

Establishing a process for identifying the need for course correction can help make sure both that opportunities to share best practices are not missed and that poor performance does not go unnoticed. For instance, a company might establish some thresholds for action based on dashboard or scorecard performance—a point of performance at which some action will be taken. Two months of yellow performance, or one month of red performance, may prompt some action. Three months of green performance might prompt the identification and communication of best practices.

The prompts will vary, but the important thing is to develop, document, and communicate these thresholds so that action is taken when necessary. When a threshold has been met, the following steps can be taken:

- Define the situation

- Recognize the cause

- Identify necessary next steps

- Verify actions

- Evaluate results

As you can see, the evaluation process is ongoing. Even as shifts are made in strategies, tactics, and action plans, the process of measuring, monitoring, and reporting on performance will continue.

Steps Involved

A car dealership that has perfected this process takes the following steps to make course correction as necessary:

- Throughout the year, as items are accomplished, priorities shift, or performance levels indicate the need for improvement, plans are modified.

- Action plan status is monitored monthly by the president and general managers and quarterly during division meetings.

- Changing conditions may indicate that action plans should be modified to accomplish objectives or that other action plans should be developed to meet those conditions.

- When changes occur, appropriate departments or groups develop the new or revised action plan, including resource needs.

- This new action plan becomes part of the ongoing strategic plan cycle and is measured and reviewed appropriately.

- If resources needed to accomplish the plan are not available, and the plan is of high priority, appropriate resources are shifted from other, lower-priority actions.

Every element of your strategic plan should have measures attached so that performance can be monitored. While this may initially sound like a daunting task, chances are that you already have a number of measures in place that you use to manage your business. The strategic planning process just helps you tie those measures together in a way that drives performance toward the accomplishment of the overall plan.

Rather than having individuals or individual parts of your organization engaged in activities that may or may not be critical to your success, your strategic planning measures will document all of the critical outcomes that indicate whether or not you are achieving your results. And, believe it or not, you'll find that monitoring these measures over time can become extremely motivating, even when the measures are not performing as you would like them to.

The ability to focus on real information to generate real results can help employees see more clearly how their day-to-day activities impact the business—and the effectiveness of your strategic plan.

Execution is everything. Using key measures and communicating results in ways that are easy for employees to understand can significantly impact your ability to realize your objectives.

The Least You Need to Know

- A combination of leading and lagging measures can provide early warning signs of performance that may negatively impact the business.
- Measuring isn't what's important—acting on the measures is!
- Establishing a process for reviewing and responding to measures is an important best practice.
- Course correction may involve the creation of new action plans.

Communicating Progress

In This Chapter

- How strategy relates to communication
- Using strategic planning techniques to develop your communication plan
- Keeping the lines of communication open
- Offering options for feedback
- Keeping important audiences up-to-date on progress

Strategic plans that work are strategic plans that are communicated effectively—not just when they're first introduced, but throughout the process of putting strategies and tactics in place to achieve the goals and objectives of the plan. Plans that are kept secret and not shared with members of the organization are plans that fail. Effective plans involve and inform everyone from front-line staff to mid-level managers—and sometimes even to external audiences, as you'll see.

As one businesswoman notes, "Over the years, I'd have to say the biggest mistakes have been in not communicating the strategic plan beyond the executive suite. Until company leadership understands that everyone in the company will play a part in the success of the company and its strategic plans—and communicates to them in a manner they can understand—they will not see positive results."

In this chapter, we'll take a look at some best practices for communicating progress, including developing a communication strategy, incorporating opportunities for feedback, and options for regular updates on plan progress.

Developing Your Communication Strategy

Your communication strategy is really nothing more than a mini-strategic plan that will incorporate all of the same elements and considerations! At the outset, it's important to establish responsibility for communicating the plan. You might think of the responsible party as the team leader for the strategic communication planning process. For companies large enough to have a communication or marketing department, this is a likely place for this task to fit. For those that don't have these departments, responsibility for communicating the plan could be assigned to an administrative assistant, perhaps, or to someone in the company who is generally perceived as an effective communicator, both verbally and in writing. That individual could work with the planning team (or a subset of the team) to develop communication materials and evaluate the effectiveness of these communications.

BEST PRACTICES

Don't wait until your strategic plan is complete and ready to implement before you develop your communication plan. Begin planning for communication early in the process, and communicate regularly, so you can hit the ground running once the plan is done.

Just as when developing an organizational strategic plan, the team leader for implementing communications can benefit from background information or a situation analysis. For instance, to aid in developing and implementing the plan, it can be helpful to survey employees to determine their current levels of awareness, interest, and understanding of the plan and how it impacts them. It might also be helpful to poll employees to determine what communication tools or methods they prefer.

Communication—or lack thereof—is one of the biggest reasons that planning efforts fail to move forward. One employee reflects on the planning process in his company and why he feels it doesn't work: "Generally speaking, it's the way the plan is delivered and the follow up. First, an e-mail will be sent stating that a plan needs to be devised, a time frame will be given, and the plan will be presented with no further input sought. Then the action plan is never seen—maybe never even started. What I think should happen is that management needs to make sure that employees know the problem needing to be addressed, the root cause of the problem or issues, and the desired outcome of the strategic planning process." And, I would add, employees also need to be kept apprised on progress as the plan is implemented.

A communication plan can help to ensure that careful consideration is put into the methods that will be used to communicate the plan (and plan progress) and that nothing is missed.

Identify Key Audiences

To be effective, communication should be targeted. For example, the communication needs of those directly responsible for implementing the plan will be different than the communication needs of employees in front-line positions who will be primarily acting on the direction of their supervisors. The information you share with managers may be different from the information you share with front-line staff. You may even wish to communicate with certain customers. Even among employee groups, different messages or different communication tools may be required. For example, off-site staff may not have ready access to the company intranet and will need to receive hard copy information or information by phone.

Create Key Messages

When considering your strategic plan, what are the most important messages you want to convey to each audience you have identified? What do employees need to know? What do managers need to know? What do customers need to know? Your focus should be on the high points—the three to five main things that you want your audiences to understand. The following are some examples of key messages for the employee audience:

- We are developing a strategic plan to cover a three-year period, which will help us to focus on specific goals and objectives.

- Each employee in the company will be involved in the plan's implementation and will see its impact on their work through their individual goals.

- Updates will be provided on a monthly basis through the employee newsletter which will be archived online.

- There may be adjustments made to the plan as we move forward—the plan will be formally updated on an annual basis.

Develop a Time Line

The order in which you inform your audiences can be critical. For example, if you include an article in your employee newsletter about a change to the plan, but you haven't told your managers about the change yet, managers may feel undermined and at a definite disadvantage when it comes to answering employee questions. Carefully consider which audiences need the information first, which may need it concurrently, and how long you can afford to wait between the steps to ensure that the information won't begin to leak through unofficial channels.

You will also want to consider how often you want to communicate plan progress. Much will depend on the type of plan, the length of time it covers, and how strategies and tactics are likely to affect ongoing operations.

Develop a Plan

Considering the audiences, messages, and time lines you've developed, prepare a written plan that specifically outlines the communication tools and processes you'll be using. The plan should include the background, messages, and target audiences you've identified. You'll also want to detail the specific tactics you will use to convey your messages. Some important elements to include are audience, communication tool, timing, who is responsible, and cost (if applicable). A simple format like the following table can be a good way to present this information.

Audience	Tool	Timing	Responsible	Cost
Managers	Mgmt. meeting	Monthly	CEO	n/a
All staff	Staff meeting	Monthly	CEO	n/a
All staff	E-mail	Bi-monthly	Admin. Asst.	n/a
	Intranet updates	Ongoing	Admin. Asst.	n/a

The plan should be approved by the strategic planning team leader and, possibly, by the strategic planning team. This plan will become your blueprint for moving forward, not only helping you maintain focus but also providing a good organizational tool to ensure that you don't overlook important steps in the communication process.

Use Multiple Tools, Multiple Times

Sending out a memo to announce a major company initiative like the implementation of a strategic plan is communication, but it's probably not effective communication. Advertisers recognize that their sales messages need to be repeated multiple times before they make an impact. The same is true of any kind of communication. In addition, you need to use multiple tools or methods of communicating.

DID YOU KNOW?

While employers are often concerned about over-communicating, employees often report that they "didn't know about" various messages that were sent. The point at which you start to hear employees say, "I already heard about this," is when you'll know your message is starting to get across!

Some employees will pay more attention to an e-mail message than a memo. Others may not read your internal newsletter. Some may rely exclusively on the intranet site. To be confident that your communications will get across, use a variety of tools.

Think Circular

To develop a communication plan that will produce measurable results, you need to, as author Stephen Covey says, "Start with the end in mind." Where do you want to go? What results do you want to obtain?

The next obvious question is "How will you know when you have obtained those results?" If you're attempting to increase employee agreement that having a strategic plan positively impacts their work, you may decide to do a baseline survey to determine employees' current level of agreement with this statement. Not only will it give you information against which to measure future results, it will also let you know which areas need to be emphasized and which do not, allowing you to better prioritize your efforts. Once you know where you want to go and where you are now, you need to fill in the gaps by identifying the communication tools you will use to increase awareness among the various audiences you have targeted.

To be effective, communication needs to be part of a carefully considered process focused on achieving clearly identified, measurable results. It's not difficult to communicate effectively, but it does take some thought, a clear focus on objectives, an understanding of the tools available to communicate your messages, and a strong partnership between you and your internal customer. Does this all sound familiar? I hope it does, because your communication plan is really a mini-strategic plan!

Following the Strategic Planning Process

First, of course, you will need a goal. One possible goal for the communication of your strategic plan progress is to keep employees informed. You might also include additional audiences. Your goal may be to keep employees, board members, and even core customer groups informed of progress—it's up to you. But as with any strategic planning effort, the first step is identifying your goal. We'll work through an example in this chapter. In this case, let's say our goal is to "Keep employees informed of progress."

Our next step is coming up with objectives. Remember that objectives are SMART (Specific, Measurable, Attainable, Relevant, and Time-bound; see Chapter 14) and designed to support the goal. Some possible objectives for us here might be:

- Achieve 100 percent awareness of the strategic plan within 1 month of its introduction.

- Ensure that 100 percent of employees know which strategic plan elements impact their daily work and how they contribute to the plan within three months of its introduction.

- Achieve 100 percent agreement among employees that the strategic plan reflects how we manage the company within three months of its introduction.

Let's say our communication objective is to achieve 100 percent awareness of the plan. Our next step is to come up with one or more strategies to help us achieve this objective. These might include:

- Leverage the strength of managers' relationships with employees to deliver information about the plan.

- Use existing communication tools (the intranet, all-staff meetings) to communicate plan progress.

- Involve employees in the communication process by assigning key employees to communicate progress on specific parts of the plan.

- Avoid negativity about the plan by helping employees see how it can help them to focus their efforts on things that will make a difference to the company.

DID YOU KNOW?

Social media tools like Twitter can be used to communicate with external audiences. Companies can use similar tools to encourage internal communications between employees with services like Yammer, a microblogging service like Twitter that allows only those with the same e-mail domain to join a network. Alcatel-Lucent uses Yammer to communicate with employees around the world, and has 1,000 users on Yammer and about 200 posts a day.

As we saw when discussing the planning process, our objectives will relate to capitalizing on any strengths or opportunities we might have (in this case, our managers' relationships with employees and our existing communication tools) and overcoming any weaknesses or threats (in this case, the potential threat of employee resistance to the plan).

Finally, we develop our communication tactics. Let's focus on our objective of "Leverage the strength of managers' relationships with employees to deliver information about the plan." To support this strategy, we might use the following tactics:

- Develop an online training program for managers on how to effectively communicate the plan to employees.

- Provide managers with Frequently Asked Questions (FAQs) to help them respond to potential employee questions.

- Develop a monthly update that managers will deliver to employees at required monthly meetings.

As you can see from this example, the process of pulling together a strategic plan—in this case, a strategic communication plan—doesn't need to be time-consuming as it might be with an organizational plan. In the case of a communication plan developed for a specific purpose, for instance, it can involve simply walking through the steps to ensure that the plan is focused on a goal, that it includes measurable objectives, and that strategies and tactics are developed to achieve those objectives. The strategic planning process applies to any kind of planning activity you're engaged in.

Communication Channels

There are a variety of different communication channels that you might use to communicate with your employees about your strategic planning activities. Thanks to technology, many of these tools offer flexibility and convenience for sharing and updating information as well as the opportunity to get real-time feedback from employees.

Face-to-face communication remains the best option for sharing information with employees. It allows an opportunity for discussion, works well in situations where there are likely to be questions, and is more personal and engaging than other forms of communication. In small companies in particular, face-to-face communication can be very effective—all-staff meetings, individual department meetings, and one-on-one sessions with supervisors and managers are all options for in-person communication that can be used to share messages about strategic plan progress.

BEST PRACTICES

Despite the prevalence of technology—e-mail, intranet sites, etc.—direct, face-to-face communication between employees and supervisors or managers is still the most effective way to share information.

Traditional Communication Channels

There are a broad range of communication tools that companies have access to—many of which represent no-cost or low-cost opportunities to get information about the strategic planning process and progress to employees:

- **Print—newsletters, statement stuffers, and flyers.** The benefits are that these tools can be targeted to specific segments and they are tangible, which can signify value. Since not all employee segments will have ready access to electronic media, print still remains an important option for companies that need to communicate key messages to employees. The downside of print is the cost associated with creating, producing, and printing these documents; closely related to this is the turnaround time, which can be lengthy.

- **Posters, bulletin boards, table tents, clings, etc.** These attention-getting communication devices can help to augment an awareness-building campaign for your strategic plan. They can be placed throughout the facilities where employees work—in break rooms, hallways, or other common areas. Depending on the size, format, and use of color, cost may be a consideration.

- **Intranet.** Most companies, even the very small, have an intranet site that allows employees ready access to all sorts of information about company activities. The strategic plan is no exception. The intranet can be a great place to establish a web page specific to the strategic planning process where updates can be posted regularly and options for feedback through online forums and chat functions may also be provided. The big benefits are the low cost, ease of updating, and ability for employees to access information from off-site (if they have the appropriate permissions set up). Downfalls include making sure that the information is kept up-to-date and changed regularly to keep employees' interest and, in some companies, unequal access for employees who may not work from a desk.

- **Video.** The availability and low cost of video camera options make it easy and inexpensive for companies to quickly produce and share video with employees in live or online formats. Video can add a personal touch to communications and provide the ability to show and tell. For strategic plan communications, video can provide an option for personalized updates from leaders and team members on progress and can be particularly useful in companies where employees work in dispersed locations.

New Communication Options

In addition to the traditional communication options that many companies are likely to have ready access to, there are some new tools that can provide benefits in communicating about the strategic planning process and progress:

- **Blogs.** Internal blogs can be a good way to keep employees up-to-date on plan progress. Blogs can be maintained by the strategic plan's team leader, by individual team members, or by those assigned to move forward with specific sections of the plan. They can be a quick and relatively informal way to share information on progress and also allow for interactions through questions and comments that may be posted on the site.

- **Social media.** Tools like Facebook, Twitter, and LinkedIn may present opportunities to communicate with employees about strategic plan progress and also offer the ability to interact—ask questions, share feedback—through group functions.

DID YOU KNOW?

A 2010 poll by the Human Capital Institute's human resources membership found that, when counting both public sites such as LinkedIn and in-house applications, 49 percent of organizations use social networks in some way.

These tools can be effective for building a sense of community; however, it can be difficult to get employees to incorporate the use of these tools into their everyday habits—and of course, some companies are concerned about the potential for time-wasting. They are not yet a replacement for more traditional communication options, but social media applications can provide a good, interactive way of generating discussion about the strategic planning process and execution.

Mobile media is another quickly emerging communication option that some companies are exploring—the ability for employees to access information from their cell phones means they can stay up-to-date while on the road—or even at home. Mobile media represents a good way to communicate with employees who don't work in office settings. A drawback is cost—from the users' standpoint.

Each company will have its own communication tools and preferences. The key is to recognize the wide range of options available and to use these tools in combination to ensure that messages are getting out widely and regularly to employees.

Here's how a small printing company communicates its strategic plan to various audiences: "Results of strategic planning are first communicated to employees through a deployment meeting. They are then discussed by leaders with their departmental teams or other appropriate members during follow-up sessions. Teams and individuals update goals and mission statements for their departments that support the Division plans, thus aligning actions, measures, and goals throughout the organization. Other stakeholders receive a variety of communications to detail our plans and strategies for informational and planning purposes. For example, we hold a supplier appreciation luncheon to provide a more direct opportunity to present our plans to key supplier partners and receive feedback on their plans for the future and their needs."

Communicating with External Audiences

Some companies will wish to communicate with external audiences, which might include board members, the community, or customer groups. It's important to consider all audiences that can benefit from being informed about and kept up-to-date on strategic plan progress. Many of the tools outlined previously can be used. In addition, companies wishing to communicate with external audiences may consider the following options:

- **Internet.** As with the internal intranet site, keeping audiences informed through the Internet represents a quick and relatively easy way to stay connected and may also allow the opportunity for interaction through posted comments and messages. If you consider this option, you will need to assign someone to monitor and respond to any messages that may be received.

- **Blogs.** A company blog can be a good way to update external audiences on planning activities. Blogs also allow for two-way communication through reader comments left in posts.

- **Community meetings or advisory boards.** Even companies not large enough, or not interested in, having formal boards sometimes pull together advisory groups or groups of community members to share information with and receive feedback from. These groups can represent a good opportunity for sharing information about the strategic plan and progress being made.

- **E-mail and e-letters.** E-mail is a convenient and inexpensive way to communicate with many people at once, providing an opportunity to update audiences on plan progress.

Incorporating a Feedback Loop

Communication about the strategic plan and its progress should not go only one way. It is important for the developers of the strategic plan to receive feedback about …

- The content of the plan.

- The format of the plan in terms of ability for employees and other audiences to readily understand it.

- Questions about the plan and how it relates to employees' activities.

- Recommendations for future plans.

Multiple feedback channels are possible through face-to-face interactions, online interactions, and traditional interactions through tools like suggestion boxes, surveys, and polls.

> **BEST PRACTICES**
>
> Social media tools like Twitter, Facebook, and LinkedIn make it possible to communicate with audiences that are distributed nationally or internationally. They can serve as a form of "virtual advisory board," allowing your company to share information on plan progress and receive feedback and input from readers.

Often, though, it's not the existence of the tools that determines whether or how feedback will be received but rather the culture of the organization and the level of trust employees have with supervisors and managers. Three things are necessary for effective communication between employees and their leaders: desire, opportunity, and trust.

First, employees need to want to communicate. They need to understand that what they think matters. This desire can be impacted through the communication activities we've already discussed. It's important for employees to understand how what they do impacts the strategic plan and to believe that what they do and think is important. Organizational and team leaders can strengthen this desire by being very explicit about each employee's role in executing the strategic plan and effectively tying strategic planning activities directly to individual goals and objectives through the employee evaluation process.

Once employees understand that what they think matters and believe that the strategic planning champions and organizational leaders want to hear from them, opportunity for communication must exist. This is where the availability of the communication tools discussed previously comes into play. Identify those tools that allow for feedback, and communicate the availability of those tools to employees. There are a variety of options:

- Town hall meetings

- Focus groups

- Polls

- Surveys

- Suggestion boxes (the traditional kind or online)

- Tip lines

- Direct one-on-one contact between employees and their supervisors, managers, and plan developers

- Forums, chat rooms, and other social media-related tools

Finally, the environment must be non-threatening so that employees feel comfortable sharing their feedback, even if that feedback is along the lines of "I think strategic planning is stupid." While managers and business owners often try to avoid this kind of feedback, it can actually serve as an opportunity to address misperceptions and provide important information about why strategic planning is important. The key is to be open to whatever employees have to offer. If an employee shares an opinion with you and you react negatively, defensively, or don't respond at all, you reduce the chances of that employee communicating with you in the future—and word will travel.

Business leaders and members of the planning team should also be alert to informal communications and comments from employees that might take place in hallway or break room conversations. What you are hearing from employees can help you adjust your communication processes, tools, and messages as well as your strategic plan.

Regular Updates

Establishing a regular process for updating the plan and sharing the update with employees can be a good way to keep the plan front and center in their minds. Making the plan available online can be a good way to provide employees with ongoing access to information on progress, but don't assume that they will just seek out that information. Even if you do make the plan available to employees online, you should still send out regular reminders with highlights about what has occurred since your last formal communication.

Earlier in the chapter I talked about sharing messages multiple times in multiple ways. Some companies worry that they're communicating too much. In reality, this is rarely ever the case. It takes repetition and varying methods of communication over a long period of time to ensure that those communications are sticking!

MISSTEPS

If you come to a reporting period where there is nothing to report, warning bells should sound. It may suggest that the plan is not being worked on because employees assigned to various plan elements don't feel accountable.

A big complaint about strategic plans is that they are created and then forgotten. In the next chapter, we'll look at ways to ensure that your plan becomes a living document that is used to drive the performance of your company, division, department, or project. For now, here are some tactics you might build into your communication plan to ensure that employees are being kept up-to-date on progress:

- Make the plan a regular focus at company and department meetings. Make it clear to employees that the plan is not just another document but a business tool that is truly used to drive action.

- Set up an internal blog hosted by the team leader (or the communication designee) to share regular updates.

- Create discussion groups led by planning team members to provide updates on progress and seek information from employees.

- Share monthly (or based on a frequency that works for your team) brief updates in a hard copy format and direct employees online for more detailed progress reports.

- Consider keeping the planning team in place year-round to serve as a steering committee to ensure that communication occurs and is meeting the needs of the organization and employees.

- Remember that, ultimately, the CEO or business owner owns the plan (if it's a strategic organizational plan) and needs to be firmly and visibly behind it and an integral part of any communication activities.

A small manufacturing company uses a communication matrix to verify that all employees have received the strategic plan, performance updates, and technical information they need. "We validate the communication methods, frequency, message, and whether the communication was one- or two-way communication. Our second quarter 'Breakfast with Joe' is an informal breakfast meeting that allows opportunity for open dialogue between all associates and our president."

A healthcare organization has identified a list of ongoing communication activities and indicated who the audiences are for each, how often they occur, and the key messages that are delivered to these audiences:

When	What	Audience	Message
Annual	Off-site planning	Senior leaders, board	Strategic plan
	All-staff assembly	All	Best practices
Quarterly	Supplier reviews	Suppliers, partners	Perf. report
	Emp. forums	All employees	Perf. report
Monthly	Dept. meetings	Employees	Perf. report
			Best practices
	Quality councils	Providers	Perf. report
			Best practices
	Report out	Leaders, teams	Perf. update
			Best practices
Bi-monthly	Newsletter	All	System stories
	Chiefs of Staff	Physicians	Best practices
Regular	CEO letter	Employees	Breaking news
			Recognition
	Global e-mails	All	Major announcement
Daily	Rounding	Customers	Feedback
		Employees	Recognition

To be effective, communication needs to be planned and—as with all strategic planning efforts—focused on achieving measurable results. See Appendix D for an example of a survey that can be used to assess the effectiveness of communication related to strategic planning efforts.

The Least You Need to Know

- Effective communication plays a critical role in plan execution.
- Assigning a specific person responsibility for plan communication is a good way to make sure communication occurs regularly.
- Strategic planning principles can be used to develop the communication plan.
- Communications should incorporate multiple messages delivered through multiple media.
- As changes occur, updates to the plan should be made and communicated to internal and external audiences.

Making Adjustments

In This Chapter

- Keeping the strategic plan front and center
- How to use a formal plan for revisions and updates
- Why a regularly scheduled planning process can help drive success
- Keeping the plan alive throughout the planning process

As we've seen, it is not the creation or publication of the strategic plan that most determines its success, it is how the plan is actually implemented and used. Execution depends on the plan being a living document that is used to guide organizational activities. That is, sadly, often not the case in many organizations. One employee recently involved in a project where the founder of the company led the strategic planning process says, "The founder didn't communicate well at all. Plans were made that were not realistic and thus not followed—plans were communicated to some team members and not others."

Effectiveness in execution requires a process that ensures that the plan will actually be used to guide individual behaviors, that there is a defined process to incorporate changes and updates, and that a regular planning cycle be implemented to keep the plan alive.

In this chapter, we'll take a look at ways businesses can use strategic plans to help guide work throughout the company and increase the odds that the plan will actually have a measurable impact.

Plans Are Living Documents

It is not enough to just develop the plan—you have to work the plan. This requires developing a process to ensure that the right people will be working on the right things at the right time, often in collaboration. We'll use a strategic organizational plan as an example as we walk through this, but the process could work the same at any level of the organization, or even with a project-based plan.

Working the Plan

In Chapter 4, I talked about the important role of the team leader and how the team leader should be, in essence, the owner of the plan—the person who is most responsible for making it all happen. We'll assume in this case that the team leader is the business owner, and we'll further assume an organizational chart that includes three levels—senior leaders, managers, and employees.

> **BEST PRACTICES**
>
> When strategic plans are built into the daily operations of the company and used to manage the company's operations, they become living documents that guide how work is done.

Let's consider a company that has an annual planning cycle that begins in October. The team leader is the CEO and all of the company's five managers are part of the planning team. The annual plan provides direction for the activities of the company during the following year:

- The strategic plan establishes the overall goals and objectives for the company.

- The objectives provide a basis for measuring the effectiveness of the plan.

- Each manager is assigned responsibility for one or more of the strategies in the plan and held accountable for achieving the related objectives.

- Managers assign specific tactics to employees in their departments. The tactics become part of the employees' annual work plans.

- All managers and employees are accountable to achieve the objectives, strategies, and tactics assigned to them and reflected in their annual performance plan.

Incorporating the strategic plan elements into the overall operations of the business and assigning specific responsibilities to managers and employees for accomplishing the plan's objectives, strategies, and tactics is the best way to ensure that the plan is executed. In this way, the plan becomes not just another thing to do but the document that provides direction for the organization.

As managers, departments, and employees work to achieve their assigned responsibilities, additional plans may be developed to help guide these activities. The marketing department, for instance, may develop a strategic marketing plan to achieve the marketing objectives in the strategic plan. The HR department may develop a strategic HR plan to achieve staffing-related objectives.

Operational Work Is Ongoing

While the strategic plan can be used to manage the organization, it is important to note that this plan will not include everything that needs to be done in your business. In addition to the strategic activities needed to accomplish the plan, you will be involved in operational—or ongoing—activities that may not show up on the plan—things like purchasing supplies, payroll, and maintenance. Employees should understand that the strategic activities that may be assigned to them do not take the place of the ongoing responsibilities they may have—the work must go on.

It is possible that, as strategic plans are initiated, some departments may not have assignments made in support of the strategic activities in the plan. The billing department, for instance, might simply be asked to continue to perform their daily work in support of the organization but may not be involved in any new initiatives or any improvement projects—and that is just fine. Even though this may be the case, these departments are likely to still have performance measures that indicate how they are doing and will still need to measure and monitor performance and make improvements throughout the year. The billing department, for instance, may be focused on decreasing the time from receipt of the service until the bill is generated.

Other departments may be called upon to support the strategic initiatives, and they will need to consider how these new assignments or expectations will impact their resources—staff time and budget. In other cases, as time goes by, changes may occur that require additions, eliminations, or revisions to the plan.

As the plan is being implemented and progress is being evaluated, the need for changes may be identified. Having a process in place to consider, evaluate, and adopt changes to the plan ensures that the plan continues to guide the company's activities and that other sub-plans don't suddenly crop up.

Planning for Revisions and Updates

A plan for updates should be established during the planning process to incorporate regularly scheduled reports on progress from those responsible for various elements of the plan. For instance, in an organization with a leadership team that consists of a CEO and six direct reports at the manager level, each of the managers could be assigned to one or more of the plans' strategies. These managers might be expected to report their progress at monthly meetings on a cyclical basis, so that one strategy was covered each month. The managers might also ask their direct reports to report to them on their progress toward accomplishing their assigned tactics in the plan.

BEST PRACTICES

When assigning responsibility for elements of the strategic plan, assign them to individuals—not co-leaders, teams, or groups. When everyone is responsible, no one is responsible. Clearly establishing accountability with one person is a best practice for achieving success in executing the plan. That individual may call upon others to assist in the execution but, ultimately, he or she is responsible.

Those assigned to specific goals, strategies, or objectives do not have to be formal managers within the organization. The key is that whoever is assigned responsibility understands what will be required and is held accountable to achieve results.

On a regular basis, the planning team should meet to review plan progress. Is progress being made? Are there areas where progress is not being made? Do measures need to be adjusted? Do new strategies or tactics need to be developed? The timing for these meetings will depend on the organization and the elements in the plan. A monthly review is typical, but companies in more fast-paced environments or that are facing more serious threats or looming opportunities may want to meet more frequently. And companies in slower-moving industries or an environment that is relatively stable may meet less frequently. The key is for the planning group, and the entire organization, to recognize that the plan is a living document that is subject to change.

Responding to Environmental Changes

In addition to changes that may be necessary to address poor performance, changes in the environment—both opportunities and threats—may require changes to the plan. Suppose you own a bakery in a small town, and you've operated that bakery for a number of years. One day you hear about a new bakery opening up down the street—a national chain that has been extremely successful in other locations. Or suppose you own a consulting firm and have relied on three key customers for the past several years. Suddenly two of the three announce that they are issuing RFPs in consideration of a shift to another consultant. Or maybe you own a fishing business on the gulf coast in Louisiana and an oil spill threatens your livelihood.

These types of situations—hypothetical yet all too real—happen to businesses, large and small, all the time. Competitors enter the market. Competitors leave the market. Customers leave. New customers emerge. Supply chains dry up. Laws change.

During the strategic planning process, you will formally be reviewing environmental impacts that could affect your business, but those impacts don't just take place during your annual planning cycle. Changes can happen at any time. Regardless of how carefully we plan, things happen. New opportunities pop up. New threats emerge. And when they do, they need to be considered, and incorporated as appropriate into the strategic plan.

There are various ways that companies can set up processes to address shifts that require changes to the strategic plan. Generally these processes are based on communication that flows in alignment with the company's organizational chart. So, for instance, if an employee hears about something that may impact the company, he or she alerts the manager. If the manager considers the issue to be significant, he or she raises it to the next level within the organization, and so on until it reaches the top of the organization—the organization's leadership team—where discussion occurs about whether and how this change impacts the strategic plan.

But information can be gathered at any level of the organization and by any member of the organization. Because of this, employees should know how they should communicate and share the information they gather. All employees—including senior-level employees—need to understand that they should not, on their own, make strategic changes or add strategic initiatives without somehow having those initiatives reviewed and approved by the planning team.

Responding to New Ideas

You should also have a process in place to accommodate new ideas that might come up at any point in your organization at any time during your planning cycle. You don't want to create a culture where employees think that new ideas are only considered once a year or you risk losing out on great new opportunities. On the other hand, you don't want a culture where new ideas pop up constantly and divert employees away from the work they've been assigned in support of the strategic plan. This is, in fact, one of the reasons that many plans fail to be executed. A balance can be struck between being too tied to working the plan and missing great opportunities and jumping at every opportunity and failing to execute the plan. But it takes discipline—most often at the top of the organization.

Consider, for instance, the small business owner who went into business primarily because of the autonomy that it represented. Who likes to work in a bureaucracy where new ideas have to pass through multiple channels before anything happens? But as many small business owners eventually learn, even they need to have some type of filter to gauge the wisdom of making a significant change or taking on new activities.

MISSTEPS

The business owner should not be immune to following the identified process for making changes to the plan. Business owners can sometimes be their own worst enemies by choosing not to follow the plan that has been put in place and that they have approved. Actions speak louder than words!

One important filter is "If we follow through on this new idea, what will it keep us from getting done?" If the answer is "Nothing; we'll still be able to accomplish our plan," go for it! If, however, the answer is "Something will need to go," it's time to call the planning team together for a discussion.

Every organization has limited capacity, and trade-offs must be made. If something new is taken on, something else obviously will not be done—or additional resources must be created to accomplish the new task (new staff or external resources).

Responding to Performance Issues

Performance issues will also impact the plan—either performance that is not meeting expectations or, believe it or not, performance that may be exceeding expectations! While exceeding expectations can often be good, it's important that progress is monitored so that the impacts of performance that is greater than expected can be considered by other areas of the organization and their plans adjusted accordingly.

Here's an example to illustrate. A woman worked for a publishing company that regularly issued revisions of existing titles. After a conversation with one of the authors, a member of the department had a great idea to do a promotion targeted at those who owned a previous edition of the book, offering a discount on the new edition. They tried it and it worked phenomenally—response rates were literally 10 times what they normally would be. The department quickly began making plans to send out promotions for all of the revisions that had been released in the past year. Fortunately, the CEO got wind of the plans and said, "Wait a minute. Before we move forward with this, we're going to need to discuss whether we can handle this additional activity."

"What?" exclaimed the woman. "You mean you don't want this new business?" "I can't answer that yet," said the CEO. "I don't know what the new business will cost." They went on to discuss the additional impact that a sudden increase in orders would cause for the small company: the need to print more books, which would require the purchase of supplies (paper and ink) and possible overtime for already stressed-out print shop staff; additional shipping demands for a small shipping department, with the resulting increase in shipping costs; a possible increase in returns if some of the titles hadn't changed enough for customers to feel a new edition was worth the cost; and on and on. The moral of the story? Even strong performance may require the attention of the planning group to determine the impact on the organization.

DID YOU KNOW?

Performance should be reviewed on a regular basis by the planning team with discussion geared toward whether and how to respond to areas where performance is not meeting expectations. The team should also consider opportunities to celebrate success in meeting objectives by recognizing the efforts of employees and the company as a whole.

The Annual (or More Frequent) Planning Cycle

While your plan should be reviewed regularly and updated as necessary, you should also build in a formal planning cycle to update the overall plan. This update should not involve starting from scratch; you should use the existing plan as the starting point for the next planning cycle. The steps will be very much the same but should take less time in subsequent cycles once your initial plan has been developed. (See Chapter 20 for details on communicating updates.)

Even if your team leader changes, if members of the team change, or if you decide to hire outside consultants to help with your plan, your existing plan can still serve as a starting point. The steps will involve the following.

1. Gathering information to update the situation analysis.

2. Reviewing the mission, vision, and values.

3. Reviewing and updating the SWOT analysis.

4. Reviewing the existing strategic plan to identify those things—based on the SWOT analysis and the year's activities—which should be dropped (either because they are no longer relevant or they have been accomplished) or continued (because they are still relevant and have not been accomplished). Your key questions for each plan element will be as follows:

   Met or not met?

   Ongoing or dropped?

In some cases, ongoing items will become operational and will not show up on the plan. For instance, suppose one year's strategic plan included an objective to install a new HRIS (Human Resource Information System). Once accomplished, this becomes part of how HR is managed and will no longer show up in the strategic plan.

There may be items on the plan that were not achieved. For instance, perhaps there was an objective to increase market share by 25 percent, but market share remains the same. The team will need to consider whether this is still an important objective given the organization's goal, situation analysis, and the knowledge gained over the course of the last planning period. Perhaps the objective was too lofty and needs to be adjusted. Perhaps the strategies in support of the objective were not the right strategies and will need to be changed. Perhaps the team believes that the strategies were the right strategies, but the tactics were not.

Each element of the existing plan should be reviewed, with some elements being eliminated. Then the team will go back to identify areas where new objectives, strategies, and tactics may be needed. Again, the team may decide that its work stops at the point of assigning strategies to departments or individuals outside of the planning team. Tactics would then be developed by work groups or individualss.

Keeping the Plan Alive

The best way to keep the plan alive is to incorporate it into how work gets done at your company. I've talked about how this might occur through the assignment of strategies and tactics to departments and individuals and by incorporating the evaluation of their success in completing their assignments through the employee review process. But the employee review process, if a company has one (and many small companies may not), generally only occurs on an annual basis. How can the plan be kept alive in between these evaluation periods? One way is to develop individual *work plans*.

DEFINITION

A **work plan**, also called a project plan, is a plan that outlines in detail how a task will be accomplished. Most plans include a list of people participating in the project, a list of equipment needed, specific project tasks, a schedule for completion, and a budget (as appropriate).

Using Work Plans

Work plans can be very complex and may make use of project planning software both to create the plan and to track progress. But work plans can also be very basic, representing simple task lists that visibly tie individual activities to department and organizational activities.

One company that successfully used work plans to guide the work of its employees—4,000 of them!—incorporated a deceptively simple format of green (organizational), blue (departmental), and red (individual) arrows to help employees clearly see the connection between their work (red), their department's work (blue), and the work of the organization (green). (See Chapter 18 for more on this system.) First the planning team would assign strategies (green arrows) to departments. More than one department might be assigned the same green arrow. For instance, a strategy of increasing market share might be assigned to the marketing department (responsible for communicating about the company's products and services), the sales department (responsible for sales and business development), and the product development department (responsible for ensuring that the product is of high quality to meet customer expectations).

Once departments were assigned their green arrows, they were tasked with identifying the department activities that would occur in support of those green arrows. Generally, departments would do this as a group. Then, individuals in each department would identify the specific activities that they needed to do to ensure that department arrows were supported.

The following example shows how an individual's work plan ties back to the department and organization plans.

Organizational	Department	Individual
Increase market share	Implement ad campaign	Hire ad firm
	Increase media coverage	Build media list

As individuals in the department met with their managers on a regular basis (often weekly), they would bring their individual work plans and review their progress on their individual plan items. The department manager would gather information from all employees and, when meeting with the VP, would provide an update on progress toward accomplishing the department—or blue arrow—items on the plan. Vice presidents, in turn, would gather all of the information and updates from their managers and report overall progress to the CEO. In this very simple way, the plan was kept alive, and everybody in the company could see how the things that they were working on contributed to the accomplishment of the overall plan.

Time for Celebration!

Accountability for achieving strategic plan objectives should focus not only on revising plans or increasing efforts when measures are not performing up to expectations, but also taking the time to recognize and celebrate when measures are achieved—or exceeded.

"During my tenure as a director at a health-care center in a large metro area, we produced an all-staff event each year to educate, engage, and energize staff about the corporate business plan," says one woman. The event was in a trade show format that, in addition to providing recognition, offered an opportunity for communication and education about the planning process. Previous events had included staff-performed skits, which told stories that helped explain why the work was important.

There are a variety of things—from the simple to the more elaborate—that organizations can do to celebrate their strategic planning successes. Here are some ideas:

- Track progress in some graphic way as strategic plan objectives are met—use a thermometer, for instance, or a car headed toward a finish line.

- Provide updates in the company newsletter and on intranet sites, recognizing individual and group performance.

- Food is always a good way to celebrate and can range from bringing in treats to recognize a milestone to sponsoring an ice cream social where planning team leaders serve staff and offer their thanks for the hard work that has been done.

- Give movie tickets, gift certificates, or other small forms of appreciation.

Celebratory events don't have to be elaborate. The important thing is that steps are taken to recognize the efforts of staff members and to celebrate successes along the way.

The Least You Need to Know

- Be prepared for environmental changes (internal or external) that may require a change in your plans, such as a new competitor, economic shifts, or employee changes.

- Having a well-defined process in place is important to ensure that the plan will be executed and that all involved will understand what is expected of them.

- Not all company activities are strategic activities. Operational work is ongoing and equally important.

- It's important to take time to celebrate successes to provide recognition and motivation for the continued support of employees for future planning efforts!

Glossary

action plan   A step-by-step, specific list of the actions that need to be carried out to accomplish a tactic.

Balanced Scorecard (BSC)   A tool used to track business performance across four broad categories: financial performance, internal business processes, learning and growth, and customer satisfaction. The tool is designed to help organizations balance the measures that they monitor, recognizing that these areas have relatively equal importance.

BHAG   An acronym for Big Hairy Audacious Goal, a BHAG is an extremely challenging goal that pushes an organization beyond its comfort zone.

business plan   A document prepared for an external audience which is specifically designed to achieve funding and support for a new business initiative.

competitive analysis   The process of identifying and researching relevant competitors to determine their strengths, weaknesses, and differentiating factors. Competitive analysis will yield ideas for positioning a business and its products and services to provide different—and hopefully, better—products, service, pricing, and access to customers.

competitive intelligence   Gathering and analyzing information about competitors and their products and services. Competitive intelligence is legal; industrial espionage is not—but the line between the two can often be blurry.

consensus   Reaching general agreement, not unanimity, among members of a group.

control chart   A tool that is used in statistical process control. It shows data points over time and how these data points vary from the mean (or average). The variation gives an indication of whether a change is statistically significant or just a random occurrence.

core competencies   Those things that you do better than anybody else. They are things that hold great value for your customers and that competitors would have a difficult time replicating.

core values   The shared beliefs of members of an organization that guide their behaviors and actions.

dashboard   A method for tracking performance on measures that uses a red, yellow, and green coding system to quickly communicate whether performance is meeting expectations.

demographic information   Information that defines the observable or quantifiable characteristics of a customer—gender, age, income, where they live, etc.

disruptive innovation   Describes an unexpected change that impacts a product or service either by making the product or service obsolete or by introducing a change that appeals to an entirely new market.

disruptive technology   *See* disruptive innovation.

facilitation   Leading a group of people through a process toward an agreed-upon outcome by encouraging participation, involvement, and commitment from all participants.

facilitator   An individual who is responsible for leading a meeting or discussion. The role of the facilitator is to move the discussion forward; the facilitator is not an active participant in the discussion.

fiscal year   The 12-month time frame a company uses to calculate its financial statements. For most companies, this coincides with the calendar year, but not always. Companies may choose when their fiscal year begins and ends.

focus group   An in-depth interview conducted in a group setting with 6 to 10 people. The input from participants in the focus group session is based on their opinions and preferences and is often influenced by the discussion that occurs during the focus group session.

goal   A general statement of desired performance that indicates what an organization would like to achieve.

groupthink   A term used to define the tendency of groups that have worked together over a period of time and that are very cohesive to avoid critical analysis and conflict. This leads to the acceptance of ideas raised readily without adequate testing, analysis, or evaluation.

industry analysis   The process of evaluating the factors that are impacting a particular industry—the industry the business conducting the planning activity is in—by looking at data and information related to the size and number of businesses, their sales, and the regulatory and other issues that may impact them.

intellectual capital   The collective value of the knowledge resources that your business has, generally represented through what people know, or have in their heads. In a heavy service economy, intellectual capital can be as valuable as—if not more valuable than—financial capital.

internal analysis   The evaluation of factors internal to a company, and under its control, that may impact its future success. Internal analysis generally focuses on customer, employee, and financial considerations.

iterative   An adjective used to describe a cycle of activity that is ongoing and that changes from cycle to cycle as new information is gained. An iteration reflects one cycle in the process.

key performance indicators (KPIs)   Measures used to monitor what a company determines are its most important indicators of success.

Malcolm Baldrige National Quality Award   A government program that helps companies focus on achieving measurable business results by focusing on six process areas (leadership, strategic planning, customer focus, measurement, workforce focus, and process management) through a series of specific criteria-based questions. The seventh category asks for results in support of the six process categories.

market analysis   The process of identifying and analyzing factors in a specific geographic area to forecast market demand and identify issues that may either positively or negatively impact sales.

market share   The percentage of the total available market that a business serves. It may be measured based on number of customers, revenue, or unit sales.

marketing-mix strategy   A plan that indicates how a company will align all of its decisions related to product, price, placement, and promotion activities to achieve maximum success.

matrix   A grid that allows planners to consider the relative value of various items based on identified criteria.

mission   A brief statement developed by a business to describe its purpose, identifying its core business and whom it serves.

mission statement   A statement of the reason your business exists and reflects both who you wish to serve (a definition of your customers) and the value that you hope to provide them with.

NAICS codes   Six-digit classifications created to represent businesses in North America—Mexico, the United States, and Canada. They provide a framework that allows businesses to access and apply comparative statistics and data relevant to the business they are in.

nominal ranking   A process used to prioritize items based on individual rankings. Nominal ranking is frequently used during the SWOT analysis to prioritize the items in each category. *See also* SWOT analysis.

objectives   A measurable and time-based action that will be necessary to achieve a goal. Objectives are the only truly quantifiable element of the strategic plan. *See also* process objective.

opportunity   An opportunity is something favorable in the world outside your business that you can leverage to your benefit. It is something that you have not yet taken advantage of but that, if explored, could have the potential to improve your business in some way.

outcome measures   Outcome measures reflect a final outcome or result. The number of stories run by the media is an outcome measure. *See also* process measures.

outcome objective   Objectives that identify a specific outcome or result; for example, "Achieve a 100 percent pass rate on the customer relationship management system efficiency exam by June 1." *See also* process objective.

polarizing   When two opposite positions are taken and held strongly between members of a group. Once the positions have been taken, it can be difficult to find neutral ground.

poll   A quick survey designed to get a sense of the opinions or feelings of a group of people.

Porter's Five Forces analysis   A framework for analyzing industry impacts based on five key forces designed to provide an indication of the competitive environment, and consequently, the overall profitability potential for the business. The combination of the five forces will either support or drive down profitability.

process measures   Measures that tell you about steps along the way to some final outcome or result. *See also* outcome measures.

process objective   Objectives that indicate a process to be completed or activities to be accomplished. The measure of whether they have been achieved is based on a yes or no evaluation, not a specific outcome measure. *See also* outcome objective.

project plan   *See* work plan.

run chart   A tool that is used in statistical process control that shows data points over time and the variation of these data points from the mean (or average), which gives an indication of whether a change is statistically significant or just a random occurrence.

situation analysis   The evaluation of the environment in which a business, or business unit, operates. It is used to provide input to the strategic planning process.

SMART   An acronym for Specific, Measurable, Attainable, Relevant, and Time-bound, used to describe specific criteria for evaluating whether or not objectives are appropriate.

stakeholders   Individuals or groups that are impacted or affected by the activities of your organization and its ability to fulfill its mission and vision.

statistical process control (SPC)   A method of tracking measures over time to determine whether change is random or due to some statistically significant change.

statistical significance   The degree to which you can rely on the information you gather to accurately predict an outcome.

strategic plan   A document that outlines the steps a company will take to achieve identified goal(s) consistent with its mission, vision, and values.

strategic planning   The process used to create the strategic plan, generally involving a team of people who review background information and develop goals, objectives, strategies, and tactics to be implemented by the organization in support of its mission, vision, and values.

strategy   A statement that indicates, generally, how you will approach meeting your objectives. Strategies are directly related to leveraging the strengths and opportunities and overcoming the weaknesses and threats you identified during the SWOT analysis.

strength   Something distinctive that sets your business apart from the competition, a differentiating factor that you have or a key business metric that is performing exceptionally well.

SWOT analysis   A review of an organization's *strengths, weaknesses, opportunities*, and *threats*, often used as an early step in a strategic planning process.

tactics   Specific "to-do" items that are designed in support of strategies.

team leader   The individual assigned responsibility for the strategic planning process.

threat   Something in the external environment that has the potential to affect a business negatively. Threats may emerge from competitors, the economy, government regulations, or environmental impacts.

value chain analysis   A term that was popularized in 1985 by Michael Porter in his book *Competitive Advantage: Creating and Sustaining Supervisor Performance*. It is the process of looking at the series of steps that lead to the delivery of a product or service and identify areas where there may be weak links in the chain that might represent opportunities for process improvement.

values statements   Statements that describe the core behaviors that guide the work that your business does and the actions that employees take. They define how all members of your business will act, consistent with your mission in pursuit of your vision.

vision   An aspirational statement developed by a business outlining hopes for the future.

vision statements   Far-reaching statements that provide an indication of what the company hopes to be or achieve over the long-term.

weakness   A deficiency or problem that exists in your business. It might be something tangible, like a mass exodus of customers or high turnover among employees. Or it could be something more cultural or attitudinal, like an unwillingness to expand or poor customer service attitudes among employees.

work plan   A plan that outlines in detail how a task will be accomplished. Most plans include a list of people participating in the project, a list of equipment needed, specific project tasks, a schedule for completion, and a budget as appropriate.

Resources

Books

Aaker, David A. *Developing Business Strategies* (Wiley Publishing, Inc., 2001).

Allison, Michael, and Jude Kaye. *Strategic Planning for Nonprofit Organizations.* Wiley Publishing, Inc., 2003.

Fogg, C. David. *Team-Based Strategic Planning: A Complete Guide to Structuring, Facilitating and Implementing the Process.* AMACOM, 1994.

Kaplan, Robert S., and David P. Norton. *Alignment: Using the Balanced Scorecard to Create Corporate Synergies.* Harvard Business Press, 2006.

————. *The Strategy Focused Organization.* Harvard Business Press, 2000.

————. *The Balanced Scorecard.* Harvard Business Press, 1996.

Napier, Rod, Clint Sidle, and Patrick Sanaghan. *High Impact Tools and Activities for Strategic Planning.* McGraw-Hill, 1997.

Porter, Michael. *Competitive Advantage: Creating and Sustaining Supervisor Performance.* Free Press, 1998.

Stern, Carl, and Michael Deimler (eds.). *The Boston Consulting Group on Strategy: Classic Concepts and New Perspectives*, Wiley Publishing, Inc., 2006.

Websites

Association for Strategic Planning
12021 Wilshire Blvd., Suite 286
Los Angeles, CA 90025-1200
Website: www.strategyplus.org

ASP is a nonprofit association that provides information on strategy development for nonprofit and for-profit businesses and government organizations.

The Balanced Scorecard Institute
975 Walnut Street, Suite 360
Cary, NC 27511
Website: www.balancedscorecard.org

The Balanced Scorecard Institute is the official site related to Kaplan and Norton's work on strategy formulation and management. It provides access to training and certification and is a resource for consulting services.

Baldrige National Quality Program
100 Bureau Drive, Stop 1070
Gaithersburg, MD 20899-1070
Website: www.nist.gov/baldrige

The Baldrige Program educates individuals and organizations on performance excellence management. It administers the Malcolm Baldrige National Quality Award, based on criteria in six broad categories, and an additional category focusing on results.

Mind Tools
Hardwick House
Prospect Place
Swindon
Wiltshire
SN1 3LJ
United Kingdom
Website: www.mindtools.com

Mind Tools' mission is to help people around the world learn the practical skills needed to excel in their careers. The site offers a wide range of information and resources on tools useful for career and leadership success, including tools related to strategic planning.

Sample Strategic Plans

Organizational Plan for a Health-Care Organization

The following represents a summarized version of an organizational strategic plan for a nonprofit health-care organization that is run through a Foundation. The plan is being developed by the Foundation and represents a three-year planning time frame.

Overview

Over the next three years, the branding and awareness goals of the Foundation center around cementing our reputation among key stakeholders. We want to become known and recognized by all people who suffer from XYZ disease, as well as by those who participate in their care, as a force for improvement in their quality of life.

To accomplish this, we must increase our exposure online and in more traditional media, such as print, radio, and television. We must also carefully conduct these communications within the messaging platform created during the rebranding process, which will occur in the summer of 20XX. Our marketing efforts will focus on Foundation products (such as the Information Resource Center) that facilitate education, awareness, and patient empowerment while raising important funds for research.

Goal

By June 31, 20XX, greatly increase the number of people who recognize the Foundation as the leader in the fight against XYZ disease, as well as the most authoritative, useful, trusted, and unbiased source of information on the disease.

Objectives

- Increase the number of people who recognize the Foundation as the leader in XYZ disease by 50 percent nationally, by June 31, 20XX.

- Based on the results of the annual consumer survey, increase the percentage of people who recognize the Foundation as the most authoritative, useful, trusted, and unbiased source of information by 30 percent, 25 percent, 50 percent, and 30 percent, respectively, by June 31, 20XX (two year objective).

Strategy	Tactics
Strengthen brand through consistent logo, etc.	Provide all Foundation name chapters with brand standards
	Create brand standard access on website
Leverage use of website for awareness	Redesign website
	Promote website through consumer media
	Develop Facebook/Twitter accounts
	Develop YouTube account
Strengthen impact of national events	Hold national walk
	Hold national online funding program
	Gain PR for national events

Strategic plans can range in length from one page to more than one hundred pages. Some are professionally designed and produced as full-color, bound and printed documents. Others are much shorter—some as brief as one page. Many, given today's technology options, are created and communicated electronically, allowing the planning team to provide extensive background information at minimal expense. The common elements in most plans are:

- Introductory message or executive summary.

- Mission and vision of the organization.

- List of the planning team members.

- Goals, objectives, and strategies (and sometimes tactics).

- Appendixes. Plans often include appendixes that contain the background materials, or summaries of the background materials, used in the development of the plan. This might include elements of the situation analysis, the SWOT analysis, meeting minutes, etc.

Following are some examples to provide a sense of the typical format and content of these plans. The plans have been sanitized to remove any identifying information or data.

Organizational Plan for a Library

The following organizational plan is developed for a library. This plan is designed to be shared with the library's audience—its patrons—and the focus on the external audience is evident.

Message from the Board President

"Our Guide to Tomorrow" is a strategic plan for the XYZ Public Library to offer improved library services for our joint community over the next few years and beyond. It is the result of the collaboration of the library staff, Board of Trustees and community volunteers. Under the direction of consultants from Library Consultants, our planning committee focused on the integral role we have as an information center for our towns, and we gained insight into ways to promote lifelong learning and literacy.

This plan is an outline to address the changing needs of library users and the increased services offered to them. A vast collection of data was gathered by Library Consultants in an effort to let us know what the public wants from their library, and much thought was put into ways to fulfill these requests. Now that "Our Guide to Tomorrow" is complete, our real task begins—implementing the proposed changes so that the community receives only the best library services.

The Planning Process

Library trustees, members of the planning committee, library staff, and many residents contributed time and energy to this planning process and the developing of the strategic plan. Library Consultants, a library consulting firm, assisted with the effort.

Data Analysis

The following methods were used to gather data for this plan:

- Focus groups and surveys
- Staff discussions and meetings
- Space analysis
- Meetings with planning committee

SWOT Analysis

(Top items presented in a four-square matrix. The actual SWOT analysis is not provided here, but it would be presented in a table format, with strengths in one box, weaknesses in another, and so on.)

Our Strategic Plan

Mission: The XYZ Public Library, the community's hometown library, provides resources to help people realize their dreams.

Goal: To make sure every visit to the library is enjoyable and that users are satisfied.

Objectives:

- To increase library visits by 10 percent over the next year.

- To increase satisfaction with the availability of materials by 30 percent by the end of the year, as measured by our annual patron survey.

Strategy	Tactics
Develop great library collection	Increase materials budget by 15 percent each year
	Develop a gift program and a "buy, read, donate" program
	Increase number of available best-sellers
	Develop rapid read collection
Increase assortment of materials	Assess new popular digital and print formats
	Develop a Spanish language collection
Establish reader advisory service	Promote library acquisitions to community
	Use web page to highlight recent purchases
	Write local newspaper column on new books

Marketing Plan for a Health-Care Organization

The following example outlines a plan developed for a business function—marketing—in this case, in the health-care industry. Note the connection made between this functional plan and the organization's overall strategic plan.

Background and Purpose

XYZ Health Care is a fully integrated health delivery system that provides primary, secondary, and tertiary care to a broad geographic region. The purpose of this document is to provide a comprehensive situation analysis, to review and assess historical marketing efforts, and to formally outline (1) specific marketing goals and objectives; (2) market-based strategies and tactics for achieving those goals and objectives; and 3) success criteria that will be used in evaluating the effectiveness of our efforts.

Relationship of Marketing and Strategic Plans

The XYZ Health Care system recently published a strategic plan, which is the cornerstone for future operational activity. This marketing plan was developed to support the major goals of the strategic plan. This relationship carries through all sections of the marketing plan.

Situation Analysis

The external environment includes the health-care industry as well as the business, social, and economic conditions in which XYZ Health Care and other health-care providers operate. This information will help create a context for interpreting the specific business conditions facing XYZ Health Care. A review of health-care trends will present a big-picture industry overview in addition to anticipated activities and actions that may impact the organization. Regional trends will describe events and conditions on a more localized scale.

Health-care industry trends:

- Outpatient visits continue to increase while hospital admissions have plateaued and lengths of stay have decreased.

- Systems created by mergers and consolidations are expected to undergo intensified community and regulatory scrutiny to ensure that the public interest is being served.

- The driving force behind integrated health systems is market pressure—particularly pressure from large employers demanding better value. Integrated health systems must: manage total costs; focus on populations rather than individuals; and become customer-centered, data-driven, and process-oriented.

- Several early entrants into the hospital-based system fray are now in extremely serious financial and organizational trouble. Some experts believe that the economies of scale and coordination that exist in multi-hospital systems in theory may be unachievable in fact. Furthermore, many not-for-profit boards are looking at sales to investor-owned companies as a face-saving strategy for abandoning their community trust.

- Hospitals will be increasingly unable to raise prices to generate additional volumes from the commercial market due to rising managed care penetration and significant excess capacity.

- The managed care industry anticipates improved premiums in (year), but not for all companies, products, or markets. There is continued, strong industry enrollment.

- Most of the growth in HMO enrollment has been in point-of-service plans; the percentage of managed care patients who are enrolled in group-model HMOs has declined steadily since the early 1980s.

- *Managed care* has a negative meaning to most consumers. Consumers want choice, quality, access, control, information, affordability, and preventive care.

- Providers are at risk from new Medicare constraints on rapidly growing post-acute and outpatient programs, continued inpatient restraint, and growing managed care market share. Medicare payment constraints are predicted to negatively impact providers' revenues, margins, and earnings outlooks, particularly in the context of rising managed-care penetration.

- All buyers—employers, business coalitions, and government programs—are driving cost competition among HMOs and insurers.

- Traditional indemnity insurers will continue to sell their health businesses to managed care companies.

- Key factors that contribute to rising health-care costs include:
  - Use of sophisticated, expensive technologies
  - Duplication of tests
  - Increases in variety and frequency of treatments
  - Increasing number and longevity of the elderly

- Regulations that result in cost-shifting rather than cost reduction

- Increasing accidents and crimes that require emergency medical services

- Restrictive work rules in the health-care delivery system

- Labor intensiveness and earnings growth for health-care professionals and executives

- Built-in inflation in the health-care delivery system

- There is increasing demand among providers for advanced information technology.

- Organized health-care labor will continue to take an activist stance.

Competition

XYZ Health Care's key competitors include individual providers (hospitals, clinics, etc.) in addition to integrated delivery systems. Detailed profiles of each of these competitors are included in this section. A map that indicates each site is also included.

Competition in the primary market area has intensified greatly, particularly over the past year. The providers in the market are basically in two camps—ours and theirs.

Consumer Perception of Key Providers

A correspondence analysis was performed using current health-care consumer study data. This technique helps determine the qualities and attributes most closely linked to each organization.

Consumers in the primary market area believe:

- XYZ Health Care is the tertiary care provider for full-service health-care needs.

- Competitor A is the specialty care provider with highly skilled doctors.

- Competitor B offers basic services and is the low-cost provider.

- Competitor C is the more service-oriented, secondary-level care provider.

Strengths, Weaknesses, Opportunities, and Threats (SWOT)

Strengths	Weaknesses
Organizational commitment	Lack of customer and market focus
ABC affiliation	Operational issues
Market position	Patient loyalty
Service delivery for patients	Insurance company strategy
Business orientation	
Opportunities	**Threats**
Emphasize ABC affiliation	Competitive activity
Develop target market areas	Declining Medicare reimbursement
Focus on key market segments	Increasing managed care penetration
Build relations with external physicians	
Develop insurance company strategy	
Enhance community relations	

Goals and Objectives

Goal: To retain current and generate additional patient activity, especially in outpatient clinics, by influencing existing and potential customers to choose XYZ Health Care for their health-care needs.

Objectives:

- Over the next year, increase XYZ's total clinic encounters to 600,000—this will be an increase of approximately 3 percent.

- Over the next year, enhance consumer preference by increasing the proportion of consumers who believe that XYZ Health Care is best for: heart problems (increase to 45 percent from 39 percent); serious injury or trauma (to 35 percent from 29 percent); cancer (to 30 percent from 25 percent); and primary care (to 38 percent from 36 percent).

- Within 18 months, increase the percentage of clinic patients who say they would recommend XYZ Health Care to 85 percent (from baseline of 78 percent).

- Elevate consumer perception of XYZ Health Care as being rated best for its concern for the community to 35 percent (from 24 percent).

Strategies, Tactics, and Resource Requirements

Strategy #1: Identify and remedy reasons for dissatisfaction among clinic patients who say they would not recommend XYZ Health Care.

Tactics:

- Through ongoing clinic patient satisfaction study, identify patients' specific reasons for not recommending XYZ Health Care.

- Develop and implement a plan to remedy the problems identified above.

- Conduct on-site, ABC-based customer service training for all employees.

- Establish core customer service standards for: phone abandonment rate, appointment access and availability, billing errors, and reschedule rates. Communicate standards, implement new procedures, monitor activities, and take corrective actions (if needed).

Strategy #2: Position XYZ Health Care as the overall provider of choice for health-care services in the market area, including primary and specialty care services (cardiac, trauma, cancer).

Tactics:

- In communication materials targeted to patients, consumers, employers, and insurance companies, as appropriate, focus on XYZ Health Care's key differentiating feature by highlighting the connection to ABC Affiliate.

- Develop, produce, and promote quarterly community health-education classes on topics of interest to consumers (which emphasize targeted programs).

- On a monthly basis, increase non-paid media exposure by targeting pitches to local media related to cardiac, trauma, cancer, and primary care services.

- Highlight XYZ Health Care's expertise in targeted services and programs in all existing consumer publications.

- Explore the feasibility of development and full promotion of the Chest Pain Center in the emergency department as a focal point for cardiac services.

- Offer evening hours and Saturday hours at clinics; notify clinic patients through newsletters and print ads.

- Develop direct mail program targeted to new residents in A and B counties.

- Design a display or kiosk (for lobby or high-volume waiting areas) that describes the ABC connection to XZY Health Care.

- Develop and implement a plan for toll-free numbers at all sites.

- Place materials in waiting areas of clinics, hospitals, and regional locations to send message about the ABC affiliation.

- Highlight successes in disease management in consumer newsletter.

- Develop and implement multimedia advertising campaign.

- Consistently pitch human-interest stories to local media that demonstrate appropriate and effective medical care to local residents treated at XYZ Health Care and ABC affiliate.

- Develop and implement a non-paid standing column for local newspapers, especially in target communities.

- Educate medical staff about importance of patients' recommendations (word-of-mouth).

Strategy #3: Inform health-care consumers about health plans that allow selection of XYZ Health Care providers.

Tactics:

- List health plans and other products that allow selection of XYZ Health Care as a provider in print and broadcast advertising and other communications materials to patients and health-care consumers.

- Identify open enrollment periods for larger employers. During these times, increase advertising frequency and explore feasibility of on-site visits and staffed information booths at local employer sites.

- Explore feasibility of joint marketing with 123 Health Plan.

Strategy #4: Increase employers' likelihood to either continue offering or to offer a hew health plan for their employees that allows access to XYZ Health Care.

Tactics:

- Further promote occupational medicine services to larger employers via direct mail and business advertising.

- Identify and make visits (sales calls) to larger employers in the area who do not offer a health plan that allows access to XYZ Health Care.

- Create and maintain a database of top area employers.

- Have key administrators make service calls to large employers offering health plans that allow access to XYZ Health Care.

Strategy #5: Market directly to member representatives at HMOs and other insurance organizations to increase their awareness and knowledge of XYZ Health Care.

Tactics:

- Host annual tour of XYZ Health Care for member representatives.

- Include insurance company and member representatives in distribution of all relevant communications materials.

Strategy #6: Position XYZ Health Care as a caring, concerned, and involved corporate citizen.

Tactics:

- Motivate key staff to participate in high-profile community activities.

- Develop and produce periodic community service reports that describe staff activities and involvement; distribute internally and externally using ongoing communication vehicles.

- Partner with additional key employers in market area to address employee health information needs through on-site employee seminars.

- Identify a single, high-visibility community health need to champion.

Outcome Measures

Outcome measures and responsible parties:

- Total clinic encounters (review semi-annually)—Administration; Finance

- Volume of encounters for trauma, cardiac, oncology, primary care (review semi-annually)—Administration; Finance

- Consumer preference and perception ratings—ABC Affiliate; Marketing

- Patient satisfaction with overall experience—ABC Affiliate; Marketing; Quality

- Clinic patients' willingness to recommend—ABC Affiliate; Marketing; Quality

- New patients' reasons for selecting XYZ—Patient registration

Evaluation of the Planning Process

Gathering ongoing feedback about what worked well and areas of opportunity for improvement of the strategic planning process is important. One way of doing this is to conduct a planning assessment such as the following on a regular basis to provide input to the next planning process. Distributing the assessment can provide insights about how different audience segments (for example, employees compared to supervisors) view the process.

Assigning a numerical scale to your responses can aid in scoring and provide mathematical weightings. Generally, a 1–5 scale ranges from "strongly disagree" (1) to "strongly agree" (5). The higher the resulting average scores, the higher the level of agreement.

Strategic Planning Assessment

Please indicate your position:

- ❏ Vice President
- ❏ Department Director
- ❏ Manager
- ❏ Staff

Organizational Level Planning

1. I have a clear understanding of where the company is headed and how we will get there.

- ❏ Strongly agree
- ❏ Agree
- ❏ Neutral
- ❏ Disagree
- ❏ Strongly disagree

2. The planning process allows for enough input from all levels in the organization.

   ❏ Strongly agree

   ❏ Agree

   ❏ Neutral

   ❏ Disagree

   ❏ Strongly disagree

3. I have a clear understanding of the planning process and what my role in planning is.

   ❏ Strongly agree

   ❏ Agree

   ❏ Neutral

   ❏ Disagree

   ❏ Strongly disagree

4. Measuring progress on key objectives is an important part of the process.

   ❏ Strongly agree

   ❏ Agree

   ❏ Neutral

   ❏ Disagree

   ❏ Strongly disagree

5. There is adequate communication about the planning process and results.

   ❏ Strongly agree

   ❏ Agree

   ❏ Neutral

   ❏ Disagree

   ❏ Strongly disagree

6. The company is focused on the right things to ensure short-term success.

   ❑ Strongly agree

   ❑ Agree

   ❑ Neutral

   ❑ Disagree

   ❑ Strongly disagree

7. The company is focused on the right things to ensure long-term success.

   ❑ Strongly agree

   ❑ Agree

   ❑ Neutral

   ❑ Disagree

   ❑ Strongly disagree

Department Level Planning

8. Having a departmental work plan has resulted in measurable strategic improvements in my department(s).

   ❑ Strongly agree

   ❑ Agree

   ❑ Neutral

   ❑ Disagree

   ❑ Strongly disagree

9. The work and goals in my department(s) are aligned with organizational objectives and work of other departments.

   ❑ Strongly agree

   ❑ Agree

   ❑ Neutral

   ❑ Disagree

   ❑ Strongly disagree

10. The members of my department(s) clearly understand the department role and their individual role in achieving results.

   ❑ Strongly agree

   ❑ Agree

   ❑ Neutral

   ❑ Disagree

   ❑ Strongly disagree

11. My department work plan(s) reflect the most important things we are working on.

   ❑ Strongly agree

   ❑ Agree

   ❑ Neutral

   ❑ Disagree

   ❑ Strongly disagree

12. The departmental leadership team (Vice President/Director/Manager) work closely together to evaluate progress in achieving goals.

   ❑ Strongly agree

   ❑ Agree

   ❑ Neutral

   ❑ Disagree

   ❑ Strongly disagree

13. The departmental work plan is used for prioritizating resources such as staff time, training needs, and capital equipment.

   ❑ Strongly agree

   ❑ Agree

   ❑ Neutral

   ❑ Disagree

   ❑ Strongly disagree

Suggestions for improving the strategic planning process:

_____

_____

_____

_____

_____

_____

_____

_____

_____

_____

_____

_____

_____

_____

_____

_____

_____

_____

_____

_____

Return to _____ by _____ (date)

Thank you.

Index

J–K

L

Q

W-X-Y-Z

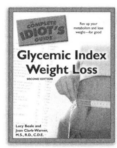
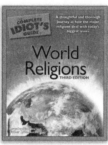

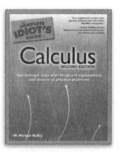

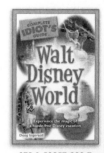

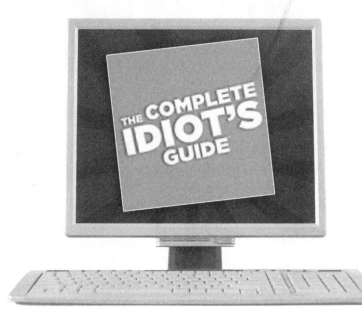